MY
REMINISCENCES

Da Capo Press Music Reprint Series

MUSIC EDITOR
BEA FRIEDLAND
Ph.D., City University of New York

This title was recommended for Da Capo reprint
by **Frank D'Accone,** *University of California at Los Angeles*

MY
REMINISCENCES

BY

LUIGI ARDITI

DA CAPO PRESS · NEW YORK · 1977

Library of Congress Cataloging in Publication Data

Arditi, Luigi, 1822-1903.
  My reminiscences.

  (Da Capo Press music reprint series)
  Reprint of the 1896 ed. published by Dodd, Mead, New
York.
  1. Arditi, Luigi, 1822-1903. 2. Composers—
Biography.
  ML410.A67A3 1977   780′.92′4 [B]   77-5500
  ISBN 0-306-77417-8

This Da Capo Press edition of *My Reminiscences* is an unabridged
republication of the first edition published in New York in 1896.

Published by Da Capo Press, Inc.
A Subsidiary of Plenum Publishing Corporation
227 West 17th Street, New York, N.Y. 10011

MY REMINISCENCES

BY

LUIGI ARDITI

With Numerous Illustrations, Facsimiles, etc.

EDITED AND COMPILED WITH INTRODUCTION AND NOTES

BY

THE BARONESS VON ZEDLITZ

NEW YORK
DODD, MEAD AND COMPANY
1896

University Press:
John Wilson and Son, Cambridge, U.S.A.

MY REMINISCENCES

Luigi Arditi.

CONTENTS.

———•———

CHAPTER IV.

CHAPTER V.

CHAPTER VI.

CHAPTER VII.

CHAPTER VIII.

CHAPTER IX.

CONTENTS.

CHAPTER XIV.

CHAPTER XV.

CHAPTER XVI.

LIST OF ILLUSTRATIONS.

Marie Antoinette Von Zedlitz

INTRODUCTION.

———•———

MUSICIANS have been asking for the last ten years, "Why does not Arditi write his memoirs? The record of his professional career could not fail to be rife with interest to virtuosi and dilettanti alike. . . ."

And musical people are right in desiring to possess the life-story of a man whose deep love and intimate knowledge of music have placed him in the front rank of contemporary musicians, and whose association with celebrated personages,[1] many of whom, alas! are dead and gone, render him socially an interesting and distinguished personality.

Arditi has known everybody of note in the musical world throughout the past six decades. From his earliest childhood upwards he has deserved and obtained encouragement and support, and his recollections of bygone days are full of kind and affectionate memories.

There can be no doubt that the early influence of great men and admirable musicians, acting upon the sensitiveness and susceptibility of his highly-wrought artistic temperament, has had a great effect upon his after-life, and stamped it with that *cachet* of refinement which is so marked a characteristic of the man and his works.

Luigi Arditi has at last been persuaded to jot down his personal recollections, and it is with these that we hope to interest his readers in the following pages.

His life, like that of many talented composers, has not been devoid of struggles, disappointments, and cares. It was by ad-

[1] *Vide* Appendices.

venturous experience that he acquired such practical virtues as courage and perseverance, and, above all, the capacity (of which he is justly proud) of confronting and surmounting difficulties.

He is indisputably one of the most popular orchestral conductors of Italian Opera in the world at the present time; and of the many foreign musical artists who have established their domicile in our country, there is no one more deserving of the esteem of the profession and the public.

Luigi Arditi was born at Crescentino, a small picturesque town which nestles in the lap of Piedmont, on the 16th of July, 1822. Whether his mother, whose maiden name was Colombo, was in any way related to the descendants of the discoverer of America I am not aware; but certainly her son has always shown a marked preference for that country. From his earliest childhood he had always evinced a great love for music, and at the age of seven he begged his father to give him a violin in preference to any toy.

At that period there existed in Crescentino a society of amateurs and dilettanti, headed by the well-known Dr. Chiò and Signor Rossignoli. These gentlemen, noticing the boy's ardent inclinations towards the study of music to be combined with unquestionable talent, prevailed upon his father to make whatever pecuniary sacrifice might be requisite to provide the gifted lad with adequate musical instruction.

Arditi first learnt the rudiments of the Divine Art under the guidance of Carossini and Capitani, and he made such marked progress that after four years' arduous study he managed to get together a small orchestra, — composed of two violins, one double-bass, one clarionet, and one trombone, — which he conducted in person, playing the first violin himself, as all conductors in those days were obliged to do. Being a very little fellow, he always had a stool put on his chair in order to raise him above the other musicians. At the age of twelve (1834) young Arditi was allowed to occupy a place in the well of the orchestra at the theatre in Crescentino, and on one occasion a trivial incident occurred which brought about the first really great grief of the little fellow's childhood.

"Aristodemus" was being performed, and the youthful violinist, as usual, occupied his "practicable" compound seat in the orchestra. Suddenly a loud noise was heard among the musicians, the piece stopped for a few seconds, audience and actors alike advanced towards the footlights in order to ascertain the cause of the unexpected disturbance, when a little shamefaced boy, whose dark eyes were suffused with tears, was picked up amid the *débris* of broken upholstery, and, what was infinitely worse, of a shattered violin.

The pain and mortification of this calamity proved for the time quite overwhelming to the boy's sensitive nature. All the pleasure and happiness of life seemed to fade into impenetrable gloom at the sight of the broken treasure — the companion of his hours of toil and recreation — that lay dumb for ever at his feet.

What had happened was this. The boy had fallen asleep, whether overcome by hard work or wearied by the play, who shall say why the tired eyelids closed ? He himself cannot remember; he only recalls — not without emotion to this very day — the angry scene which he had with his father on his return home, the bitter tears he shed when he was sternly informed that the punishment for his negligence would take the form of a three months' absence from the orchestra, and his utter prostration of spirits by this pronouncement of what to him appeared to be Fate's cruel decree. After a month's repining, the lad's dumb misery appealed so deeply to the father's heart that he was finally induced to let him resume his studies, and, what was more, to buy him another violin.

Luigi was sent to Turin in order that he might study technique under Signor Caldera. There his artistic capabilities and faculty of musical expression on the violin were greatly appreciated at all the performances of church music in which he took part, while his execution of Mayseder's variations in E major created an unusual display of enthusiasm, considering the youth of the artist. In this town he also conducted an amateur orchestra, giving great satisfaction to his master, Signor Caldera, who, prompted by the knowledge of the boy's exceptional talent, persuaded Luigi's father to permit him to enter the Conservatoire at Milan.

At the Conservatoire Arditi's chosen companions and chums were Luigi Yotti, Bottesini, and Piatti.

Here the musician had but one course to follow, and that was to study incessantly.

Professor Ferrara was Arditi's instructor in violin playing, while Maestro Vaccai gave him lessons in composition. Indeed, the latter master took the greatest possible interest in his young Piedmontese pupil, and missed no opportunity of bringing him to the front ; whenever Vaccai conducted the orchestra at the Conservatoire, he placed Arditi in close proximity to himself, thus enabling the lad, then only fourteen years old, to enjoy many exceptional advantages.

In 1838, Arditi took his first prize at the Institute of Music in Milan.

On this occasion, in conjunction with his friend and fellow-student Yotti, he gave a very admirable rendering of a duet composed by Maurer for two violins, and was, moreover, encouragingly praised and affectionately embraced by the venerable and much revered Alessandro Rolla.

At the time of the Emperor Ferdinand's first coronation, Bottesini, Piatti, and Arditi were among the favoured artists whose solo playing was enthusiastically applauded at the Austrian court festivities.

In 1840 Arditi wrote his first orchestral work, — an interesting event in the life of a composer. It was an Overture dedicated to the Director of the Institute, Count Renato Borromeo, who awarded to him the first prize, at the Conservatoire yearly examination, as violinist and composer.

Arditi's first opera, " I Briganti," was written in 1840, and was performed in public at the Milan Conservatoire during the same year.

When the young musician was eighteen, he decided to relieve his father of any further expense, by passing his final examination and leaving the Institute, in order to begin his career as violinist, composer, and orchestral conductor.

His masters, Ferrara and Vaccai, were much affected when they became cognisant of Arditi's project, knowing as they did how materially another year at the Conservatoire would add to the maturing of his already well-developed talent. Anxious to avert a stumbling-block in the boy's career, they consulted with

LUIGI ARDITI.
(*From a daguerreotype taken in Havana in 1846.*)

Count Borromeo, who, on hearing his reason for wishing to leave the Institute, immediately offered most liberally to pay all his expenses for another year's tuition, so that he might have every facility for perfecting himself in the knowledge and practice of his Art.

Very naturally and justifiably, young Arditi accepted his kind friend's magnanimous offer with joyful alacrity. He showed his deep sense of gratitude to his benefactors by the ardour and earnest zeal with which he pursued his studies during the last year of his tuition.

In 1842 Arditi bade adieu to the Conservatoire. It was with a heavy heart that he parted with his kind masters and fellow-pupils — for he had been the recipient of much affectionate consideration at their hands — and turned from loyal friends and pleasant associations to a world of new ventures, and one which was destined to be fraught with many perplexing struggles.

Another year, consecutive to that last mentioned, brings us to an important event in the musician's career, *e.g.*, his first conductorship of opera during Carnival time in Vercelli, at which time he was elected honorary member of the Philharmonic Society.

Of the old Italian days, Arditi always thinks with fondness. Then a young man, full of hope and resolution, he was determined to make a name for himself, and succeeded in doing so by dint of sheer perseverance and manful fortitude. A spirit of adventure, however, has always marked his life's course, as he will show his readers in the following chapters, and has added enormously to the enjoyment of the enterprises he embarked upon.

From Vercelli, Arditi went to Turin, where he gave concerts; later to Arona, on the occasion of the opening of the theatre, and to Varese for the autumn opera season.

Paying a short visit to Milan, he played to delighted audiences at the Canobiana, and also composed a duet for the celebrated Sisters Milanollo, which they performed with much success at La Scala.

A great compliment was paid to him in 1844. Arditi's old master, Ferrara, hearing that his pupil had made such big strides in the direction of musical distinction, offered to him the post of conductor of the orchestra at the Teatro Ré, Milan, which important post Arditi accepted, and occupied most creditably for two years. Distinguished honours were being conferred on the rising musician by this time, as the following little story will show.

At Varese, where Arditi conducted, he found an ardent supporter in the person of the Duke Antonio Litta, who steadfastly patronised the opera house.

One night the Duke informed young Arditi that he wished him to perform an important solo, the next day, at a certain musical *réunion*, at which the Countess Samayloff had promised to assist. The violinist was nervous, fearing that the inadequate instrument he possessed would not do justice to his playing, and begged to be excused on that plea.

The Duke, however, would take no refusal, and told him that if that were his only trouble he would gladly give him a violin, inviting him to the Palazzo Litta, in order that he might make a selection from instruments which the Duke would cause to be shown to him. An Amati, a Guarnerius, and several other fine violins were submitted to his choice, but Arditi's thoughts drifted back regretfully to a certain sweet-toned Stradivarius which had been lent to him by a Milanese nobleman on one occasion when he played at the Conservatoire examination, and he wished ardently that he might borrow the same instrument once more, if only for an hour, to play upon to his distinguished patron.

The Duke recollected the occasion perfectly, and divined the lad's thoughts.

"I understand," he said, smiling, "you are thinking of the Stradivarius. If it can be obtained, you shall have it. . . ."

No time was lost in seeking out Signor De Carli, the possessor of the "Strad" in question; and, unhesitatingly paying an enormous sum for the instrument, the Duke presented it to the overjoyed Arditi, whose emotion on becoming the possessor of such a — to him — priceless treasure was the best proof of gratitude he could convey to his kind benefactor.

After ten years' absence in America, Arditi once more visited the Duke, whose first inquiry was for the violin. He supposed that Arditi had not unnaturally been induced to sell it, and was much delighted to see the musician take it reverently from its case.

Here I must pause. Having endeavoured to give our readers

a mere sketchy outline of Signor Arditi's early career, I will retire, and let the Maestro relate his Reminiscences for himself. Were they recounted in his own graceful and plastic vernacular, their value would be enhanced by the impress of his genial individuality and by the charm of his bright and idiomatic humour; but these attractions must necessarily be foregone in an English rendering of a typical Italian's written memoranda and verbal utterances.

The shortcomings which may be detected in the matter or manner of this book are attributable to inefficiency in the medium through which Signor Arditi has been pleased to impart his recollections to the English reading public.

It is to be hoped that indulgence will be accorded to all such shortcomings, in gracious consideration of the many difficulties inevitably inherent to the translator's task.

MARIE ANTOINETTE VON ZEDLITZ
(*née Beatty Kingston*).

MY REMINISCENCES.

CHAPTER I.

A Long Retrospect — Two Months from Genoa to Havana — A Demolished Theatre — Impressions of Havana — Francesco's Love of Music — Ten Years in America — Julius Benedict — Alboni's Superstitions — Room No. 13 — I try to wear a Wig without Success — "Il Corsaro," My First Benefit — A Broker's Bankruptcy.

FIFTY years ago it was my firm intention at the age of twenty-three, buoyed up with great hopes generated by my so far successful musical career, to come to England with Giovanni Bottesini, my dear old friend and comrade, in order that we should give concerts and opera together.

But however felicitously man may propose divers enterprises, Providence often steps forward and intervenes with cool decisiveness to frustrate them.

So it happened in my case. At a farewell dinner given to us by the Duke Antonio Litta, in Milan, in honour of our proposed departure to England, we met Badiali, Don Francesco Marty's agent, and brother of the famous baritone, Cesare Badiali, who made us so excellent an offer to accompany him throughout a concert and opera tour, beginning with a visit to Havana and continuing to other parts of the New World, that we relinquished our former plans, and over a jovial glass of sparkling wine we promptly closed an engagement to try our luck under Badiali's auspices.

In those days long journeys were accomplished by means of sailing vessels, and it took us exactly two months to travel by water from Genoa to Havana.

Previous to our departure I had never, almost incredible as it seems, set eyes on the sea. The effect of the magnificent stretch of water, with its huge waves and foaming billows, upon my surprised senses was an overwhelming one; it almost took my breath away.

Our journey had for some reason or other been delayed, most luckily and providentially, for had we started on the day originally fixed upon, this book would never have been written. A tremendous and disastrous cyclone had passed over the coast of Cuba and across the Atlantic, devastating land and property on shore, and wrecking many ships at sea, among which, no doubt, our little craft would also have foundered.

We started on the 2nd September, 1846, from Genoa, with the orchestra, of which I was conductor, and chorus, and my recollections of those two months spent in tossing about on the ocean are anything but pleasant. Fortunately, I was a good sailor, or the discomfort of poor and insufficient accommodation, wretchedly bad food, and rough weather would have been augmented by the same sufferings Bottesini endured. How ill he was, poor fellow! His face grew thin and his body emaciated, but the eyes appeared to become larger and more melancholy as the merciless sea made our small bark dance incessantly to its strident music. And when I come to think of it, the food we were served with was so unfit for human consumption that we almost lived on the rich, pure, and luscious wine alone, of which we had a large quantity on board that was being transported to Havana from Italy.

I believe our captain had sinister views with regard to the edibles, and wanted to sell the tinned meats, etc., on our arrival at Havana. However, I own that the stuff that was placed before us was invariably thrown overboard, with the accompanying forks, knives, and spoons, and many infuriated expletives, so that towards the end of our voyage there were about three forks and knives left for the use of company and crew alike!

On quieter days, when the company was not quite prostrate with seasickness, we rehearsed our music, and having a piano on board, we managed to pass agreeably some of the time that hung wearily on our hands.

The days seemed to us like years, until finally we were informed, to our inexpressible joy, that our arrival at Havana was no longer a question of days, but of hours.

Needless to say, we were all on deck, anticipating with the greatest possible excitement our first glimpse of the land, which, by the aid of opera glasses, telescopes, and binoculars, was bit by bit unfolding itself to our enraptured eyes.

As we approached nearer and nearer, and our arrival practically became a matter of minutes, we all noticed that our agent, Badiali, grew restless and uncomfortable. He danced about the deck backwards and forwards like a man suddenly bereft of his senses, wildly gesticulating with his telescope, and uttering unintelligible exclamations. At last we pinned him down and asked him to explain his extraordinary conduct, which, when we learnt its cause, also filled us all with dismay.

"*I can't see the theatre*," he screamed excitedly; "IT'S GONE!"

"What?" shrieked some one, "the theatre gone? Are you crazy?"

" No, alas ! " he moaned dejectedly, " the café which adjoined it, and which was my property, is no longer visible either. *Dio mio*, what can have happened? It must have been burned to the ground ! "

Now it was our turn to get excited. No *theatre !* Then what was to become of us ? we asked, turning pale at the horrible anticipations that besieged our minds. It was not long, however, before we learnt the worst possible news that could have been conveyed to us. The theatre had been literally swept away, carrying with it the adjoining house, including the distracted Badiali's precious café, by the fearful cyclone that had raged with such unwonted severity all over the south of America, and to which, but for a fortunate interposition of Providence, we should also have fallen victims.

That was a pretty pasticcio !

The entire company was obliged to remain on board (it seemed as though we should never land) until arrangements had been made to accommodate us in another theatre. A subscription was speedily raised, and after much mental anxiety as to our fortune, which only a few days previously had apparently smiled so benignly, we and our belongings were transported to the principal theatre, The Tacon, a much finer and more important building than the one in which we had been originally destined to appear.

At last we settled down in Havana; Bottesini and I took rooms together, where we lived in perfect amity, and the rehearsals commenced for " Ernani," the first opera we produced in Havana, which was performed eventually with great success. Perelli was " Ernani," and Mdlle. Tedesco sang " Elvira " with all the *élan* and bell-like clearness that characterised her vocalization, for she had a most lovely voice, which, at that period, when

she was still in her girlhood, was at its best in respect
to quality and flexibility.

.   .   .   .

Foreign visitors to Havana are usually assured by
the natives on their arrival that "they cannot fail to be
pleased with the place," and, of course, a man's first
experience of life in the tropics is charmingly full of
striking novelty and unexpected incident.

The entrance of the bay called "the finest in the
world" is decidedly imposing, and the city which lies
to your right, opposite the famous forts of El Moro and
Cabañas, stretches along the shore and presents a cheerful, exhilarating spectacle, with its houses displaying
almost every colour of the rainbow, and its profusion of
church steeples and domes in several varieties of
architectural style.

We lived in a quaint little house, Bottesini and I, the
doors and windows of which were cut down to the
ground, and presented a fresh, gay appearance, in spite
of the iron bars which are used in lieu of crystal panes, —
the glass trade being quite unknown throughout Cuba
at that time. Our attendant was a Creole, a frivolous,
poor-witted fellow, whose figure was long and scrawny,
and who possessed a conspicuous predilection for getting
into scrapes.

In those days the surveillance exercised over the
negroes was terribly severe, and the laziness and insub-
ordination that they would constantly have indulged in,
had they not been constantly under terror of the lash,
created a state of things that was anything but pleasant.

For instance, our black servant was continually dis-
obeying the law by stopping out later than the hour
notified to him by the police; on which occasion, sad
to relate, either Bottesini or I had to bail him out of
custody. We were far from being rich in those days,

and were compelled to come to the unpleasant conclusion that Francesco was a very expensive luxury.

However, Francesco was musical, and that was his
redeeming point. Music would always touch him when
all else failed, and I have often, aided by my violin, lured
the truant home just in the nick of time. His ear for
sound was very keen, — so correct, in fact, that I have
sometimes relied upon his judgment upon a particular
Spanish melody when I myself felt dubious.

Francesco was a character; but he was kind to our
pets, — we had innumerable parrots and dogs, — and so
we forgave him many of his shortcomings.

From the social point of view, Havana is a city practically without ladies.

Hardly any other than negresses are to be seen
about, while ladies who have any pretension to youth
and beauty never venture out of doors unprotected.
The charms of café and club life, such as they are,
completely wean the Havana husband from a home
where real feminine accomplishments are as unknown
as saltspoons, hearthrugs, or fire-irons. A box at the
Tacon theatre, or a drive along the dreary Prado, is all
the Havana citizen can enjoy in common with his wife
and daughters; and for the rest, the women are left to
mope at home or to watch wearily through the window-
gratings, like so many sisters Anne waiting for those
who are tardy in coming.

In short, Havana may be summed up in a very few

Signor Arditi became celebrated for his Creolian dances, all of which
were composed in Havana. The most famous of these particular compositions was the one entitled " L' Incendio, e los Tamburos," which was continually being played at the Tacon Opera House. A good story is told in
connection with the first performance of this music. So realistic was the
treatment of the tambourines, and so suggestive of the " cry for help " in
case of fire adopted by the Cubans, that the firemen in attendance at the
opera were completely taken in by the sounds, and rushed in in a body,
believing the Tacon Opera House to be on fire. — EDITOR.

Giovanni Bottesini   Luigi Arditi

words: it bristles with liveliness and reckless extravagances. But let no poor man, bent on small economies and afflicted with a meagre purse or sensitive nerves, seek to fix his residence there.

Contrary to my expectations, I did not return to Europe until ten years after my first visit to Cuba.

The "Havana Italian Opera Company," under Marty's management, steadily increased and flourished, and not only did full honour to the Tacon theatre, but enjoyed the highest reputation for general excellence all over the United States.

When I look back to those *ensembles*, in which we were proud to include such first-class artists as Stéffenone, Bosio, Salvi, Geremia Bettini, Badiali, and Marini, all of whom achieved complete and brilliant successes in Europe later on, I have no hesitation in saying that never, for the time and place, would it have been possible to secure more admirable operatic performances than those rendered by this particular company.

Marietta Alboni, who was accompanied by her husband, Count Pepoli, came to America about this time (she must have been about thirty years of age), and the

recollection of her lovely voice and facility of production
still lingers vividly in my mind.   Many pleasant memories recur to me as I speak of her, for we became the
best of comrades later on ; but as her name will often
figure in the subsequent pages, I shall deal with her
incidentally whenever she passes across the horizon of
my career.

San Giovanni, who afterwards became renowned as a
teacher of singing in Milan, and Camilla Urso, the child
violinist, also accompanied us on our concert and operatic tours in the States.

I remained with Marty for about five years as orchestral conductor.   The company performed at the Tacon
theatre, Havana, during the winter months, and in the
spring it was our custom to give Grand Opera in
New York and many other important cities in the
States.

It was during one of our winter sojourns in Havana,
in 1850, that the late Sir (then Mr.) Julius Benedict, in
conjunction with Jenny Lind, visited Cuba for the purpose of directing a series of concerts which were to be
given by the " Swedish Nightingale."   Julius Benedict
was then about forty-six years of age.   His abundant
dark hair, and shrewd, clever face of pallid hue, gave
him a quiet air of distinction, while his manner was
extremely courteous and kindly to all who came into
either business or social contact with him.

His reverence for Weber, whose only real pupil he
was, and whose kindness to him when a boy was almost
paternal, was a keynote to his character.   A deep and
lasting sense of gratitude to the great master had taken
a firm root in his heart, and he constantly spoke of
Weber's encouragement and sympathy.

I well remember our first meeting in Havana, when I
was able to render him a slight service, as it led to a

record of unbroken friendship between us, which lasted all his life.

Benedict was in a great dilemma, for at the last moment his first violinist failed him on the occasion of one of his orchestral concerts, and I shall never forget his profound gratitude to me when I offered to take the place of the truant artist. It was really so genuine and heartfelt that I was more than amply repaid for my trouble.

My first concert tour and subsequent musical relations with Alboni are among the pleasant recollections of my life. She was a most charming and amiable woman, and it was impossible to know her without liking and respecting her. Unlike many *prime donne* I have since known, who find it hard to stand the wear and tear and trying ordeal of rehearsal and study of opera without losing their serenity of temper, Alboni was a veritable embodiment of immutable good nature and affability. She never allowed anything to put her out of humour, and invariably took the brightest view of trouble and worries, many of which fell to her share.

Singing was a second nature to her. She loved her work, and revelled in her triumphs. Her vocal compass was perfectly marvellous. I wrote some variations for her once, wherein she trilled on the high B flat with the greatest facility, immediately passing to the lower G; and although she suffered from intense nervousness at such a marvellous feat, considering that her voice was practically a contralto, she acquitted herself so brilliantly of the passage in question that her audiences, on every occasion of her singing the music, were stirred to the greatest enthusiasm.

Alboni was a martyr to superstition. She would never sing on the thirteenth of any month if she could possibly avoid it, or sit down thirteen to table, or travel or sign a contract on a day signalised by that inauspicious number. Like most singers, she was subject to acute nervous attacks, and any incident in connection with this dreaded date always filled her mind with misgivings of impending ill-luck.

Once, on the occasion of our first visit to Chicago, — a very small and insignificant town in those days, colonised, as far as I could judge, largely by pigs, — we arrived late, and just in time to retire for the night. A great quantity of luggage had been sent on by train in advance, and our business manager had secured a bedroom at the best hotel for Alboni.

The proprietor had been informed of Madame's painful superstitiousness, and had been implored not to give her Room No. 13. As it happened, however, Room No. 13 was the only empty and suitable apartment for the *prima donna* on that particular occasion; and in order that she should not become aware of this unlucky fact, the hotel manager caused a piece of paper to be carefully and deftly gummed over the painted number outside her bedroom door. All went smoothly at first. Alboni was ushered into her room, her boxes were unpacked by her maid, and she was served with supper preparatory to going to bed.

Suddenly she started up, agitated by the thought that it would be just as well to know the number of her room. She picked up a candle, and peered out into the darkness of the corridor in order to reconnoitre. In a far shorter time than it takes me to write these lines the house was in a fearful uproar, bells were ringing, and the hotel people and guests rushing about in a state of panic, thinking that they were about to be burnt alive in their beds.

Alboni was discovered standing in front of her door in the attitude of a tragedy queen, with the candle in one hand and the fatal piece of paper bearing the fictitious number in the other! And, what is more, she was not to be beaten. No persuasion on earth would induce her to retire quietly to rest in No. 13. No one could resist her pleading eyes and piteous face; so finally an elderly gentleman was politely but firmly asked to give up his room, which had to be thoroughly re-arranged, while he stood about shivering and discomfited, awaiting the signal to take possession of the room bearing the fatal number.

I don't believe that any of the people had much sleep at the hotel that night; but, at any rate, Alboni gained her point.

Another good story occurs to me in connection with Alboni; but this time I think my readers will laugh at my expense. I was unfortunately doomed to baldness in consequence of a bad attack of typhoid fever which assailed me at a very early age. No matter what lotions or outward applications I used in order to elicit a hirsute covering for my head, I was unable to produce the desired effect. No amount of coaxing would induce my hair to grow, so at last I thought of an easy way out of the difficulty.

Why not wear a wig? Of course; the very thing!

Speedily the *toupée* of the latest style was ordered, and I was delighted with it when I tried it on for the first time.

This occurred previous to a spell of conducting in New York, and I thought it would be a good opportunity to adopt my new *coiffure.*

Alas, I was counting without Alboni, whose superstitious instinct was only equalled in intensity by her abhorrence of wigs!

We were tuning up in the artists' room, — the orchestra was getting over its momentary surprise at my novel appearance, — and I was beginning to feel quite com-

fortable in my new head-gear, when Alboni's laughing
face looked roguishly in at the door.

" *Où est Signor Arditi?* " she inquired of one of the
company.

" *Me voici,*" I cried, stepping forward rather shame-
facedly.

She stood looking at me for a moment, and then
burst into an uncontrollable fit of laughter.

" *Comment, Arditi,*" she exclaimed, " *c'est vous, avec
cette perruque-là? Jamais de la vie; voyons, mon bon
ami, je n'aurais jamais pu chanter avec cela devant moi;
allez!* " and with one bound she seized upon my unfortunate *toupée;* she dragged it off my head in spite of the
springs, which clung to me with excruciating persistency,
and threw it to the other side of the room !

So much for my wig; I never tried to wear another
one in public, although I often put it on at home in
the privacy of my humble rooms, and wondered, somewhat sadly, why the pleasure of wearing it should have
been denied to me. My wife tells me that I seem to
have clung to it with curious persistence, since it was
the uppermost object that revealed itself to her startled
gaze when she unpacked my portmanteau for the first
time after our marriage.

I forgot to mention that I composed an opera, " Il
Corsaro," in 1847, which was performed in Havana for
my benefit, Tedesco singing the principal *rôle.* My
first engagement with Marty came to an end in 1848,
whereupon Bottesini, Desverniné (a pianist), and I
visited the principal towns in the United States, giving
one or more concerts in each place. At the close of
1850 I had, however, again returned to my conductorship, under Marty's management, at Havana.

This season of 1850 had been a particularly brilliant
one, and in recognition of my services Marty most

generously made me a present of my first entire benefit performance. The sum produced thereby, amounting to 2,500 colonnati, was presented to me, and I, feeling as though I were a " made man," proudly deposited the money (it seemed such a pile, being all in *gold*) with great care in my trunk.

A friend drew my attention to the fact that it was highly injudicious to leave so large a sum carelessly packed in a trunk, and advised me to place the same in a bank without delay. This was on a Saturday. Taking my friend's counsel, I immediately packed the entire sum of gold into a bag and proceeded to take it to a firm of bankers which had been recommended to me. Alas, on my arrival there I found the bank closed. In order to be on the safe side, and fearing to take my money home again, I left the same with a broker of whom I had heard speak. My mind had been relieved, I felt no further responsibility, and so I hurried off to my rehearsal on the following morning (we were mounting Rossini's " Otello "), not giving the 2,500 " colonnati " another thought. Such is the semi-distraught, tangled condition of a musician's brain !

Picture, then, my amazement, my horror, when on the next day I opened a newspaper, and my eyes caught sight of the name of the broker who held my money in trust, and of the formal announcement of his sudden bankruptcy ! Oh, the mortification resulting from my folly on that occasion still causes me despair even now, after so great a lapse of time !

CHAPTER II.

IN 1851, after giving a concert in which Angiolina Bosio (of whom I shall speak later) and Bottesini joined me, we visited Trinidad, Matanzas, and Cienfuegos; I once more returned to New York, and was engaged by Maretzek as conductor of the Academy of Music.

Some of Francesco Marty's most excellent artists joined the company, such as Bosio, Geremia Bettini, Salvi, and a charming singer, Madame Bertucca, who made a successful appearance as Desdemona in Rossini's " Otello." Madame Bertucca created a great sensation in her rendering of "*Assisa al piè d' un salice*," the famous willow song, in which she accompanied herself upon the harp, and this certainly was as propitious an occasion for achieving a triumph as any musician could desire.

Later, she married her Impresario Maretzek, and her career, both as an intensely sympathetic singer and a harpist of considerable talent, was crowned with conspicuous good fortune.

I signed an engagement to accompany Alboni on an eight months' tour in 1852, after which I became joint Impresario with Madame Devries, an epoch I cannot look back upon with anything like pleasure or satisfaction. The position itself involves a terrible responsibility. Apart from the loss of money, and of one's normal allowance of good temper, an Impresario is compelled to make enormous sacrifices (*sous entendu* to the complete exclusion of his own interests) in order to bring about a satisfactory issue to his efforts.

We hear a great deal of abuse launched at Impresari in general; but I often wonder whether the public, who speak without any real knowledge of the circumstances connected with a musical fracas or disagreement, really know what some unfortunate Impresari have to contend with. I DO, and the vivid remembrance of what I suffered in that capacity has endowed me with a lenient and considerate feeling for those most harassed individuals.

However, I don't want to remember anything unpleasant just now. I think one ought to try to efface from the tablets of memory all the disagreeable events of one's life as though one's mind were a school-slate; I shall carry a damp sponge about with me. mentally in future, in order to obliterate every recollection that does not bear the gentle burden of a smile, or a tender thought wherewith to smooth and soothe my furrowed brow.

The happy reminiscences are not long in presenting themselves, I am glad to say, and here, for instance, is one which is particularly gratifying to me.

The manager of the Broadway Theatre in New York, Marshall by name, came to me one day during my conductorship of Italian Opera there in 1853, and the following conversation, as nearly as I can remember, took place between us: —

2

Marshall. Signor Arditi, I want you to do me a favour.

Arditi. Well, what is it?

Marshall. You must use your persuasive powers to induce Madame Alboni to sing " Norma."

Arditi. Dio mio, that 's a heavy order. How can you expect a singer who is now singing such a vastly different work as Rossini's " Cenerentola " to attempt " Norma "? Impossible, *caro mio;* she cannot do it. I will ask her, of course ; but I have no hope whatever of being successful.

Marshall, persuasively (are not *all* Impresari persuasive ?) Well, I guess you had better try, anyway. And I 'll tell you what, — the night you conduct " Norma " with Alboni, I 'll give you the handsomest bâton to be bought in New York. There! Now I 'll leave the rest to you.

He was off like a flash of lightning, and left me to my perturbed reflections. I wanted that bâton badly. Don't misunderstand me, though : I wanted to hear Alboni sing " Norma " still more badly; it was an artistic triumph which I greatly desired to see her achieve. I knew the extraordinary extent of her command over her vocal powers; her figure was not nearly so unwieldy as it afterwards became, and — well, to make a long story short, I went to see her and pointed out the success she would no doubt obtain. We tried the music over together, she permitted herself to be persuaded, and finally we produced " Norma " at the Broadway Theatre to an enthusiastic and delighted audience.

Marshall kept his word with regard to the bâton. I have it still ; it was a little work of art in its way. Beautiful as it was, however, I only conducted with it once in my life ; after that day I laid it reverently aside with countless other bâtons and souvenirs which have since been presented to me. The bâton was made of Malacca cane, with a topaz of great beauty set at the bottom of it, while at the other extremity a little golden Apollo playing on a harp headed an inscription alluding to the production of " Norma."

I was very proud of this bâton, and must have struck up the opening bars of the overture with unusual energy; at all events, the Apollo became loosened, and flew off straight in the direction of one of the members of the orchestra, striking him with terrific force on his bald head.

He looked piteously at me, but did not allow the accident to interfere with his share of the overture; and all through the first act my attentions were divided between my score of " Norma " and the hideous lump on the head of my unfortunate flute-player, which seemed to grow larger, and larger every minute. I was terribly concerned at this unexpected mishap, and made up my mind never to run such a serious risk again.

I remember also that when I took my seat in the orchestra the next evening vivid signs of uneasiness were manifest among my musicians, many of whom were looking askance at me, while they brushed and rubbed their handkerchiefs solicitously over their heads, wondering, perchance, which of them would be favoured that night with a burst of Apollo's violent attentions. I noticed, however, that they all smiled comfortably when I produced a perfectly plain and unornamented wand, which since that event I have invariably used.

Cutting from a New York paper on the occasion of Alboni's last appearance in America, October, 1852. — EDITOR.

MUSICAL — ALBONI'S LAST CONCERT.

The last concert of Madame Alboni, at Metropolitan Hall last night, was attended by an audience of some three thousand persons. The

Yes, Alboni's " Norma " was a very great success, and
I have often felt proud that I was the means of bringing to pass this great musical treat in America.

I must not forget to mention that in 1854 the celebrated Madame Henriette Sontag urged me to accompany her to Mexico on her concert tour. We were
at New Orleans at the time, and it was with a heavy
heart that I saw her, regardless of all remonstrance
on the part of her many friends, persist in undertaking
this ill-starred journey. Typhoid and cholera had been
raging at Mexico with unabating fury; but, alas, Sontag,
whose health had always been delicate, was not to be
dissuaded from her plans. I confess that the prospect
of this visit was horribly ominous to me at that time, —
so much so that I refused her offer to go with her as conductor. I went to see her off at the New Orleans Har-

programme, from the overture to the final rondo from " La Sonnambula,"
was executed to the largest satisfaction of the house. The cavatina, " Casta
Diva," from " Norma," was realised in all its beauty, appearing as good as
new, notwithstanding it has become almost as old as " Old Hundred." The
grand variations from Hummel drew down the house, however, with
greater emphasis, for here the thorough discipline, skill, flexibility, and compass were most strikingly exhibited, and its repetition was even more exquisitely done than that which at first appeared to be the involuntary perfection of
art. Sangiovanni and Rovere, it is quite enough to say, maintained their reputation, although there was no manifest attempt to rise above the standard which they have attained. Altogether it was a pleasant concert, not the
least agreeable features of which were the orchestra and chorus. The latter, by contrast, threw Alboni's voice into fine relief, like the full moon
shining among the stars.

ARDITI'S COMPOSITIONS.

Arditi's grand variations, entitled " Musical Difficulties Solved," expressly
composed for the greatest lyric artist living, our delicious Alboni, were repeated last night, and were received with unprecedented enthusiasm by the
large audience which filled the spacious hall. Little or nothing has yet
been ventured upon by the musical critics respecting this beautiful composition of the young *maestro*, probably for the reason that they have not felt
themselves equal to the task of criticising it as it deserves. It is necessary
to hear a new musical composition several times before even the most experienced critic can possibly analyse it. Now that we have been favoured

bour, and remember that her eyes were full of tears when she bade adieu to her many friends who were sadly wishing her good-bye and God-speed.

The last time she placed her hand in mine on parting, she said, raising her veil, " Not good-bye, Arditi, — *au revoir;* " but something seemed to predict to me, as she passed slowly out of sight, that we had indeed bidden her a final farewell.

It was during that fatal visit to Mexico that she was attacked with virulent cholera one night after a performance of " Lucrezia Borgia." She passed away after a few hours' illness, on the 17th of June, 1854, together with several members of her company, thus cutting short a brilliant artistic life which had hitherto been signalised by uncheckered prosperity and ever-growing fame.

with a repetition of it, we feel authorised to say that its author has achieved something never yet attempted by any of the great masters. Signor Arditi may well be proud of the effect produced by his really grand and magnificent composition. At the same time it is necessary to say that no one but the unrivalled Alboni could do justice to it; for no other singer in the world possesses the extent, volume, and flexibility of voice, and the perfect *gusto* of singing, the utmost resources of which she exhausts in this piece.

These variations were suggested by an original and graceful little song, upon which Arditi has founded a new world of musical thoughts and feelings, expressed with unwonted energy and fire. In fact, the production of these variations alone shows that Arditi is no common composer, but a *maestro consummato*. They are full of difficulties, and we almost trembled for Alboni when she commenced them; but the *maestro* had well studied the extraordinary range and power of the wonderful songstress, and the result proved that he had not over-estimated nor overtasked them. The effect of this splendid and unapproachable effort of vocal power and faultless execution was of the most enthusiastic nature, and was long noticeable among the excited audience. She ran through the most difficult passages with the greatest nonchalance; octaves, double octaves, and from *sol* to *si*♭ in the violin clef were all disposed of with equal facility, and convinced the almost frantic public that nothing in the way of musical difficulties can come amiss to her. Both *artiste* and *maestro* were most enthusiastically applauded, called before the audience, and received with tremendous cheers. Indeed, a greater or more gratifying triumph could not have been obtained.

My acquaintance with Henriette Sontag, the Countess Rossi, was not of long duration, for she only spent two years in the United States prior to her untimely death. In appearance she was *petite*, her hair was of an auburn tint, and her eyes were large, lustrous, and of a melting softness. Her voice was a soprano of delicately pure timbre, and her range, enabling her to reach the high E with perfect ease and power, was particularly fine in its upper notes.

HENRIETTE SONTAG.

She always impressed those who knew her with her marked individuality; for in spite of her comparatively humble origin — her father having been a tolerably good actor and her mother an actress of some small repute — she bore herself with the dignity and elegance of manner which was suitable and becoming to the wife of Count Rossi, a diplomatist of distinguished family. The romance of her life was concentrated in her devotion to her husband, which was most faithfully reciprocated. It was feared that the young count's brilliant future might be clouded by reason of his marriage; but her husband's appeal to obtain the sanction of his court to his union with Henriette Sontag was successful, the King of Prussia bestowing a patent of nobility upon her, so that she was thenceforth known as *née* de Launstein, and was obliged in return to give up her artistic life and accompany her husband to the Hague, where he represented the Sardinian court. For his sake she gladly relinquished her art, although she cherished the hope that she might not lose her lovely voice; and when later she and her husband met with disastrous reverses, which seriously impaired their fortunes, she bravely took up the thread of her work where she left it, eager to try her luck on the operatic stage again with a view to making money.

When she came to America, several years later, her voice and beauty were as fresh and delightful as they had been when she made her *début* in Paris as " Rosina " in 1826, and her completest success was achieved after her first appearance in the States. Berlioz once said of her: "*Elle est absolument la première dans son genre, mais son genre n'est pas le premier;*" and, indeed, her many sweet qualities, happily combined as they were and united to her admirable talent, won her the special favour and admiration of all the eminent musicians of her time.

MARIO.

The arrival of Grisi and Mario for the first time in America marks another most eventful epoch in my career.

I was engaged as conductor to their company, and it was with them that the New Academy of Music was inaugurated with the performance of " Norma."

Grisi was then in her prime, and was reputed to be very much like Pasta in appearance, only handsomer and more refined looking. From the waist upwards she was absolutely and perfectly beautiful. She, too, like many other singers I have known, may be described as having been a "bundle of nerves." Her love for Mario was so violent that she became a prey to fits of passion-ate jealousy at times. She was never envious of his artistic successes, but she could not bear the thought that he was being admired by other women, — a fact which undoubtedly was of con-tinual recurrence, for Mario was one of the finest and noblest-look-ing men of his epoch.

GRISI.

Mario had an ardent admirer in the person of a maiden lady of great fortune, who used to follow him about — at a certain distance, of course — in silent adora-tion. No matter when or where Mario was an-nounced to sing, the mysterious lady would infallibly apply for her box at the ticket office; and at night, as surely as I raised my bâton to conduct the music, I would see the gaunt, gray figure of a plain, unattractive woman, about thirty-five years of age, sitting bolt upright in her box.

It was not long ere Grisi discovered that Mario was the chief attraction to this eccentric lady, and with flaming cheeks and rage at her heart she watched her *bête noir* from behind the scenes, while the latter used to sit intently gazing at Mario with her sad, colourless eyes.

One day during a rehearsal Grisi could bear her worry no longer, so she poured her grief into my ears, and asked me to help her.

"What can I do?" I asked, smiling at her anger; "surely *you* have no cause to be jealous of such a plain, unattractive person?"

"She drives me *mad*," whispered Grisi, laying her hand on my arm, and pinching it black and blue; "I can't sing if that ghostly woman is in the house again to-night. . . ."

I tried to calm her with the assurance that the mysterious lady was only an intense lover of music, and that there was really no need to be alarmed about her; but Grisi was obviously much disconcerted at her continual presence in the theatre when Mario was announced to sing. I can still recall the flashing glances which Grisi used to launch at a particular box, — glances which, if looks could kill, ought to have withered the occupant by their scorching intensity.

Looking over some old paper cuttings, I have come upon the following, and subjoin it in order to show my readers that I have not exaggerated my account of Mario's admirer. This article was written in a New York paper, and after a little wholesome chaff at Mario, describes an evening at the opera. Speaking of the eccentric lady in question, it says: —

"Poor thing! everybody but Grisi must pity her in their hearts. There she sits, 'solitary and alone,' in her spacious box, dressed in the costliest of laces and brocades, perfectly indifferent to everything but Mario. The ladies of the chorus look curiously at her, lorgnettes are levelled towards the place where she sits from all parts of the house, and the bearded gentlemen of the orchestra look wonderingly up at her. But she heeds nobody; and when not looking over the fringe of her splendid fan, or through the parted petals of the white camellias of her bouquet, at the object of her burning passion, she sits like a sphinx, a tremendous riddle, which nobody has yet been able to solve. But we have lately had the pleasure of meeting a gentleman recently from London who knew her well and all her antecedents, from whom we learned the following particulars : —

" Her real name is Giles, not Gyles, as has been often said. She is a native of Gloucestershire, in England, and has lived some years in London, keeping house in a quiet way at the West End, and going but little into society, though a constant attendant at the opera and the theatres. Her income is but £2,000 a year, or $10,000, which is too small a sum to make a show with in London. At one time she conceived a passion for Charles Keen, whom she haunted in the same way she now haunts Mario, until happening to meet the latter she transferred her affections, and he has been the idol of her idolatry ever since. What will become of the poor lady when Mario retires into private life and goes to live on his estate in Italy, unless she should in the mean while find some other fascination, it is not easy to conceive. Perhaps some handsome Yankee may succeed in attracting her young affections, and put an end to her unhappy passion. It is said that while Mario was indisposed at the Metropolitan Hotel she used to call there every morning in her carriage, and when the waiter brought her word that Mario was better, she rewarded the lucky Mercury with a double eagle.

" The ' Musical World' says that a lady who came over in the same steamer with Grisi and Mario relates that Mario's affectionate shadow (the hypothetical Miss ' Coutts') followed him on the embarkation, and alighted upon the deck of the steamer, arrayed in a lilac-coloured silk, with flounces embellished with feather trimming, over the whole of which was work-lace. Upon her head was a fragile breath of a bonnet, trimmed with orange blossoms. The lady advanced to the saloon, placed her hat in the hands of her maid, and reclined gracefully upon a lounge, whereupon the maid covered her with lace. A lady passenger entered into conversation with her, and asked if she did not think Mario was handsome. Thereupon she burst into a fit of laughter so contagious that everybody in the saloon was constrained to laugh with her.

" Grisi afterwards playfully said that she wished a committee of gentlemen would incontinently drop her into the sea; adding, more earnestly, however, that she really had for her the ' evil eye.' She had followed them wherever they went, — had gone with them to St. Petersburg. Twice, in such instances, had they met with comparative failure. If they failed in the United States it might be ascribed to the same ' evil eye.' "

Mario, it must be added, was curiously impervious to such flattering attentions, and was for his part most devoted to Grisi.

I have seldom seen an artist more felicitously gifted by nature than was Mario with beauty of face and figure, elegance of bearing, and amiability of temperament. His style and method of song was purely Italian, although he told me himself that he had not devoted much time to study. His masters had been Michelet, Ponchard, and Bordogni, the last-named a famous singing-master; and in spite of his want of experience on the stage, his innate artistic feeling, his delicious voice and particularly winning manner won the hearts of his audiences immediately.

A capital story occurs to me in connection with the vicissitudes to which artists are often subjected.

It was during my first long stay in America, and our company was announced for one night, during a terribly cold winter, at Washington. Shall I ever forget the bitter cold of that season? It was as though we had suddenly been transported to the Arctic regions; and the theatre in which we gave our performance was as inadequate to cope with the frost as though we had fixed up a summer tent for the purpose. " Norma " was the

opera; and Grisi, instead of appearing in her traditional
white robe with flowing folds, was compelled to come on
the stage wearing a huge fur cloak in which she was
huddled up almost to her eyes.

The house only really rose to the occasion with loud
bursts of laughter when Mario made his entrance holding
a coachman's umbrella over his head, — he, as Pollio,
being confronted by Norma in their tragical meeting,
— under which prosaic safeguards both artists cowered
while singing their grand duo.   The roof of the theatre
had given way under the weight of a heavy fall of snow,
and its coating of ice, melting under the heat of the gas,
was streaming down on the artists.

I have treasured a long and pleasant remembrance
of the hours I spent later on in London in the society
of Mario and Grisi, which, like that of Alboni, will serve
me as I gradually unfold my reminiscences.

In 1855 I was engaged by Madame La Grange, and
Mirate the tenor, to conduct opera for the season in
New York, and during that period several important
works were produced.   My opera " La Spia," founded on
Fenimore Cooper's novel, was performed in the spring
of 1856 for the first time at the Academy of Music, and
was given for five nights consecutively.   Madame La
Grange, Mdlle. Hensler (who afterwards became a mor-
ganatic wife of the King of Portugal), and Signor Brignoli
were in the cast.

One evening during this season " Lucia " was announced, and as
Signor Arditi climbed up to his seat to commence the opening bars of
the prelude, it was discovered at the last moment that all the band parts
were missing, evidently purloined by a trick that had been arranged on the
part of the opposition house.

The *maestro* did not, however, lose his presence of mind, and without a
moment's hesitation he took his seat and struck the first few opening bars
on his little piano. The orchestra followed suit, and played the entire
first act from memory, for which courageous action the audience applauded
vociferously as soon as they became aware of the *contretemps*. — EDITOR.

Madame La Grange, as the tragical mother of " The Spy," was very impressive, both as to her singing and acting, and all the other parts were admirably sustained to my complete satisfaction.

" La Spia " was never performed in England, owing to the nature of the subject ; but the song " Colli nativi " became very popular in after years, and was sung by Mongini and almost every tenor of note, Brignoli and Giuglini included, the last-named artist often introducing it into various operas.

If I have not hitherto alluded to my excellent friend Madame La Grange in a more than cursory manner, it is not because I have forgotten her merits, but rather because a propitious occasion for this pleasurable task has been tardy in presenting itself.

Of this admirable artist's qualities and gifts as a singer my readers are probably aware. For many years she enjoyed a long and well-merited reputation on the Continent, and later on she obtained a considerable and lasting recognition in England. She was undoubtedly a great acquisition to Her Majesty's

I subjoin the Dedication to Wm. H. Paine, Esq., Director of the Academy of Music. — EDITOR.

Dear Sir, — With your kind permission, I desire to dedicate to you my first operatic essay, and that on a truly American subject, — Fenimore Cooper's " Spy." The public of America in general, and the dilettanti of New York in particular, owe you a deep debt of gratitude for your energetic exertions in endeavouring to establish Italian Opera as a fixed and permanent fact in our midst. Your time, your talent, and your purse have alike been devoted to carrying out this one great idea; and if the patronage of the public did not at first respond to your efforts, I have reason to believe that it has now learned to appreciate them, and that your liberality, gentlemanly courtesy, and untiring desire to promote the cause of the lyric drama will meet with its well-merited reward,— a more brilliant and prosperous operatic career than has been awarded to any previous director.

I have the honor to remain,

Yours very obediently,

LUIGI ARDITI.

Theatre under Lumley's management, and it can only be regretted that such exceptional talent should have been brought into prominence at the time when persistent ill-luck so relentlessly blighted the career of that admirable institution.

To me 1856 was fraught with stirring interest and incident, for it was the year of my marriage to Virginia, daughter of William S. Warwick, of Richmond, Virginia. Her dear companionship throughout my eventful career has been a great help to me in smoothing many a stormy wave of strife, and in teaching me how to " trim my sails " and to keep an ever watchful lookout for a favourable breeze that might haply waft me into peaceful havens.

A criticism of " La Spia," from " The Dispatch," 1856. — EDITOR.

" LA SPIA."

We rarely agree with the musical critic of the " Dispatch," nor is he a favourite of ours. This, however, will not prevent our giving him credit whenever he deserves it. We copy, therefore, what he says of Arditi's new opera : —

"With no small pleasure we listened yesterday, for a couple of hours, to extracts from Signor Arditi's new work of ' La Spia ' (The Spy), a lyrical drama, in three acts (after Cooper's novel of that name), libretto by Filippo Manetta. Although we have, for years past, fully appreciated Signor Arditi's great talents as an artist and conductor, we never believed him so great, genial, and clever a composer as this opera proves him to be. To the dash and brilliancy of Verdi he unites the flowing harmonies of Donizetti, and the *savoir faire* of Meyerbeer's effects. The subject of this opera, as the reader may know, is strictly American ; and it is so treated, brilliantly and tellingly so. In the introduction, and sometimes repeated in the course of the opera, is a martial liberty chorus for which we predict the most extensive popularity. There is a beautiful and artistic quintette, without accompaniment, which the best living composer might be proud of. There is a soldier's march and chorus, with fife and drum accompaniment, as quaint and clever as it is original. There are a *finale* to the first act, a mother's malediction, one or two prayers, and some duos, which are perfect gems ; and the truly artist-like way in which the melody of ' Hail Columbia ' is worked in with the last grand *finale* of the opera, will, we are sure, create a *furore* on its production. But we must not, just yet, give a description of the work."

To her I owe much gratitude for the careful and untiring way in which she has helped me to preserve my reminiscences, which I fear, without a wife's loving

Virginia Arditi

and unselfish care, would have failed me at this important moment. We were married on the 20th June, 1856, and sailed for Liverpool on the morning of the 21st. Our voyage, which occupied exactly fourteen days, was considered to be an excellent passage, and we arrived in London, having thoroughly enjoyed a tranquil, unbroken spell of bliss, unclouded and unmarred by any infelicitous occurrence. There was a French hotel in Leicester Square situated to the left of the present site of the Alhambra, called the " Sablonière," where we stayed, but not for a very long period, for we moved to Golden Square a few days later, and there occupied the apartments formerly tenanted by the famous singer Rubini.

It was interesting to me to watch the effect on my wife of the sudden plunge into the vortex of artistic and musical life; the rough-and-tumble, roving career of a musician, with its unsettled, changeful aspects, was one, of course, affording a new and exciting experience to her.

We had brought many letters of introduction with us from America, addressed to some of the very highest and most distinguished members of the art world in London, and were received with that generous hospitality and courteous kindness that always characterises the English.

Our trip to London was purely one of pleasure, and on that occasion we saw more of the metropolitan sights than we did during all the subsequent years, after England had become our home.

Opera for that year had been transferred to the Lyceum Theatre, in consequence of Covent Garden having been burnt to the ground during the night succeeding a masked ball given by the " Wizard Anderson," and there we witnessed a grand performance of " Rigoletto " with Bosio, Mario, Ronconi, and Nantier-Didiée, which was superbly conducted by Costa, and which, for all-round excellence, it would be

Bosio

hard to surpass even now. Angiolina Bosio had, at that time, just reached the summit of her fame, and was tremendously sought after by the *élite* of the *beau monde*.

Bosio's appearance was full of contradictions. Her face was intelligent and gay in character, her eyes were bright, her figure winsome, and yet one could not have called her handsome, — no, not even pretty; but she was most attractive, notwithstanding, by reason of her excellent stage appearance.

Virginia had never seen Bosio off the stage, and had pictured her as a dignified, elegant, and supremely beautiful woman, commanding in her gestures and cold in her demeanour. I shall never forget her amazement and shocked expression of countenance when, one evening at a dinner given at her house, Bosio pulled out a snuff-box, together with a huge — not particularly clean — bandana handkerchief, and straightway helped herself to a hearty pinch of snuff.

Violetta, in "La Traviata," was one of Bosio's most remarkable performances. She met, however, with extraordinary success as "Elvira," in "I Puritani," and perhaps it was in this opera that she reached the highest point in her career, during one of Gye, senior's, seasons at Covent Garden in 1852. Grisi had been cast for the *rôle* of "Elvira," but she, for some reason, had declined to sing.

Bosio being available, seized her opportunity, and made such an irresistible appeal to the susceptible hearts of her audiences that her deliciously fresh voice remained enshrined in their memories for ever afterwards, and she was, there and then, added to the number of the chief stars glittering in the operatic firmament.

CHAPTER III.

IN August, 1856, after a pleasant sojourn in London, during which we became very intimate with Grisi and Mario, my wife and I went to Paris, where we renewed our friendship with Tedesco and Alboni, who received us with open-hearted kindness and hospitality during our brief stay in that city. Thence we proceeded to Milan, taking the St. Gothard route, where I presented my wife for the first time to my parents. We made a trip to Crescentino in Piedmont, my birthplace, at this period, and it was with very keen interest that I went over the old ground of my childhood, seeing the associates of my boyish days, who, like myself, had grown up to manhood, and visiting the dear old house where I was born, with its old-fashioned gardens, by that time, alas, grown wild through continued neglect.

My wife could not then speak Italian, and the French spoken among the Piedmontese was primitive, to say the least of it. Our arrival caused no little excitement among the villagers, who had known me as a little child, some of whom rushed forward to meet us with outstretched hands, while others stood deeply engrossed in watching the new arrivals who had come " all the way across the Atlantic," and said to one another in awe-stricken whispers, while gazing at Virginia, " *Come, viene dall' America, e non è nera?* . . ." [1]

My arrival in Milan was speedily followed by several offers of professional engagements. My consideration was divided between the proposed conductorship at the Teatro del Oriente in Madrid, Teatro Reggio in Turin, and the Theatre Naum, in Constantinople, of which three offers I chose the last, as it was not only the most lucrative proposal that had been put before me, but it also afforded me the opportunity of seeing something of Eastern life and its manners and customs. Consequently I accepted the six months' engagement for Constantinople, and prior to starting in September for the East we visited Turin and Venice.

It had always been my wife's wish and ambition to visit the latter lovely city, and, indeed, the night of our arrival was so idealistic that I will venture to let her describe her own impressions of that occasion in her own womanly way. I subjoin the letter which she penned to Mrs. Warwick after our trip to Venice, in which she also describes our subsequent arrival at Constantinople : —

August 31st, 1856.

MY DEAREST MOTHER, — Congratulate me with all your heart, for at last my fondest wish has been realised, — I have seen Venice !

Oh, mother, you can't think how beautiful and romantic our arrival was !

A gondola, guided by a handsome young Venetian, who was standing in the stern of his boat, conveyed us and our luggage to the hotel.

---

[1] " What ! you have come all the way from America, and are not black ? "

I could not make up my mind to go to bed until I had persuaded Luigi to take me to see the Bridge of Sighs; and there
I stood, watching the strange, fantastic scene, while I pictured to
myself some of the sufferings of body and mind that had been
undergone by the poor doomed wretches who had passed over
it when bidding the world an eternal good-bye.

The streets are full of picturesque suggestions. The shops,
the houses, the enchanting colours and dresses of the Venetians,
— all the aspects of Venice are calculated to awaken one's sense
of the ideal.

Our week spent in the lovely sea-girt isle seemed to me to be
a dream of passing enchantment, and we left this exquisite spot
with the utmost regret.

September was drawing to a close when we started for Constantinople from Trieste, spending a day at Corfu.

On the morning of our arrival in the magnificent Golden
Horn, the sun shone brilliantly on the gleaming minarets and
spires of the gorgeous mosques. This gave us a foresight of
Oriental luxury as we had pictured it to ourselves; but, alas
for the fond hopes that were engendered by distance, which lent
a *great deal* of enchantment to our view, and by the glorious
sunshine which made all dazzle and glitter under its magic rays.
No sooner had we set foot in Stamboul, the ancient part of
Constantinople, than the miserable squalor of our surroundings
made itself apparent.

Our destination was Pera, the European quarter; and when
we discovered, to our dismay, that vehicles were unknown luxuries in those parts, we were compelled to tramp up an inter-
minably steep hill, preceded by extremely odoriferous hamals,
who carried our luggage on their shoulders, while swarms of
wretchedly hungry outcast dogs followed us closely.

At last we reached the opera house, and were ushered into
the presence of the brothers Naum, the Impresari, who, to do
them justice, were apologetic with regard to the conspicuous
absence of carriages, while explaining that those used by the
ladies of the harem were constructed without springs, and consequently quite impossible for us to use.

We were tired out from our voyage, and being requested to
be seated in a semicircle, were regaled with a white sweetmeat,

which, handed to one on a spoon, together with a glass of water, reminded me of nothing so much as the powders of my childhood.

The brothers Naum are Armenians, and have become sincerely attached to Luigi already. They are doing all they can to make us comfortable, but we are surrounded by a fearfully rowdy set of Italians, who are capable of any outrage if Luigi does not accede to their demands.

Our apartments are quite close to the theatre, whither I wend my way in fear and trembling lest we should be shot at "from round the corner," as it has been hinted to us more than once will be the case if we excite the ire of any of our bloodthirsty *compagnons de théâtre*.

We are certainly experiencing a great deal of anxiety and discomfort in consequence of the bad food, the dirt, and, I grieve to say, the fleas! Over the latter horrible affliction I must draw a veil; it is better imagined than described.

Some very charming people, called Fossati, have tendered us the utmost hospitality here, and are introducing us to the Russian and Italian embassies.

The opera company is very good on the whole, and [1] the *prime donne*, among whom are Donatelli and Murio Celli, are all public favourites. The latter was chosen to sing before the Sultan.

The performances are always well attended. Smoking, contrary to our custom in America, is allowed during the performance, and it greatly amuses me to watch the ladies of the harem peeping timidly out of their *loges grillées*.

The Sultan, Abdul Medjid, never comes to the opera now, since one night he and his suite were alarmed by the news that a murder had been committed within the precincts of the building. His Majesty, entertaining a horror of bloodshed, has since preferred to command the presence of artists in his palace for the purpose of giving selections of operatic music.

The other day the Sultan sent for Luigi and his orchestra, and we all adjourned to the palace at the appointed hour.

---

[1] Murio Celli (now a celebrated teacher of singing in New York) is a devoted friend of both Signor and Madame Arditi. He often speaks of her conspicuous success in "Norma" and "Luisa Miller" during our season in Constantinople. — EDITOR.

Imagine my surprise when informed that I should not be admitted to the performance, and that I should have to wait for Luigi in the visitors' drawing-room! That was too much to bear, mother. Fancy an American woman allowing herself to be " sat upon " by a Turk! I instantly resolved to enter the music room by hook or by crook, and, quietly awaiting my opportunity, I successfully squeezed myself into the glittering *salon* with the aid of the player of the double bass, behind whose instrument I practically hid myself. Was not that a triumph?

Through the whole performance I sat within a very short distance of the Sultan, and of the grating behind which the members of his harem were ranged, whose flashing jewels were, alas! all that I could see, owing to the closeness of the bars.

Luigi looked splendid in his fez, and was requested to play several violin solos, which were encored by the imperial party, and gave so much pleasure to the Sultan that he sent his drago-man, or Oriental interpreter, to Luigi, requesting him to salute his Imperial Majesty according to Turkish fashion, a very elaborate undertaking.

At the end of the performance exquisite coffee and sweets were served to us in cups and plates of pink enamel, which were positively studded with diamonds and other precious jewels. I must own I thoroughly enjoyed my visit to the palace, in spite of the angry glances cast at me by some of the eunuchs, whose appreciation of our sex appears to be of the lowest order.

A few days after the entertainment at the palace Luigi was presented with the diploma and order of the Medjedié, in recognition of the gratification he had afforded to the Sultan. . . .

Luigi has just completed a cantata which he has written expressly for and dedicated to the Sultan. The words are in the Turkish language, and the vocalists who have been engaged to sing it before the Sultan next week seem to have some difficulty in mastering them. After the event has taken place I will write again. Things are looking brighter, and, above all, Luigi is happy in his work, giving satisfaction to everybody, and endearing himself more and more every day to his wife, who adores him. . . . Can I say more?

.After the opera season is over I will let you know our plans for the future; until then, God bless you.

Your loving daughter,

VIRGINIA.

After the close of the opera season in Constantinople we lingered a while there, enjoying the weather, which was deliciously warm and balmy, and visiting many lovely spots on the verdant banks of the Bosphorus.

The brothers Naum were anxious to re-engage me for another year of opera in the Turkish capital; but my wife, who had borne all our petty worries and discomfitures with excellent temper, patience, and fortitude, felt, as well as I, that we had endured enough hardships during our sojourn amid Oriental life and surroundings, and we accordingly decided to return to Italy.

It was during our stay in Milan, in 1857, that we first met Madame Puzzi, who was for so many years the right hand and most judicious adviser of Mr. Benjamin Lumley, the then manager of Her Majesty's Theatre in London.

That chance encounter with one of the cleverest and most energetic women of the day — whose *salon* was the rendezvous of the fashionable and musical world in London — probably, nay, undoubtedly, influenced our future destination to a very great extent.

During the long subsequent friendship and affection which subsisted between Madame Puzzi, her dear daughters, and ourselves, Madame Puzzi was always the friend to whom we turned for advice when we had strayed or lost our way along the tortuous and intricate paths of professional life.

Not long after our above-mentioned meeting — it must have been about a month or six weeks — I received a telegram from Mr. Lumley, offering me an engagement in London. According to his proposal, which, if I intended to accept it, required me to leave Milan almost at a moment's notice, it was thought advisable by my family to leave Virginia in Milan until my plans should be matured ; consequently I started for London alone, and on my arrival was almost immediately sent in the company of Signor Brizzi (who for the time being was representing Mr. Lumley in Ireland) to Dublin.

Here I was placed at the head of an orchestra which, at that time, was comparatively unfamiliar with Italian operatic music. Brizzi, who was one of the most charming and talented musicians it has been my good fortune to meet, used to say that he was the first man who introduced me to the British public. I may add that my task in Dublin was a hard and toilsome one, requiring much patience and energy, and I feel that it was greatly due to my perseverance in Ireland that I established my subsequent position with Mr. Lumley in a comparatively short time.

Maria Piccolomini, the Tuscan *prima donna*, was then at the beginning of her brief but brilliant career, having scored a decided success in the " Traviata." Her voice was the subject of much controversy, for some people asserted that its quality was weak and its register limited ; but I found it fresh and juvenile, her personality agreeable and full of charm, and her acting on the stage exceedingly realistic.

For a time the rage she created in London spread like wildfire. It became contagious. Every one was talking about the romantic details connected with her operatic career,[1] while her youth, beauty, and piquant manner insured her a favourable reception wherever

---

[1] Piccolomini became a singer and artist against the wishes of her family, and was compelled to resort to stratagem in order to arrive at her heart's desire. — EDITOR.

she sang. From the moment of her *début* at Her Majesty's Theatre, its fortunes were secure for the season.

Her vocalisation, notwithstanding her immense success, was far from being perfect. She knew this herself, and was not blind or deaf to her own shortcomings. Modesty was one of her charms, and I recollect an incident illustrative of this very characteristic.

One night after she had achieved a great hit in "L'Elisir d'Amore," some of her ardent admirers made an attempt to drag her carriage home; but not having been in really good voice that night, and feeling that such an honour would be misapplied, she had the tact and spirit to protest against a doubtful

PICCOLOMINI.

triumph, and, veiled and unrecognised, she escaped in a cab from the crowd that surrounded her carriage.

People used often to ask themselves, "What is the secret of Piccolomini's charm?" Wherein lies her attractive power? It must have been the indescribable *chic* of her appearance, the melting liquid of the clear brown eyes, the little coquettish toss of her graceful head that fascinated every one. Piccolomini's attractions lay not so much in her talents as in the fascination of her whole being, and in the display of pathos, which, at times, was wonderfully genuine, and unquestionably superior to any kind of art.

A French critic once described her characteristically. He said : " She sings with infinite charm, but she is not a cantatrice. She acts with great talent, but is not an actress. She is a problem — an enigma. . . ."

GIUGLINI.

The great tenor, Giuglini, at this time also penetrated the hearts of his audiences with the subtle fascination of his exquisite voice. People were fairly entranced with his singing, and hung upon his notes as though spell-bound, awaking only to overwhelm him with applause.

I have always found the English public placid and self-contained in the matter of new artists, but Giuglini instantly dispelled all doubts that might have been raised as to his right to be considered a singer of the very first calibre, and thus it happened that when on that memorable night of April 14th, 1857, he appeared for the first time at Her Majesty's Theatre as Fernando, in " La Favorita," he was at once established as a tenor almost unrivalled since the brilliant days of Rubini, and was placed on a pedestal from which he was never subsequently deposed.

I must not forget to mention the first performance of " The Bohemian Girl " given in Italian, entitled, " La Zingara," which was produced under the immediate superintendence of the composer Balfe. Giuglini, Piccolomini, and Belletti were the principal artists. As usual, we were restricted as to the number of our rehearsals, and at the last of all Balfe came to me agitatedly, exclaiming, " My dear Arditi, that opera will *never* be produced to-morrow night ! " I did my best to allay his fears, promising to have an extra rehearsal with orchestra and second parts on the following morning. The performance took place as announced, and Balfe, overjoyed at our brilliant success, embraced me with a combination of Irish and Italian fervour, allotting to me the triumphs of the evening for having surmounted all the difficulties appertaining to the hasty production.

Piccolomini and Giuglini achieved great successes in their respective parts; but I do remember that on one occasion the *prima donna's* patience gave way owing to a little fit of jealousy. Giuglini's rendering of the song, " When other lips and other hearts," was so exquisite that he was invariably encored.

At the time of Giuglini's great social and artistic triumphs in London, a gentleman, very much resembling him in face and figure, used to pass himself off as the great singer.

On one occasion Giuglini's double obtained an *entrée* to a distinguished house under pretence of being the artist, and was invited to a large dinner which was to be given in his honour. Giuglini, hearing the facts of the case, made inquiries as to the name of the people who had been duped, ascertained their address, and suddenly appeared on the scene like a skeleton at the feast, at the moment when the *soirée* was at its height. — EDITOR.

On this particular evening *one* encore was not sufficient for the public, and Piccolomini, whose part obliges her to remain listening to his love song on the stage, grew weary of the reiterated calls for a repetition, and calmly fetched a chair and sat herself down, with a resigned look on her face, much to Giuglini's disgust.

Lumley's provincial Operatic Company subsequently visited the provinces, and among other towns were Manchester, Liverpool, Birmingham, etc., the tour lasting until the end of October, 1857.

At the approach of Christmas I determined to send for my wife, who, it will be remembered, remained in Milan at the time when Mr. Lumley first summoned me to London. Having anxiously awaited my signal to join me, she started for England on receipt of my telegram, only to find, much to her dismay, that a company had suddenly been organised for Germany. Piccolomini, Giuglini, Aldighieri were among the stars of this company, and we visited Berlin, Amsterdam, Rotterdam, Dresden, and Hamburg, etc., remaining abroad until close upon Christmas Day.

Our *tournée* was not destined to be of long duration. Notwithstanding the artistic success we met with everywhere, — and here I must say, in parenthesis, that the German orchestras were excellent wherever we went, and that I have always been excessively proud of the praise bestowed upon my conducting by German musicians, — it was rumoured that the financial state of Germany was uneasy, banks were described as being "shaky," and consequently the tour, which otherwise might have been extended until the spring, came to an abrupt close. Lumley having wired us to "return to Liverpool without delay," the entire company embarked for England, and on our arrival at Liverpool we gave a performance of "Traviata" without a single rehearsal!

In 1858 a very important event in the history of Her Majesty's Theatre took place, namely, the marriage of the Princess Royal Victoria, in honour of which occasion three festival performances were given, — " Macbeth,' the music of which was conducted by Mr. Benedict; " The Rose of Castille," conductor, Mr. Alfred Mellon ; and " La Sonnambula," conducted by myself.

" Macbeth " was arranged and given under the management of Mr. Charles Marshall.

At the conclusion of the tragedy acclamations resounded all over the house, and her Majesty the Queen, with the Prince Consort, the Princess Royal, and the then Prince of Prussia, graciously acknowledged the display of loyalty by rising and bowing with a smiling countenance to the enthusiastic audience.

The second festival performance took place on the following Thursday, the 21st, and was superior to that of the preceding Tuesday.

Balfe's " Rose of Castille," with Louisa Pyne as Elvira and Harrison as Manuel, was given, and went off with an *élan* and brilliancy that delighted every one present.

The Queen, the Prince Consort, and her illustrious visitors appeared to be well pleased with the acting and singing, and when the final curtain had dropped and risen once more, the whole operatic company was discovered on the stage, Mr. Alfred Mellon raised his bâton, and the National Anthem was given with the accompaniment of full chorus.

" La Sonnambula," with Piccolomini and Giuglini as Amina and Elvino, completed the trio of festival nights on the 23rd of January.

It was Piccolomini's first attempt to play Amina, and considering the difficulties of the part, and the brilliancy and power required to sustain the *rôle*, she acquitted herself more than creditably.

Giuglini's Elvino was, in many respects, one of his most remarkable achievements, and, if anything, reached an even higher pitch of favour than on the night of his *début*.

The gathering was a brilliant one, the orchestra and artists combining to give the highest satisfaction, and Her Majesty the Queen, who appeared to be delighted with the performance, gave evident signs of her satisfaction by her gracious smiles and bows.

TITIENS.

The next important event was the *début* of Mademoiselle Thérèse Titiens, the afterwards celebrated German soprano, which took place on April 13th, 1858, in " The Huguenots."

Giuglini was to be Raoul de Nangis, and Titiens Valentine; and owing to the wonderful rumours which had already reached the English shores concerning her, the tension and excitement which prevailed both before and behind the scenes on that occasion was such that no one who was present will ever forget.

Mr. Lumley very generously kept a box in reserve for the three nights of the festival performances at Her Majesty's Theatre for the wives of the artists and their friends. Fifty pounds was offered him on each occasion if he would sell it, but he steadfastly refused to disappoint the ladies, and consequently lost £150 by his magnanimous conduct. — EDITOR.

Mr. Lumley came to the artists' room shortly before the curtain was raised, and informed the company that Her Majesty would be present. Titiens and Giuglini were both horribly nervous; and the former, who was evidently labouring under a supreme effort to be calm, clasped her hands convulsively, and whispered: " The Queen will be there; Heaven grant that nothing will occur to spoil our success! . . ."

Far from their success being marred, I can't recall a more fully triumphant result than that of the 13th of April. Titiens' fine dramatic presence and imposing voice struck home at once; and ere she had sung half a dozen pages of music, significant looks passed amongst the audience, murmurs of approval grew into exclamations of pleasure, and when that never-to-be-forgotten high C, in the finale of the first act, soared high and brilliantly above the other voices and orchestra, a roar and thunder of applause broke forth from the whole house that has seldom been equalled before or since.

Titiens established her fame that night once and for all; and the greatest care and elaboration had been spent in doing every possible justice to the German *maestro's* work, and a venture which, to all appearances, at first was hazardous, proved an enormous and brilliant success, and Her Majesty's Theatre added yet another name to the list of her triumphant vocalists.

CHAPTER IV.

THE curtain had fallen on the last act of "The Huguenots," and had terminated the protracted season of 1858. It had fallen, moreover, upon the last performance destined to be directed by the able and judicious hand of Benjamin Lumley.

Her Majesty's Theatre was thereafter doomed, for want of capital, to remain closed for two years; and since I, as well as several of the "stars," was still engaged to Lumley under contract, we were "let out" to touring companies, of one of which Willert Beale was manager; and thus, in the spring of 1859, he sent an operatic company, of which I was nominated conductor, to Ireland.

At the head of our programme stood such attractive names as Mario, Grisi, and Viardot, sufficient in themselves to warrant successful performances for us in spite of our oft-times inadequate orchestras. It must be borne in mind that at the epoch of my first visit to Dublin

Italian operatic music had been little practised there; hence the difficulties and wearying rehearsals which we had to undergo for many hours a day, lasting in some cases until shortly before the curtain rose.

On the occasion of the production of Verdi's "Macbeth" in Dublin, the whole performance was so far from being perfect that all the singers and members of the orchestra had to remain hard at work in the theatre from early morn until the last available moment.

Madame Viardot filled the *rôle* of Lady Macbeth, and her performance was a very remarkable one. There was a picturesque weirdness about her appearance, a quiet, mysterious calm that excited a good deal of comment when she first appeared on the boards.

Her knowledge of music, too, and love for her art, as well as her deep interest in all matters connected with creative genius, were extraordinary. I cherish, and am delighted to reproduce here, in facsimile, a wonderful letter she once wrote to me *à propos* of her wishes respecting the transposition of an opera, — a letter which was illustrative of her clear knowledge of notation and composition, as well as of her lucidity in dealing in a practical way with the parts which she required to be transposed: —

4

28 Rue de Douai
15 Marzo. 1859

Caro Maestro,

Ecco le transposizioni che fo' nella antichissima parte di Lady Macbeth. La più difficile, quella che domanderà qualche cambiamento nell'istrumentazione sarà quella della cavatina. L'andante ℳ recit.va in Re bemol, l'andante "Vieni t'affretta" in Si b, ed l'allegro "Or tutti sorgete" in Re b, per conseguenza il tutto una 3ª minore sotto. Non è male! tutto il resto dell'atto come è scritto. La cabaletta "trionfai" non si canta. Nell'atto 2do Scena del banchetto, ci vorrà una passata dopo le ultime battute del coro che finisce con le parole "come ci detta il cor" per

attaccare al brindisi in la bemol
L'Allegro si fa come scritto in
fa (dopo la scena col sicario).
Per la 2.da strofa del brindisi si
passa un tono sotto 5 battute
prima del Brindisi, mettendo
la bemol nell'accordo di fà che
precede.

il Brindisi lieto di nuo-vo u...

e siamo sulla strada di <u>la bemol</u>

finito la replica del Brindisi, o
bisognerà fare una passata per
arrivare alla settima battuta
(All.^o agitato)
dove ci ritroviamo in la
oppure si potrebbe subito prendere
quella battuta sul "va!" di Macbett,
cioè tagliando le sei prime.

La scena del Sonnambulismo un
Tono sotto — c'est a dire ritornello
e Recit.ᵛᵒ in mi b minore — e l'and.ᵗᵉ
in si maggiore — Mi par di veder
l'orchestra fare la grimace alla
vista orribile "dei bei 66666 e dei cinque ######!
Caro maestro, bisognerà far
copiare le parti di questi tre pezzi
perché l'orchestra che avremo non
ama a trasportare ... che il pubblico.

Molto mi dispiace che non
sarà con noi la di lei amabilis-
-sima consorte, alla quale
le prego di dar my kindest
love. Sarei stato veramente
enchanté di vederla — Non
mi fermerò affatto a Londra.
Vi ... caro

[Facsimile of handwritten letter in Italian]

TRANSLATION.

15th March, 1859.

CARO MAESTRO, — Here are the transpositions which I am making in the part of Lady Macbeth. The most difficult of all, which will necessitate certain changes in the instrumentation, will be that of the *Cavatina*. The recitative in D flat, the Andante, " Vieni, t' affretta " in B flat, and the Allegro " Or tutti sorgete " in D flat, consequently the whole scene must be a minor third lower. Not bad! All the rest of the act may be given as written. The *cabaletta* " Trionfai " is not sung.

In the banquet scene (Act II.) there must be a transition from the concluding phrase of the chorus finishing with the words " Come," etc., in order to get into A flat, the key of the drinking song. The Allegro as written in F. For the second verse of the *Brindisi* it must be taken a whole tone lower, five beats before beginning the melody, by inserting A flat into the preceding chord of F ; thus : —

(*Vide facsimile.*)

In this way we approach the key of A flat.

After the repeat of the *Brindisi*, a transition must be introduced at the seventh beat of the Allegro Agitato, where we again find ourselves in the key of F major.

.   .   .   .

(*Vide facsimile*.)

Or we might take the beat of Macbeth's "Va!" exercising the six previous beats.

The sleep-walking scene must be a tone lower; that is, the melody and recitative in E flat minor, and the Andante in B major. I fancy I see your orchestra making faces at the horrible aspect of the six double flats and five double sharps! Dear maestro, you must have the parts of these numbers copied, because the orchestra we shall have only likes to transpose (transport) the public.

I'm so sorry that your amiable wife will not be with us; give her my kindest love; I should have been charmed to see her. I shall make no stay in London. *Au revoir, cher maître.* If I should be incomprehensible, write to tell me so, and I will endeavour to make myself clearer to you.

Believe me, dear Signor Arditi,

Yours ever affectionately,

(Signed)   PAULINE VIARDOT.

But to return. The final rehearsal of "Macbeth" augured no good results at first; but the unwonted energy and really eager perseverance that every one exhibited on that occasion led us to hope at seven o'clock — when we all parted to rush in search of sandwiches and of liquids wherewith to moisten our parched throats — that we stood a good chance, after all, of pulling the opera through safely. And so we did. Viardot's wonderful voice and artistic singing were alluded to in enthusiastic terms in all the leading papers, and the orchestra, having collected its scattered wits, acquitted itself very creditably on the whole.

A funny incident occurred that night during the performance, and one which, although it had well-nigh escaped my memory, is worthy of record. In the sleep-walking scene of Lady Macbeth, when the nurse and the doctor appear on the stage together and confabulate with one another, a loud voice suddenly called out from the gallery, causing a roar of laughter in the middle of a most serious scene: " Hallo, doctor! Well, is it a boy or a girl?"

During the period of my hopes and fears in connection with the orchestras which I conducted in the early days I must say that I always found my artists anxious and willing to learn and listen to good counsel. I used my most persuasive powers of eloquence — true, my English was sadly broken, and my language forcible, to say the least of it — in my endeavours to teach them discipline and the cultivation of solidarity in playing, while I always urged students to gain as much experience as possible by minutely studying the available scores of all the best composers. I maintained, and still maintain, that it is most essential for the imagination, simultaneously with the ear, to portray the exact sounds as correctly as they are given on paper, so that the student is able not only to read music, but to hear it in his imagination as well.

Early in April, 1859, the sudden death of Angiolina Bosio, in St. Petersburg, came upon us all not only as a severe shock but as a universal calamity. No tidings of her indisposition had reached us; on the contrary, all her friends — and their name was Legion — had been rejoicing at the welcome news that she had obtained the honour of being elected " première cantatrice " to the Imperial Court at St. Petersburg, when she was called away, just as she had reached the very zenith of her brilliant powers and reputation.

During the period of our uninterrupted friendship, which lasted from the happy time of our first meeting to the day of her death, her career was always characterised by strenuous and arduous study, and she earned the sincere affection of thousands by her simple, sincere, and unaffected manner.

Madame Bosio's gigantic efforts to please the public were prompted by her devotion to her art, not by personal vanity or ambition, and during our many hours of work and rehearsing I was often struck by the indomitable will she invariably exhibited in her endeavours to master technical difficulties.

How well I remember, on the occasion of my benefit in Havana, the almost superhuman exertions she made to learn her trills in " Sonnambula ! " A powerful cast was announced for that night, and Bosio, who had been immersed in floods of tears for days previously, with anxiety and fear lest she should be eclipsed by the more familiar stars which were to appear in conjunction with her, had worked herself up into a sort of frenzy, from which she happily emerged gloriously triumphant. She positively vaulted over her vocal obstacles with a dash and sparkling vivacity which were irresistible, and many critical amateurs, who had previously perhaps failed to appreciate her talent at its true value, were obliged to bow before the enchantress ; indeed, her impersonation of Amina, in Havana, was from that date generally looked upon as the culminating point of her career in the States.

Madame Bosio's success later on in London, under the elder Gye's *régime*, led to further triumphs, and she continued to progress steadily and surely in the estimation of the public until the year in which she died, when, without offence to Grisi, she might in truth have been styled the " Queen of Song; " indeed, her death caused a vacuum which for many years remained unfilled.

The next event of interest to me was one of a domestic nature, — a daughter was born to us on the 13th of July, 1859.

We were in London, and occupied apartments in Regent Street, not a hundred yards from the Sun Fire Insurance Office, which is situated at the corner of the Quadrant. The happy event was announced to me in the evening towards seven o'clock, and my informant discovered me engaged in an exciting conflict with an unusually limp tie, in front of a very shaky looking-glass at Her Majesty's Theatre, where I had for some time been occupied in heartily grumbling at and anathematising my laundress with regard to the lack of starch in my linen.

The christening of our daughter, Giulietta, took place a few days later at our tiny rooms, which were as full as an egg (to use a familiar adage) on that occasion of operatic celebrities and general musical talent. Thérèse Titiens, Liebhardt, Aldighieri, Giuglini, Mario, and Grisi were present, besides many others; and the kindly gathering of all my excellent comrades around me on such

Signor Arditi received many kind congratulations from his friends and comrades on the occasion of the birth of his daughter. I take leave to insert the following letter which he received from Mr. B. Lumley, for it is one of which Signor Arditi is especially proud. — EDITOR.

July 16th, 1859.

MY DEAR ARDITI, — Allow me to congratulate you and Mrs. Arditi on the happy event which has just made you a father.

I avail myself of this opportunity of thanking you for the talent and zeal you have shown during the past season, and during which you have increased the high reputation already gained by you. I had intended to present you with a little souvenir to mark my appreciation; but as I might in my selection possibly be presenting you what you already possess, I ask you to allow me to enclose you a draft for £50, which you will please apply in the manner most agreeable to you.

I remain, dear Arditi,

Yours very sincerely,

(Signed) BENJAMIN LUMLEY.

an occasion was a happy assurance to me of the affectionate regard in which they held me.

Mario and Grisi had promised to stand sponsors to
the child; and as Mario had never, within the memory
of man, been known to arrive in good time at any function whatsoever, we anticipated his advent with anxiety,
not unmixed with apprehension. Imagine, then, our surprise and delight when, at a quarter of an hour *before*
the time appointed for the ceremony, Grisi and Mario
arrived together, laden with flowers for my wife and
several beautiful silver presents of unusual splendour
for my firstborn.

Grisi sailed into the room with a face like a sunbeam,
and gave us each a hearty kiss.

" There," she said triumphantly, pointing to her husband, who stood at the door, beaming all over his face
with evident self-satisfaction (what a handsome, splendid-
looking fellow he was!), — " there, this is the first time
Mario has ever been known to be punctual. I hope you
appreciate such an unheard-of event, for I feel sure it
will never happen again!"

I really do believe that never before or since that
occasion was Mario known to have positively been " up
to time."

In the autumn of 1859 we again visited Ireland on
tour under the management of Willert Beale, this time
my wife accompanying me. It was during this tour that
I first conceived the melody of " Il Bacio," the *valse*
which, in later years, was destined to become the most
familiar of my works. Perhaps, in view of this fact, it
will not strike my readers as being egotistical if I give
them, in a few words, the true story of how I came to
write it.

One evening after dinner at the Queen's Hotel, Manchester, I sat myself down to the piano, while my fingers

strayed almost unconsciously over the notes. I played a little air to myself, and Piccolomini, who was chatting to my wife, looked up quickly and said, " What is that you are playing? It is charming. Please note it down, or you will forget it." I did so on an old envelope, merely jotting down a few notes, and then thrust the paper into my pocket. From that moment to the following year I thought no more of the tune.

Piccolomini had gone to America in the meanwhile, and it had been a promise on my part that I would compose a song for her to sing at the first concert in England on her return from the States.

Time flew, as it is wont to do, with amazing rapidity; and although Piccolomini was on the point of returning to London, I had not as yet composed the promised song.

There was no time to be lost, and I found myself in a fix for want of words, as well as of an inspiration.

A happy thought occurred to me. The very thing! Why not hunt up those notes which I had jotted down on an old envelope the previous year in Dublin? I appealed to Virginia, — I always did so when in doubt, or need of sound counsel, — and asked her what had become of the precious slip of paper. She had fortunately taken care of it for me, and knew where to lay her hands upon it at a moment's notice. So far I was safe; *but what about the words?* There occurred the next hitch.

Destiny, in the shape of a very good friend, came to my aid in the nick of time, however, and the words were written for me on the very day on which I began to arrange the music.

A high baritone of the name of Aldighieri, and a very excellent singer to boot, was practising with me one morning, and I told him that I was greatly in need of words for my song.

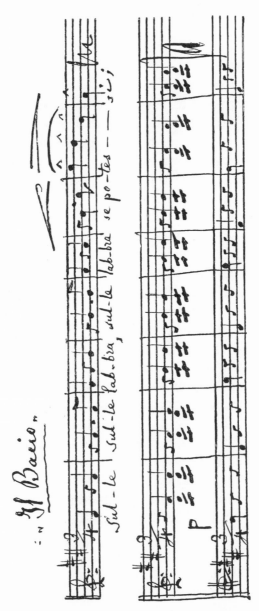

FACSIMILE OF THE OPENING BARS.

"I will write you some verses if you will give me an idea," he answered promptly. "What subject would you like?"

Virginia, who was sewing at the other end of the room, answered ere I had time to think of anything, and said, "Why not write about a kiss? There's a good subject for you!"

Aldighieri thought the idea an excellent one, and forthwith set to work and wrote the words to "Il Bacio," which have since become famous. I can't tell how it was, but the music of "Ill Bacio" came to me so spontaneously and naturally that it was written in an incredibly short space of time.

On Piccolomini's arrival in England I took the music to her house. Madame Puzzi was there, as well as several of Piccolomini's relations, in the presence of whom we tried over the song for the first time. Piccolomini was delighted with the music I had composed for her, and although her first concert, which she was about to give in Brighton, was to take place on the very next day, she set herself to learn the song, and acquired it to perfection in a few hours. Never had a song been written under so many difficulties, or in so short a space of time; never was a song learned so rapidly or delivered more admirably than "Il Bacio" was when sung in Brighton by Piccolomini in 1860.

Although I was fortunate in "hitting off" the public taste so conspicuously with regard to this song, incredible as it may seem, *I sold "Il Bacio" to the firm of Cramer, together with three other compositions, for the sum of £50.* From that day to this I have never increased my profit to the extent of sixpence in connection with that song! Flaxland, of the Place de la Madeleine, who gave 400 francs for the French copyright, on the contrary, made a fortune of 400,000 francs

out of the transaction, and boasts that the beautiful
business house he was able to build in Paris was the
outcome of the enormous profits he derived from
my composition, while I heard lately that the copper-
plates and copyright of " Il Bacio " were sold a few
years ago in London for the sum of £640.

That is the simple and true story of a song which,
if it did me no pecuniary good, was, at any rate, the
means of providing me with good publishers for
my subsequent works.

To return, however, to the subject of our periodical
visits to Ireland and the provinces. Touring in those
days was a very different sort of institution from what
it is now. The Impresari paid all expenses which
were incurred, and the artists generally stayed at one
and the same hotel. We occupied general drawing
and dining rooms, and were always accompanied
by a manager, or major-domo, whose business and
pleasure (?) it was to be the perplexed recipient of all
complaints — musical, culinary, or personal — which
aroused ire within the breasts of his flock. I cannot
say that his position ever struck me as being an
enviable one. The poor man positively lived in a
permanent atmosphere of apprehension in anticipation
of artistic ructions, which were in the habit of occurring with distressing frequency among the members of
the company.

Our provincial journeys to Ireland and Scotland
became hideously monotonous to us, particularly as we
had to go through the same routine twice a year.
From an artistic and pecuniary point of view these
tours (Ireland in particular) were very successful:
but, be the truth confessed, we used to long for "foreign
messes," as the British cook is wont to term the
harmless necessary dish of steaming macaroni and the

luscious " stuffato ; " for the everlasting English dinners, excellent as they were, wearied our palates beyond endurance. Piccolomini used to be the life and soul of those journeys, and she, in conjunction with Giuglini (when they were not engaged in vigorous chaff and banter), kept us in shrieks of laughter with their wild fun and high spirits.

Shall I ever forget those dreaded meals at the hotels, at which we used to appear with funeral mien, while each individual fondly nourished the vain hope that something other than the regulation boiled fowl or veal cutlet was nestling under the gorgeous plated covers that gave such an air of importance to the dinner table !

Those hopes, never, alas, realised, were straightway nipped in the bud as soon as the waiter, with due pomposity, removed the covers ; and then, with groans and exclamations of despair, we cried, "*Toujours perdrix,*" and proceeded to apply our teeth to the insipid meat with which we had been served.

Titiens, too, was a merry, pleasant companion, and an artist whose popularity increased enormously after each successive visit to Ireland and Scotland.

She was noted, *entre nous autres artistes*, for carrying an enormous superfluity of luggage about with her when on tour. Stage dresses which she never wore were, I was told, packed into her trunks, and on one occasion some members of the company determined to play her a trick in consequence.

Mdlle. Titiens always took a room at the hotel for exclusive use as a *garderobe*, and one of the gentlemen (I believe it was Willert Beale) obtained access to this apartment during her absence one day and promptly stuffed out all the dresses, put heads with wigs and painted faces on to the shoulders, and seated the figures on chairs (there were twelve or fourteen) in a dim religious light around the room.

Need I say more? Titiens, on her return home, wanted to change her dress, and she proceeded to this room. A minute later she came shrieking down the stairs, having been frightened out of her wits at the strange sight that met her gaze. She thought she must have suddenly gone mad, and that the ghosts of her different impersonations had appeared to torture her.

On the 10th of April, 1860, Her Majesty's Theatre was reopened for the season by Mr. E. T. Smith. During the previous season he had managed Italian opera at Drury Lane; but a marked improvement had been achieved in the direction of the orchestra and chorus in 1860, with such artists as Molique and Blagrove leading the violins, and the first night was inaugurated with "Marta" and "Fleurs des Champs" (a ballet), Thérèse Titiens being the Lady Henrietta, and Giuglini impersonating Lionel. "Almina" was produced on the 28th of April of the same year, with Piccolomini in the part of Almina. The composer of the opera, Signor Fabio Campana, came to London just as Piccolomini was about to retire, and implored her to sing the title *rôle*.

At first she was not to be persuaded; but Campana's entreaties, to which I added my own, proved finally victorious, and Piccolomini, in conjunction with Giuglini as the lover Biondello, carried off the honours of the stage.

To the universal regret of the public, upon whom Piccolomini had made a profound impression, she decided to retire from the stage at this moment, and a handsome testimonial was presented to her at her farewell performance of "Traviata" by her many admirers.

It would be impossible to mention otherwise than cursorily the chief musical events during my conductorship at Her Majesty's Theatre. The operatic season of 1860, under Mr. E. T. Smith's management, had brought several important works to the fore, among which "The Huguenots" and "Oberon" were the chief and most popular novelties. Titiens and Giuglini may be said to have caused an undiminished sensation every time they appeared before the footlights together. The nightly receptions accorded to these great singers amounted well-nigh to a frenzy, and one which lasted until the close of the season. Mr. Benedict divided with me the arduous duties of conducting; but why we should have been driven in double harness was a matter which gave rise to much comment at that time.[1]

This production of "Oberon" was, of course, absolutely left in the hands of Mr. Benedict. I heartily concurred in handing over this duty to my excellent *confrère*, to whom it was but a just compliment, both as the beloved pupil of Weber and as the one who had been selected to compose the necessary recitatives. Nevertheless, I may as well take this opportunity of

[1] Said the "Musical World": "We cannot recognise the necessity of *two* conductors. Why Mr. Benedict and Signor Arditi should both be retained it is impossible for us to make out. We can understand that a conductor who has other engagements to attend to might find it inconvenient to preside in an orchestra where performances are given every night, as at Drury Lane last year, but at the regular performances of three or four nights a week there can be no difficulty. Besides, as no servant can serve two masters, so no band can follow two conductors.

"Mr. Smith is fond of duplications (witness the harlequinade of his Drury Lane pantomime); but if he would desire his Italian opera to flourish, he must be simple and observe the unities. Let him eschew two conductors as he would two coachmen on the box of his chariot, if he would wish to be driven straight and escape upsetting." — EDITOR.

saying that I do not approve of the system which now prevails of employing three and sometimes four conductors during a single season. Such a thing was, at the time of which I am writing, quite unknown, the particular case of "Oberon" proving the exception to the rule.

Six operas per week, with attendant heavy rehearsals, is likely to prove too arduous a task for one conductor ; yet it is highly advisable to leave, as far as it is practicable, the control of orchestra and chorus in the hands of one man.

During our many tours in Ireland some of our experiences in connection with our musical associates are worth recording. Here again I must ask my wife to step in and lead me by the hand.

One of many letters written to her attached friend, Madame Puzzi, may throw a little light on the impressions that particularly fixed themselves upon her mind during our short periodical visits thither. At any rate, I have made a few extracts, which I have ventured to add to my own prosaic records : —

" In the midst of our excitement in Dublin," she wrote, during the month of September, 1860, " I have isolated myself for a few moments from the whirl of our *entourage* to send you a few lines, dear Mama Puzzi. It is such a pleasure to me to address my thoughts to you; you seem to understand just what I think and feel.

" We are greatly amused over Giuglini's latest *grande passion* just now, and when he is not raving in despair about some imaginary wrong, he pours his eulogium concerning Mdlle. X—— into my ears.

" I am a sort of social reservoir, into which all our company empty their confidences, and, what with one and another, my mind is kept busily at work smoothing and patching up little feuds and disagreeables which are continually occurring.

" Luigi likes his conductorship in Dublin immensely.

" The Irish public is an intensely appreciative one, and there seems to exist an excellent feeling of good will in the orchestra towards its leader, who, in his turn, is devoted to all his students. They don't seem to mind one bit when Luigi, after the manner of Italians, storms and tears his few remaining hairs out at their roots during rehearsals, and they show him a marked respect, too, in attending to his counsel, and in following his word of command.

" Luigi's sphere of interest and action has greatly extended itself since he has become more intimate with the orchestra and singers. He has a way of merging himself, as it were, into their individual feelings, and seems to be much liked by all. His propositions for the increase and improvement of the orchestra are being adopted, and we anticipate very felicitous results if his musicians continue to work with the same ardour and precision.

" Titiens, Giuglini, Luigi, and I were invited to Dublin Castle the other night, on the occasion of one of Lord Carlisle's receptions. As luck would have it, I forgot to take an evening dress with me from London, and was, at the last moment, perplexed as to how to put in a presentable appearance.

" Imagine to yourself the anxiety I experienced when, having at the eleventh hour borrowed a white ball dress from an unusually stout lady, I was obliged to sit up half the previous night *taking it in !* I snipped and pinched it until it was greatly reduced, and finally I succeeded in making it fit !

" The *soirée* was a great success on the whole.

" I had previously been warned that Lord Carlisle is very fond of embracing some of the ladies who attend his receptions, if they happen to meet, in appearance, with his approbation, and it was with a sort of dread that I attended the party that night, earnestly hoping that such a *contretemps* would not befall me.

" We learnt, however, on our arrival at the castle, that his Lordship was too unwell to appear, and that he begged to be excused, so my fears were at an end in that respect.

" A good story was told to me about Lord Carlisle the other day.

" It has been rumoured in Dublin that his Lordship entertains a very deep admiration for a certain American lady, called Miss

Manners. Having absented himself on a public occasion when his presence had been expected, he greatly excited the ire of many people who were interested in his attendance.

" Stepping into his loge on the following night at the theatre, a cheeky student took upon himself to call out, ' Where was your Lordship last night?' or words to that effect; to which a smart youth, evidently on the alert to distinguish himself, promptly ejaculated, without a moment's hesitation, '*Manners*, my boy, *Manners !*'

" I must, ere I close, give you a specimen of Irish naïveté, which to you, as a *maestro di canto*, will appeal irresistibly. 1 was asked the other morning to interpret for a lady who had called upon my husband in order to request him to hear her daughter sing, as she was anxious that the latter should go on the operatic stage. Luigi, who was very busy at the time, yet loath to refuse the lady's request, promised to see the girl, and fixed upon a date to receive her.

" The girl's mother, however, thought she would save time; and jumping up, she said, ' If you will hear *me* sing, Signor Arditi, it will do just as well; her voice and mine are exactly the same ! ' Tableau !

" Much as I love to chat with you, dear friend, I must say good-bye. I have a serious duty to perform, and you will agree with me that it is one which must not be neglected. Giuglini is about to fly his new kite, and you know that if we don't, one and all, humour him by taking intense interest in his hobbies, he considers that he has been ' upset,' and then we have the greatest difficulty in reconciling him to the performance of his duties.

" Giuglini is quite mad on the subject of kites, but never mind; with all his faults and little peculiarities, he is thoroughly goodhearted and kind.

" *Au revoir ; à bientôt,*

"*A toi de cœur,*

" VIRGINIA."

CHAPTER V.

I HAVE now reached an all-important event in
connection with my career, and the music of the
nineteenth century to boot, namely, the *début* of Adelina
Patti in London. This event in itself is one which
has been written about *ad lib.* by far more capable pens
than mine; but the affectionate terms upon which the
Diva and I have stood since I first saw her, then a little
dark-eyed, roguish maiden, with red, pursed-up lips, and
quick, rippling laughter, seemed to justify my dwelling
upon the beginning of her wonderful career.

The first time I ever set eyes on Adelina was in New
York, when she and her mother visited the hotel at
which I lived, in order to eat the macaroni which was
always excellently prepared by an Italian *chef* of renown ;
and her determined little airs and manners then already
showed plainly that she was destined to become a ruler
of men.

Madame Salvador Patti, *veuve* Barili, Adelina's mother,
was anxious that I should hear the child sing, and so
she brought her little daughter to my rooms one day.

Bottesini and I were highly amused to see the air of importance with which the tiny songstress first selected a comfortable seat for her doll in such proximity that she was able to see her while singing, and then, having said, "*Là, ma bonne petite, attends que ta Maman te chante quelque chose de jolie,*" she demurely placed her music on the piano, and asked me to accompany her in the rondo of "Sonnambula."

How am I to give an adequate description of the effect which that child's miraculous notes produced upon our enchanted senses? Perhaps if I say that both Bottesini and I wept genuine tears of emotion, tears which were the outcome of the original and never-to-be-forgotten impression her voice made when it first stirred our innermost feelings, that may, in some slight measure, convince my readers of the extraordinary vocal power and beauty of which little Adelina was, at that tender age, possessed. We were simply amazed, nay, electrified, at the well-nigh perfect manner in which she delivered some of the most difficult and varied arias without the slightest effort or self-consciousness.

Having heard such artists as Bosio, Grisi, Sontag, Alboni, and many other great singers, including her own mother, in the prime and *apogee* of their careers, and having, so to speak, been born on the stage (since Madame Salvador Patti was singing "Norma" upon the very night of Adelina's birth), her extraordinarily impressionable nature turned to music and melody as naturally as a babe seeks its mother's lips in the first perfect kiss of life.

Little Adelina's vivacity when quite a tiny girl was remarkable. Nothing ever escaped her notice, and if she observed curious mannerisms in any one, years afterwards she would remember them and imitate them perfectly. She could enter the room as bright as a ray

"This is my Portrait when
I was eight years old,
and had already been
singing a year in
public"—

Adelina Patti Nicolini

of sunshine, all smiles and sweetness ; but if any one had had the misfortune to ruffle the pretty brows or thwart My Lady Wilful, her dark eyes would flash, her tiny fist would contract with anger, and clouds would speedily gather across the surface of her laughing face and burst forth in torrents of tears almost as quickly as a flash of lightning.

I remember, one day, Madame Salvador Patti came to consult me with regard to the score of an opera that was in my possession. My little enchantress had accompanied her mother as far as the door, but there she lingered irresolutely, looking as though she were "angry with the whole house." Although I was not aware that I had in any way vexed her, she suddenly conceived the notion of venting her ire on me. I was seated at my desk, pouring forth an effusion of music to a young lady of whom I was deeply enamoured at the time, and had valiantly struggled through and reached the last bars of the dedication in question, when, without further ado, she ran up to my table, raised herself on tip-toe, and turned the inkstand completely over on my manuscript, exclaiming in a quick, peevish tone, " *Cosa fai tu brutto ?* "

The burst of temper was all over in a moment (so, indeed, was my MS.), and after the satisfaction of having carefully watched the ink trickle leisurely on to my landlady's carpet, she smiled roguishly, showing her white teeth, and danced out of the room, looking back at me, her dark, lustrous eyes full of lurking mischief, as though nothing whatever had happened, despite her mother's profuse and reiterated apologies.

Such a little wilful tyrant was Adelina Patti when I first knew her. But if a poor hungry child had crept up to her, and had begged for a silver piece in order to get a loaf of bread, or if two little frozen hands had been outstretched in search of warmth and comfort, the little

dark-eyed nightingale would have helped and soothed
that forlorn infant with her own slender means, with her
warm-hearted, childish kisses, and her simple words of
endearment; she would have given her best-loved pet
or her favourite doll away if it could have been the
means of restoring smiles to a little tear-stained face, or
happiness to an aching heart.

I was intimately acquainted with Adelina Patti's
family. Her amiable and talented sisters — Amalia,
Clotilde, and Carlotta, who respectively married Maurice
Strakosch, Thorne, and the Chevalier de Munk — were
all accomplished artists; while her brothers — Ettore,
Nicolo, Carlo, and Antonio — were devoted to music,
Carlo having as a child studied the violin with me, and
having at the age of twenty become leader at the New
Orleans Opera House, afterwards at New York and the
Wakefield Opera House, St. Louis, Missouri.

To return to Adelina, in whom for the present we are
particularly interested, she first studied singing under
the careful guidance of her brother-in-law, Maurice Strakosch. When she appeared at Covent Garden on the
memorable night of May 14, 1861, as Amina, in "La
Sonnambula," she was, comparatively speaking, unknown
in London.

The reports which had reached the English public
about her successes in America were looked upon as
exaggerated and extravagant; and I really believe that
upon the occasion on which she first laid the foundation
stone of the pedestal upon which she has reigned ever
since there were not twenty people in the house who
knew that Adelina Patti was a singer of more than
ordinary merit.

I, however, had heard her sing in America, and had
witnessed the scenes of extraordinary triumph in which
her vocal efforts had been received, cheered, and clam-

oured for; I had seen the child grow up into a beautiful
girl; I had noted the improvements which her voice
had undergone, and the rich and rapid development of
her faultless register that was about to come upon the
British public as a revelation.

I could not help smiling with some superiority when
people asked each other: "Who is this little dark-eyed
singer from America? Can she sing; or will she, like a
falling star, shine brilliantly for a time, and then fade
into obscurity for ever?"

A very few people who had been present at the hurried and shortened rehearsals knew what was to follow;
but nothing was known of Patti's antecedents, her name
having appeared only four days in advance of her *début,*
and without a single remark in the advertisements.

There was no heralding of trumpets, no fluttering
anticipations, no stir in musical circles, no sensational
outlook whatsoever to announce the advent of one of
the world's greatest singers. She came, she sang, and
she conquered. The surprise she caused after the first
recitative of "Amina" was indescribable; and by the
time she had reached a passage *di bravura,* and had
put all her soulful notes into the final rondo, "*Ah, non
giunge!*" the house rose in a roar of enthusiasm that
may be chronicled as unprecedented.

The next day the papers were full of the all-absorbing
topic, and one journal said: —

"Why should not the brilliant advent of Mdlle. Patti fill us
with hope for the renewed fortunes of Italian opera? We want
another Bosio, another Malibran, and another Pasta. May we
not indulge our imagination so far? Mdlle. Patti is a triumphant refutation of the assumption that art and genius have
deserted the operatic stage, and we may assert emphatically
'that Italian opera has obtained an accession of strength in
a certain line which we did not expect to witness in our own
time,'" etc.

But now I have diverged long enough, for the moment, from my purpose, and must leave Patti at the point of her brilliant *début* in London; for it must be remembered that she did not appear under my bâton, but at Covent Garden, under that of Sir Michael Costa, the house at which at that time furious opposition to Her Majesty's Theatre was being carried on to the utmost ability of its lessee.

Later on my pen will record many other reminiscences in connection with the Diva; but for the present I must ask my readers to accompany me to the Lyceum Theatre, where, during the month of June, 1861, Mr. J. Mapleson, the late *factotum* of Mr. E. T. Smith, opened the season of Italian opera.

It was with feelings of decided relief that all the artists looked forward to their work under this directorship; for, if the truth be confessed, Mr. E. T. Smith was more *au fait* in the capacity of an advertising agent, or in that of managing pantomimes, than he was in the delicate and intricate function of directing an operatic company.

Smith reminded us of the proverbial bull in a china shop in his alacrity for " putting his foot in it " on every available occasion. The following incident, humorous as it may have appeared to its originator, was quite unappreciated by the victims whom he had selected as butts for a very poor joke.

On the occasion in question, Mr. E. T. Smith invited several members of his company, including Titiens, Giuglini, my wife, and myself, to drive to the Oaks. We departed in grand style on a handsome coach and four, and the ladies were congratulating each other upon our Impresario's sudden outburst of generosity and unwonted attention.

Alas! at first we were blind to the subtle reason for Smith's unexpected amiability, until some one got down from the drag during the afternoon and happened to pass round the back of the coach. I believe it was Giuglini who made the awful discovery; at least I shall never forget his disgust and utter collapse when he informed our party of the trick Smith had played upon us. The latter had caused a huge placard to be hung on the back of the drag, upon which the following awful inscription hung in glaring letters: —

E. T. SMITH'S

OPERATIC COMPANY.

Remonstrance was of no avail after the mischief was done, but the ladies stoutly refused to return home on the drag unless the advertisement were removed; and so Smith, having thoroughly enjoyed his joke, was quite ready to accede to their wishes, while the rest of the company returned to town wiser yet sadder men.

Such a man was Smith. I could cite many instances in which he sorely tried the feelings and tempers of his artists; instances in which he did his utmost, in a blundering sort of way, to do good with an *éclat* which only aroused the discontent and ire of many.

When, for instance, Her Majesty's Theatre was transformed into a song-room for " Hot Codlins," and the walls re-echoed with the piercing outcries of clown and pantaloon within the very space where Pasta and Rubini had sung from their hearts and their souls to the public who adored them, E. T. Smith absolutely failed, and very justly too, to arouse an enthusiasm for harlequinade among the serious opera-loving people who had so loyally supported his efforts in the production of good music.

Under Mapleson, however, everything was changed for the better. Art, in the form of Italian opera, was zealously encouraged by him in every respect, and under his clear-sighted and genial auspices gave the Lyceum audiences great and genuine satisfaction.

I will not here enter into the subject of the long and acute rivalry that existed between Her Majesty's and Covent Garden Theatres. It is not for me to draw comparisons between the two houses which, opposed as they were to one another, gave, each in its turn, excellent performances.

Mapleson was, or rather is, gifted with rare amenity and amiability of manner. He was seldom out of humour; he knew exactly how to manage his artists, and, what is better, his creditors. There is an old saying to the effect that " *la plus belle femme ne peut donner que ce qu'elle a ;* " and I am of the opinion, that, if we change the sex, and say, " *le plus bel homme,*" etc., the saying would apply admirably to my jovial friend the Colonel.

I have known *prime donne* enter his office infuriatedly, vowing they would not depart from his presence without a " little cheque," or hard cash, and these same irate ladies would sally forth, after waiting his leisure for some considerable time, with their angry looks transformed to absolute serenity, and actually feeling, to all appearance, as though Mapleson were conferring a considerable favour upon them by continuing to owe them their hard-earned salaries. His manner was quite irresistible; there never lived the man whose suave, gentle art in calming the irrepressible creditor was more conspicuous or effective. To do him every justice, he paid his debts when he had money; but when the safe was empty, he knew how to rid himself of tiresome and embarrassing duns with remarkable graciousness and admirable tact, never letting people into the secret of his financial difficulties, or allowing them to depart uneasy at heart with regard to the sum owed to them. This was an art in itself; but a fact of far greater importance is that Mapleson was, unlike E. T. Smith, a musician.

I remember a good story of Mapleson, which opportunely recurs to me at this moment. A certain tenor who had made his *début* under Mapleson's management came to him one day in a towering rage, flourishing a daily paper in his hand, and complaining bitterly of the manner in which his singing had been criticised by that journal.

"It's shameful," cried the infuriated singer, "to have been maligned in this fashion. You, Mapleson, I know, have the greatest influence with all the newspapers in London; can't you get this contradicted, or at least an apology tendered to me for this unpardonable insult? Not being known in London makes it all the harder for me, because nobody will care to hear me sing now. I am simply ruined. . . ."

Mapleson at first assumed a pained expression, and looked thoughtful for a moment. Then a happy thought occurred to him, as it always did on such occasions.

"Let me see what paper it is in," said he. The tenor then tore asunder the opening page of the "Daily Telegraph," and thrust it into Mapleson's hands.

"Good gracious!" said Mapleson; "why, my dear boy, you're as safe as a trivet; I feared at first the notice might have appeared in an important paper, but nobody ever reads the 'Daily Telegraph,' so you need not be in the least alarmed! . . ."

A good and noble woman, apart from being a brilliant artist, was Thérèse Titiens, and she stood by Mr. Mapleson through "rain and sunshine;" it may be said, in fact, that this Impresario owed his brilliant successes as a director of Italian opera in a great measure to her valiant and effective services.

The Lyceum Theatre opened with "Il Trovatore" on the 8th of June, 1861, which was given, as far as the performers were concerned, in a manner that left nothing to be desired.

Titiens was Leonora; Alboni, Azucena; Giuglini, Manrico; while the *rôle* of Il conte di Luna was confided to a new baritone, Delle Sedie.

Of his singing I can only speak in enraptured terms. I say singing, for he had no voice to speak of; but his exquisite delivery, the passion of his intonations and utterances, were so delicious that I can scarcely recall them without re-experiencing the emotion that he originally awakened in me.

Titiens was at her very best; again triumphantly proclaiming herself a brilliant Leonora, and doing perfect justice to Verdi's music.

Giuglini and Alboni, too, were in splendid voice, and the orchestra, consisting of about fifty-two performers, materially aided the impressive effect of the performance.

Great excitement was caused at Her Majesty's Theatre when, during the time at which rehearsals of Verdi's then new opera, " Un Ballo in Maschera," were in active progress, it was reported that Mr. Gye, the then manager of Covent Garden, was about to outvie us, and produce " Un Ballo " a week earlier than we had intended doing. All our energies were naturally brought to bear upon this crucially momentous question, and it was decided, *coûte que coûte*, to score over " the opposition shop," and be " first in the field."

The pressure put upon us all was immense, but the dread of being beaten in our race for glory kept us indefatigably at our posts ; and after almost superhuman

efforts on the part of all concerned, we managed to produce " Un Ballo in Maschera " just one week previous
to its production at Covent Garden.

This production proved to be one of Mapleson's most
conspicuous successes. To quote one of the leading
papers : —

> " The cast was admirable, irreproachable, indeed ; the greatest
> pains had been expended on the rehearsals, and the execution
> throughout could hardly be surpassed. In fact, a more thor-
> oughly complete and powerful first performance of any work we
> have very rarely heard, and the greatest credit is due to all
> concerned. . . ."

Giuglini, Delle Sedie, Gassier and Madame Gassier,
Madame Lemaire, and Thérèse Titiens filled the principal *rôles*, and unqualified praise was awarded to artists
and orchestra alike.

A week later, as I said before, the same opera was
produced at Covent Garden with a brilliant cast.

Madame Penco as Amalia, and Madame Nantier-
Didiée, Mario, Tagliafico, Madame Miolan-Cavalho, and
M. Zelgar acquitted themselves admirably, and " Un Ballo
in Maschera " was pronounced to have been excellently
performed and produced at both operatic houses.

Mapleson proved, during his short and venturesome
season at the Lyceum, that he was a man of great
energy and indefatigable perseverance. Many important works were thoughtfully prepared, well sustained,
and competently managed, and it was with the unanimous good wishes and congratulations of the public
and the company alike that Mapleson's first season
came to an end on the 6th of July, 1861, on the occasion of the benefit of Mdlle. Titiens.

Our Dublin season opened in September of that
year with Titiens and Giuglini, Delle Sedie, Ciampi,

and other big stars. Our reception was, as usual, a demonstrative and hearty one. " The gods " were as noisy as ever, and expressed their pleasure on seeing the old familiar faces by vociferous shouts and whistling, which, from the foreigner's point of view, is the very opposite to the correct way of showing one's approval. Delle Sedie was terribly alarmed when his " Il Balen," in the " Trovatore " (that being the opera we opened with), was greeted with yells and tremendous whistling; it was not until he had been assured by his fellow artists that it was the Irish students' way of signifying their contentment and desire for an " encore " that he was persuaded to appear, somewhat nervously, and give a repetition of his delightful rendering.

Titiens liked the stormy exclamations of the pit and gallery that were hurled at her. She loved the Irish, and they loved her. It is quite touching, even now, to hear the deep and reverential way in which she is remembered and spoken of in the provinces, her thoughtful actions and kindnesses to the people with whom she came into contact having been fondly treasured up in the public memory, where she holds a firm seat in the regard of all who knew and survived her. Her warm-hearted, cheerful personality left most delightful impressions in the hotels where she stayed, and in some of the rooms she occupied her photographs are enshrined, and the apartments are characterised and looked upon as being worthy of especial notice, " since the great artist, Thérèse Titiens, stayed there."

My appearance in the orchestra was also greeted with robust shouting and applause, while such exclamations as, " Viva, Victor Emmanuel ! " " Bravo, Arditi ! " " Where's your wig ? " and " How's the macaroni ? " were to be heard emanating from all parts of the house.

They even cheered my wife when she entered her box, and cries of " Three cheers for Madame Arditi, and all the little Arditis!" brought down the house.

The dwellers in Olympus were really a very queer lot in Dublin. They thought nothing of singing songs and glees in the *entr'actes*. I have heard many a solo correctly and tunefully played upon an ordinary penny tin pipe.

Giuglini was interrupted in the middle of his song, " Ah si, ben mio," with roars of approval, and one enthusiastic Irishman shouted out, " Ah, begorra, and Mario 's a fine singer; but sure, we loike your singing best, and that 's the truth ! . . ."

Alas ! the good old times of genuine cordial greetings that used to warm our hearts seem to have calmed down into colder and more matter-of-fact receptions nowadays. It was perfectly delightful, to artists and musicians alike, to meet with such enthusiastic and friendly applause, and our visits to Ireland were invariably signalised by similar demonstrations.

I remember a very funny incident in connection with the performance of " Norma " at Dublin, which is perhaps worthy of relation.

Titiens was singing Norma, and Giuglini impersonated Pollione. In the last act Norma and Pollione have a dramatic scene, in which Norma, enraged with Pollione, rushes towards a gong, which she strikes with a leather-knobbed stick, in order to summon the Druids, who finally arrest her lover.

Titiens seized the stick, and as she raised it to sound the gong, Giuglini got in her way, and unfortunately received a violent knock on the bridge of his nose, causing instantly a profuse bleeding. The curtain had to be lowered in order that the injured Pollione might recover himself sufficiently to proceed with the act.

Titiens was frightfully upset at the unfortunate mishap, but Giuglini behaved excellently about it, and in spite of the swollen nose, which immediately assumed alarming dimensions, " Norma " was brought to a successful close.

Our Dublin tour came to an end, and we proceeded thence to Liverpool, where, on our arrival, the lamentable news of the death of His Royal Highness the Prince Consort came upon us with shocking suddenness.

He had always been a most liberal and intelligent patron of art in general, and of music in particular, and the sad event was deplored with the deepest feelings of sincere sorrow by Her Majesty's subjects, as well as by the foreigners who then dwelt in this country.

The Prince Consort was a first-rate judge of music, and an accomplished amateur both as composer and executant. His frequent attendances at the operatic performances were always looked upon as a guarantee of the excellence of the music and its rendering alike, while the web of powerful interest which invariably folded itself round the opera nights seemed to be incomplete without the invigorating and encouraging presence of Her Majesty the Queen and her Royal Consort.

The stars of Italian song, and, indeed, their humble musical satellites, never shone more brilliantly, or discharged themselves more adequately of their tasks, than when Royalty honoured them with its presence and its warm-hearted applause ; and from the day that this most truly excellent prince and loyal husband was taken from us, England's Queen has never again appeared publicly at either opera house, or, indeed, at any theatre.

Every loyal subject of the Queen, and every lover of this country felt the sharp and acute pang inflicted upon all classes of society by the loss of one who was so truly noble and lovable, and who rendered such admirable service to England. The Prince Consort's death left a gap in the great patrons of the musical world which has never since been filled up.

CHAPTER VI.

THE affairs of Her Majesty's Theatre were in a
most uncertain condition at the opening of the
year 1862. Every one was asking, "Who will have the
Theatre this season?" It was the year of the Great
Exhibition, and it would have appeared preposterous
had Her Majesty's remained closed. Indeed, had it not
opened that year, the star of its fortunes would probably have set then and for ever.

At first it had been rumoured that Gye was nego-
tiating to keep Her Majesty's closed; but after a long
period of indecision and deliberation the season opened
under the able management of Mr. H. J. Mapleson.

Titiens, Giuglini, Vialetti, Ciampi, Gassier, Mdlle.
Trebelli, were among the artists engaged. The last-
named, together with the Sisters Marchisio, made their
débuts that season in England. Some curiosity was
occasioned by the announcement of their appearance,
since all three ladies had earned high continental
reputations.

The orchestra was composed of excellent musicians, all members of the Philharmonic Society band, with myself at its head.

I directed the opening performance of " Un Ballo in Maschera," with Titiens and Giuglini as Amalia and Riccardo. Giuglini had previously been seriously ill; fortunately, however, he had recovered his health and voice, and sang admirably. The *début* of the Sisters Marchisio, who appeared in " Semiramide," followed shortly after the season's opening.

MDLLE. TREBELLI.

They had already become famous in concert rooms, their specialty being duets; but they each possessed vocal qualities enabling them to shine independently of each other.

The verdict on their performances at St. James' Hall was fully confirmed at Her Majesty's Theatre.

Barbara and Carlotta Marchisio possessed contralto and mezzo-soprano voices of singular charm, — that of the first-named being of extraordinary compass; the latter possessing that quality which tells so well in concerted music. Mdlle. Trebelli (who, until the day of her death, was beloved for her kindheartedness and amiability by all who knew her) also made her *début* in London under my bâton.

She was an excellent musician. How well I recall her rich, telling notes, her refined execution, and her graceful, elegant personality. She had served her apprenticeship in Spain, Germany, and France, before appearing in London, and was remarkable for her *sangfroid* and self-composure on the stage. She made an excellent *début* as Maffeo Orsini in "Lucrezia Borgia" on the 9th of May, 1862, and thenceforth created a deep and lasting impression on her English audiences. Her great talent as a singer was no less notable than her amiability and true friendship, as my wife and I can testify from long experience. There will be much to tell of her in connection with my career, for I am glad to say she achieved many of her successes while singing under my conductorship.

Miss Geneviève Ward, who at present holds a very high position as an actress and stands at the head of her profession, appeared in London, under the name of Guerrabella, in "I Puritani," during May, 1862. The fact that on the lyric stage she drew forth highly flattering demonstration from her audiences proved that her skilful vocalisation and excellent acting was greatly appreciated; and it was indeed to be regretted that "Mdlle. Guerrabella," shortly after her favourable appearance in England, lost her voice during an engagement in Havana. Had not this unforeseen trouble come upon her just at the most important period of her musical career, she would no doubt have taken her place among the singers of the century. However, she was not long in finding a sphere of art, and, as we all know, has earned laurels by her histrionic powers as a tragédienne, in which line she has found full scope for her varied and admirable talents.

At this period all "Art England" was sympathising with Verdi on account of the incivility of the royal commissioners with respect to his cantata.

Briefly, the difficulty was as follows : Verdi had been asked to compose a march in honour of the Great International Exhibition. For some reason, and, no doubt, a good one, the *maestro* composed a cantata in lieu of the march, which was, without a shadow of reason, rejected by the royal commissioners. Verdi was, not unnaturally, extremely hurt at the wrong that had been done to him, and it became a general question as to the best method of making an *amende honorable* to the Italian *maestro.*

It was arranged, after due consideration, to produce the cantata at Her Majesty's Theatre, with full band and chorus. The solo parts, originally intended for Signor Tamberlik, were arranged for Thérèse Titiens, and on the 31st of May of the same year the work was heard in public for the first time.

The feelings which were entertained with regard to the *maestro's* composition rose to a tremendous pitch of enthusiasm during the performance.[1] Titiens' solos were magnificent; indeed, they were so perfectly rendered that it was hard to realise that they had been composed for any other voice than hers.

The execution of the cantata was under my direction, aided by the chorus of the Vocal Association, while we were fortunate in securing the entire strength of the company.

---

[1] There was only one general rehearsal for Signor Verdi's cantata.

The *maestro* himself was present, and was amazed and delighted to find that the English musicians were such capable men. They read their parts so admirably, and indeed faultlessly, that the whole cantata, from the beginning to well-nigh the end, proceeded without a hitch. In the final part, however, a grave mistake occurred, and Signor Arditi for the first time stopped the orchestra.

The *maestro*, who had listened in perfect silence to the rehearsing of the cantata, could not help exclaiming, " *Che peccato !* " (" What a pity ") and afterwards warmly congratulated Signor Arditi on the efficiency of his conducting and the superiority of his orchestra. — EDITOR.

Londra 30 May 1862

Car.mo Arditi

Quando avrete un momento di tempo vi prego di far accomodare nella <u>Cantata</u> questi due piccoli squarci che vi mando. Io gli accomoderò nella partitura originale e nelle altre di Francia e d'Italia.

Altro, e pensateci; se vado in qualche cosa comandatemi e scrivete nel caso a Torino.

Credetemi con stima d'amore

G. Verdi

In recognition of the manner in which the cantata was produced, the *maestro* was good enough to speak in highly flattering terms. He sent me a fine portrait of himself, to which he added a few affectionate words. I spent many pleasant hours in his quiet retreat in St. John's Wood in those early days of our acquaintance,— days to which I look back in happy retrospect.

This production was a memorable one in many respects, and it will live long in the hearts of all who, having been present on the occasion, watched the *maestro's* subsequent triumphs.[1]

The production of "Roberto il Diavolo," which took place in June, reminds me of a good story in connection with Mapleson.

The *prova generale* was called for the evening before the performance, and I was horrified to find that the stage management was unusually backward and slow. The various stoppages we had to submit to were trying my temper beyond endurance; but when Bertram had *twice* sung his invocation without eliciting the least response from the demons, who at that moment should have appeared from below, I threw down my bâton in a rage, and shouted lustily, "Where the devil is the Impresario?"

Mapleson, whose discretion on such occasions always got the better part of his valour, did not make his appearance; and when I called out again, more frantically than before, a large black cat came calmly and leisurely

---

[1] TRANSLATION OF VERDI'S LETTER.

DEAR ARDITI,— When you have a moment to spare, pray put the accompanying two passages into the cantata, and I will insert them in the original score, and in the editions for France and Italy.

If I can be of any use to you, command me, and let me know in what, at Turin. Believe me, with esteem and affection,

Yours,

G. VERDI.

out from the wings, walked down the middle of the stage, and stood facing me, as though wishing to remonstrate with me on behalf of his master.

Of course this proved irresistible, and in spite of my impatience I was obliged to join the house and the orchestra in roars of laughter.

Mapleson saw that his emissary had averted the storm, and so came forward "*avec son plus gracieux sourire*," and promised henceforth to manage the devils himself.

I may say that that comic little incident was the saving clause of the production, for we kept the rehearsal up until two o'clock in the morning, and averted what we all thought must have been a disappointment for the opening night.[1]

"Roberto" closed the regular season of 1862, after which eight supplementary performances, at reduced prices, were given, and well supported.

The final performance was for the benefit of Signor Giuglini; and that reminds me to mention "L'Italia," a descriptive lyric in four parts, given for the first time in London, and which was composed by the above-mentioned eminent tenor. This cantata was highly creditable to Giuglini, but his talent as a composer did

---

[1] After the wearisome rehearsal finally came to an end, Mr. H. J. Mapleson drove Signor Arditi home in his brougham.

Arditi, who was thoroughly tired and worn out, despaired of being able to produce the opera on the following night.

Both Impresario and conductor were anxious and preoccupied, and on parting they shook each other warmly by the hand.

"I'll do my best," said Arditi, earnestly, "but it will be a miracle if we succeed."

Mapleson answered impressively, "For God's sake, do, old fellow! it will mean a loss of £500 to me if 'Roberto' is not produced to-morrow night. . . ."

As was mentioned before, "Roberto" *was* produced on the following night, and achieved considerable success. Very few, however, who were present were aware of the almost superhuman efforts that were exercised by all concerned in the performance. — EDITOR.

not possess the same charm as his vocal attributes. The
"Ode," however, met with a good reception, and his
rendering of the parts of "The Genius of Italy" (the
work being of a patriotic nature) was given in his own
brilliant style. Alas! that so perfect a singer should
have died at so early an age, the victim of a cruel and
relentless disease!

With the autumn of 1862 came one of our periodical
provincial tours.

In the company of Thérèse Titiens and Giuglini I
went to Liverpool to conduct a series of concerts, and it
was during our stay there that the "Foreigners' Ball"
took place, an unusually brilliant function.[1] The entertainment was the very best of its kind, the first part
being devoted to a concert, in which Titiens, Madame
Lemaire, and Signor Bossi took part. Titiens was, as
usual, the attraction of the evening.

A new *valse* of mine, entitled "L'Ardita," was enthusiastically encored when rendered by her with her usual
perfection; and after the mayor had presented her with
a diamond bracelet, as a token of the people's affectionate regard, the ball proper was opened, and lasted
until the small hours.[2]

At the latter part of the year my wife stayed with

[1] The "Foreigners' Ball" was given for a charity which was organised
in aid of all the destitute foreigners in Liverpool, and was the means of
collecting a very large sum of money. — EDITOR.

[2] "L'Ardita" was composed expressly for, and dedicated to, Mdlle.
Parepa. She sang it at first with great success, but afterwards she
appeared to prefer "Il Bacio."

One day Arditi said to Mdlle. Parepa, "You don't care for 'L'Ardita'
any more, as you so seldom sing it?"

Parepa smiled sadly, and replied: "Dear *maestro*, think of the words,
'Io so volar,' and then look at me; do I look as if I could *fly*?"

Mdlle. Parepa had grown enormously stout, and therefore feared she
might meet with derisive laughter if she sang that particular song.
— EDITOR.

Mr. and Mrs. Henry Lee in Norwood, at their lovely country seat and hospitable house, where many great musical celebrities had been entertained, and where, if I remember rightly, the famous Catherine Hayes died. Among the notorieties who visited them, Tom Hohler, of whom more anon, was a constant and welcome guest.

It was during Virginia's sojourn at Norwood that she first learnt the sad intelligence of her mother's death, which had taken place during the previous summer in Virginia, and the news of which had only just reached her, owing to the blockade caused by the American war.

In consequence of my wife's bereavement, which had greatly affected her health, I had decided that, if possible, we should go to Paris for a change; and as it so happened that Mapleson was anxious to secure my opinion on the advisability of producing " Faust " during the coming season, we were able to combine pleasure with business, and departed in February with the ostensible purpose of reporting upon the beauty and attractions of that opera.

Gounod's passionate music came upon us like a revelation. All Paris was in ecstasies over the exquisite phrasing, warmth of expression, and eloquence of the melodies. We went to hear " Faust " on two consecutive nights, and I telegraphed to Mapleson my conviction that it should at all hazards be secured for the coming season.

Our visit to Paris in 1862 was, in many respects, a memorable one. It was on that occasion that we made the acquaintance of two of the century's greatest musicians, Rossini and Gounod.

The first time I saw Rossini I was taken by Badiali to his apartment on the Boulevard des Italiens, situated at the corner of the Rue de la Chaussée d'Antin.

We found the *maestro* seated at his piano, accompanying one of his compositions, admirably rendered by Madame Miolan-Cavalho. He was clad in a very shabby loose shooting-jacket, and wore a conspicuously ill-fitting and ugly-coloured red wig.

His manner at first impressed one as being nonchalant and careless; but once seated at the piano, his eye would kindle, heart and soul merging into his fingers, and the *maestro's* guests would stand breathless, and eager round him while drinking in his intoxicating melodies. At the conclusion of the song Rossini turned and greeted Badiali affectionately. Seeing a stranger, he rose and approached us.

"Let me present Signor Arditi, *maestro*," said Badiali, "a very excellent friend of mine."

"Any friend of yours is a friend of mine," said Rossini, cordially, putting forth a hand of welcome; "but Arditi is not a stranger to me: I know his music and I am pleased to see him in my house. . . ."

Thus simply and unostentatiously we made friends on the spot.

A galaxy of witty and brilliant men and women was always to be found at Rossini's receptions, which lasted from nine till eleven P.M., that time being exclusively devoted to music and *bons mots*.

The *maestro* was often given to characteristic remarks and sharp criticisms concerning other composers, but, to do him justice, he never sought to give his opinions unasked; on the contrary, he used to evade as much as possible the disagreeable task of criticising the works of mediocre musicians.

Prince Poniatowski, for instance, who in after years became a great friend of mine, had been hunting after Rossini for weeks in the hopes of playing him selections from two of his operas. in order to elicit his opinion as to which work would be preferable for production. So persistent was he in his supplications that Rossini could not possibly refuse to listen to a recital of the music in question.

Poniatowski, highly elated at having gained his point, accompanied Rossini home, where Rossini settled himself in his own particular chair, with his feet on another, and placed a huge bandana handkerchief over his eyes.

Poniatowski seated himself at the piano, and worked away lustily for an hour or so. When, almost exhausted and bathed in perspiration, he was about to commence his other opera, Rossini awoke from a doze into which he had fallen, and touched him lightly on the shoulder so as to arrest his progress.

"*Ce n'est pas né-cessaire, mon cher,*" he said sleepily, "*faites jouer l'autre. . . .*"

On the other hand, Rossini was never happier than when encouraging and advising beginners, or such artists as had any claim to his notice, and his charming familiarity towards people to whom he was attached was a matter of renown.

He preferred the society of artists to all other, and

was always delighted when his friends gathered round him and gave him free scope for his display of caustic wit and humour.

I remember once I had rendered him a slight service, and calling on him one afternoon I found him alone. Rossini was effusive in his reiterated thanks to me, and seemed anxious to prove his gratitude in a more material manner. He glanced round the room for a moment, and caught sight of a few wigs that had been placed on stands on the chiffonier.

"I am sorry, Arditi," he exclaimed, "that I cannot give you an actual proof of my gratitude; but if you would like to possess one of my wigs, you can take any colour that you fancy would suit you. . . ."

We were chatting together one day about a now well-known passage in the overture of "William Tell," which had always been wrongly played by various orchestras in England. I told him that on my remonstrating during the London rehearsals with my Corno-Inglese player, he replied "they had always played it thus." On hearing this, Rossini rose from his chair, fetched his *carte-de-visite*, at the back of which he proceeded to inscribe the correct version of the passage in question, while he wrote my name under the photograph. I reproduce, in facsimile, this interesting souvenir:—

And I also add the bars of music in the incorrect form (B instead of A) in which I had so often heard them played.

Need I say that it was not without considerable satisfaction that, on a later occasion, when again conducting "William Tell," I was in a position to triumphantly flash Rossini's photograph and the right bar of music before the stubborn Corno-Inglese, who had formerly presumed to argue the point.

Many were the pleasant evenings we spent in Rossini's company. Virginia wrote an account of her first meeting with the *maestro* to her friend Madame Puzzi. I subjoin an extract from her letter: —

DEAREST MAMA PUZZI, — At last I have met the great man Rossini, and hasten to tell you how he impressed me.

To begin from the beginning. Luigi has, of course, met him several times, but on Friday last (my lucky day) a *soirée* was given, to which I was invited.

The Baroness de X—— promised to present me, and she called in the morning to consult with me about my toilette. As you know, I am in mourning for my dear mother, and intended to wear a black tulle dress, with a white camellia in my hair.

The Baroness told me my dress would do admirably, but a *married* woman could not go to a *soirée* with only a camellia in her hair.

I submitted to the inevitable, and was trotted off to a famous milliner on the Boulevard de l'Opéra to buy a wreath, for that is the height of fashion in Paris just now.

I considered this wreath most unbecoming, but nevertheless I wore it without a murmur.

When we arrived in the presence of the *maestro* I thought

him the queerest looking old thing I had ever seen! Such a quaint, ungainly figure; such sharp, piercing eyes; such a vivacious, quick manner with it all, that I was quite taken aback for a moment.

Rossini looked me up and down, bowed low with a pleasant smile, and said: —

" Now I realise why Arditi composed ' Il Bacio ! ' ' "

Of course he paid me a great compliment, to which I curtsied; but I could not resist the temptation of giving him a pert answer.

" I never knew, Maestro," I retorted, — the words were out ere I had hardly realised it, — " that a composer or conductor ever required an excuse for writing about or giving a *bacio !* . . ."

Rossini was not surprised. He merely patted me on the back after my little outburst, and said, " Brava, l' Americana ! "

The party was a brilliant one. All Paris was there, and not only the *élite* and really *beau monde*, but also all the best artists, who vied with one another to do honour to their illustrious host.

The music, as you can imagine, was quite a revelation; there was plenty of mental food, plenty of wit and repartee, but refreshment *none*, not even a glass of water, which I thought hard on the singers.

Mdlle. Trebelli is at her best just now, and simply entranced her listeners. She sang a new song of Luigi's, called the " Farfalletta," with which Rossini was so pleased that we are going, with his permission, to dedicate it to him.

The following is the letter Luigi addressed to Rossini, begging him to accept the dedication of his song, " Farfalletta " (the Butterfly): —

To the Great Papa Rossini.

Bright luminaries have always attracted silly moths. Mine must fulfil its destiny, but with a name on its titlepage that will serve as a talisman, and save it from perishing. Therefore, poor moth, hover about, fly in all directions, and if you may not alight upon the lip (as did the kiss, " Il Bacio "), fashion will permit thee to settle on the wreaths and head-gear of the fair Parisian dames.

Humbly and devotedly,

Luigi Arditi.

Here is a facsimile of his answer, the gist of which I give in
English : —

Carissimo Arditi

*Profetto della partenza (per
Londra) del Sig Padovani pel
quale so v'interessate molto e
fate bene .*

*La Scelta della Carta nella
quale vi scrivo è dedicata
a quel Angioletto di vostra moglie
alla quale mi ponete Schiavo.*

*Il Comune amico Bengel mi
ha rimesso la vostra Carissima
Letterina e il Pezzo Graziosissimo
di musica che vi piacque Dedicarmi
agradite addunque i miei vivi
e Sentiti ringraziamenti .*

Non infievolite il vostro
interessamento pel Padovani,
Tenetemi calda nel vostro
affetto, & Credetemi ognora
Vostro Cominatore e affto
G. Rossini
Parigi 7. Aprile 1863

DEAR ARDITI, —

    •   •   •   •   •   •   •   •

The heading of the paper on which I am writing to you is dedicated to your little angel of a wife, of whom declare me the slave. Our common friend Engel had handed to me your charming letter and the graceful piece of music you were pleased to dedicate to me. Receive my lively and sincere thanks.

Your affectionate admirer,

G. ROSSINI.

During the evening Luigi was complimenting him on his unwontedly smart appearance, for he had never seen him in evening dress before, when Rossini, looking very pleased with himself, and turning round several times, said: "*Dites donc, mon cher Arditi, ne suis-je pas un Don Pasquale idéal?*"

. . . .

Ere leaving Paris, my wife and I were entertained by Alboni, Tedesco, and all our old friends, while our last evening was devoted to Mdlle. Trebelli and her parents, who gave a *dîner de fiançaille* in honour of their daughter's betrothal to Bettini, the tenor.

On our return to London a great national event took place, which we were fortunately able to witness, namely, the arrival in England of Princess Alexandra of Denmark, on the eve of her marriage to Prince Albert Edward of Wales.

I remember that we had been attending a rehearsal at Her Majesty's Theatre, and we all assembled on the huge stone balcony of the building to witness the great procession.

Never was a bride more lovely, nor happier looking, than Princess Alexandra on that memorable day.

The weather was cold and wintry, and tiny snowflakes flitted about in the air, melting on the burning, happy cheeks of the beautiful Princess, as the procession drove along in open coaches.

Her sweet smiles and blushes warmed the hearts of all who were present at her arrival,— ready to welcome and love her then almost as fervently as they love her now.

. . . .

At the end of my season in Edinburgh the members of the orchestra of Her Majesty's Theatre, who were with me on tour, presented me with a handsome rosewood bâton, mounted in gold, bearing the following inscription: —

PRESENTED

TO

SIGNOR ARDITI,

BY THE FOLLOWING MEMBERS

OF THE ORCHESTRA

OF

HER MAJESTY'S THEATRE,

EDINBURGH, 5TH DEC., 1862.

Messrs —

Anderson.	Griesbach.	Mapleson (Alfred).
Buzian.	Handley.	Pettit.
Clementi.	Healey.	Pollard.
Gilardoni.	Lockwood.	Svendsen.
	Ward.	Wiener.

CHAPTER VII.

THROUGH the kind interest shown to me by
Mr. Anderson, who was at that period leader
of the Queen's band at Windsor, I was privileged
to play in the orchestra on the occasion of the
marriage of the Prince and Princess of Wales.

It would be quite impossible to express in a few
words the grandeur and solemnity of that auspicious
event. One face, however, amid a sea of radiant
countenances, was absent from, or at least invisible at,
the joyous gathering. It was that of the Queen,
whose sorrow, I regret to say, at the loss of her
beloved Consort, so recently taken from her in the
prime of his manhood, was too poignant to permit
of her taking part in a joyful public ceremony.

Immediately after the wedding festivities were over,
Colonel Mapleson and I proceeded to Paris to interview Gounod and his publisher with regard to the production of "Faust" at Her Majesty's Theatre during
the following season.

I had, as I mentioned before, already heard "Faust," the many beauties of which I had fully recognised. On this occasion I took a vocal score with me to the theatre so as to jot down notes of the instrumentation. The first time I called upon Gounod he received me with great cordiality, and naturally enough our conversation was confined to the important project we had in view.

Gounod was delighted at the prospect of the production of "Faust" in London, and was kind enough to express his gratification at the knowledge that I was to conduct the opera. We talked long and earnestly about the orchestration, the chorus, the singers, — in fact, about every detail of the work, and Gounod seemed surprised to find me so *au fait* of the music.

I placed my vocal score before him, and showed him the numerous notes which I had made on the margin when I heard it. Gounod looked up quickly and said : " Then you have seen the full score, Signor Arditi, since you have noted all the instrumentation quite correctly ! " I smiled and shook my head. " No, Maître," I replied, " I jotted down these notes very hastily, but I have not yet seen the orchestral score."

Gounod rose and fetched his own complete MS., which lay on the piano. " Look," he said, with evident satisfaction, " yours is almost identical with mine, even to the very tympani ! "

I was delighted to have made a favourable inpression upon the great French composer, who from that moment put his music into my hands with perfect confidence and full permission to act in all matters relating to the production as I should deem right and judicious.

Mapleson and I stayed in Paris only as long as was absolutely necessary for us to secure the English rights of production, and to settle with Gounod's publisher, Choudens, everything appertaining to the monetary part of the transaction.

Meanwhile I went over the music with Gounod very carefully and completely, and we were entirely at one about every detail, except that I urged upon him the importance of considerably cutting down the final duet in the last act. Here we had a little tussle, for the master said it would break his heart to destroy a note of one of the most important parts of the opera.

Gently, but firmly, I put before him my reasons, which, I felt, were well worthy of consideration, the chief one being that too long a finale, and the too frequent repetition of a theme, is apt to tire the audience, and to drive it away before the fall of the curtain.

Gounod listened to me patiently, but with a somewhat sad mien. It was a hard wrench for him, but ere I left Paris I had obtained not only his full consent, but his approval of my suggestion.[1]

Back in London once more, the rehearsals of "Faust" were immediately commenced.

To the lovers of Gounod's "Faust" (the opera which is certainly *one* of the most popular works of the present day all over the world) it will seem almost incredible that the music was not looked upon with any great degree of favour at the outset; however, I begged the members of my orchestra to persevere, assuring them that they would be delighted with the music on a more intimate acquaintance.

The members of the orchestra, for instance, were not at first attracted by the music, the style and

---

[1] M. Gounod was more than delighted when he heard the music in its revised form, which appeared in the later editions, and has always since appeared with the cuts suggested by Signor Arditi. — EDITOR.

orchestration being so new to them, and during the first rehearsals they were scarcely favourably impressed.

I had ardently hoped, and indeed Gounod had given me his promise, that he would himself come to London in order to superintend the rehearsals of "Faust," and it was with no small amount of trepidation that, day after day, I looked for his coming and was continually disappointed. As we progressed I noticed a marked difference in the attitude of the orchestra towards the music. They were awakening to the fact that "Faust" possessed immense charm, and at the expiration of four or five rehearsals my prediction had fulfilled itself to the very letter.

I must mention that, previous to the production of "Faust," three benefit performances had been arranged to take place in honour of an ex-director of Her Majesty's Theatre, Mr. Benjamin Lumley, whose name was for years past intimately and honourably associated with the history and achievements of that house.

Mapleson courteously placed the theatre at the disposal of the friends who were arranging the testimonial evenings, but at the last moment Lord Ward refused to lend Her Majesty's, and the performances consequently took place at Drury Lane.

To the great delight of Lumley's many supporters, Piccolomini (the Countess Gaetani), on hearing of the proposed performances in aid of her old and valued friend, volunteered to come to England and to sing gratuitously for the occasion, a proposition which was gratefully accepted by the committee. Titiens, Giuglini, Gassier, Delle Sedie, Ferranti, Vialetti, and myself also lent our aid, besides several other well-known artists, and the Lumley performances began and ended triumphantly. Universal sympathy and co-operation was liberally extended to the ex-manager by all who remembered the opera in the old palmy days, as well as by those who had only heard of its former fame; for artists and audience alike were desirous of recognising Mr. Lumley's ancient liberality and good will.

I had almost forgotten Signor Schira's opera, "Nicolo de Lapi," the work of an old friend that deserves honourable mention. It was produced in May, 1863, and was considered an attractive feature among the musical novelties of that year.

Schira's score was that of a thorough musician, and of one who had ample command of the technical resources of his art.

"Nicolo de Lapi," a patriotic opera, containing characteristic military airs and melodies, was written in the genuine Italian style, fervid, melodious, and free from pretence or assumption. The airs were simple and graceful, and betokened much creative ability.

Schira was an extraordinarily able yet oddly-minded man, one of the old school whose abhorrence of Wagner, or indeed any other than Italian music, almost amounted to a mania.

It is of him the story is told that when Gounod's "Faust" was first produced in London, he was sitting in the stalls of Her Majesty's Theatre, and during one part of the music he held up his hands to his ears so as to exclude the sound, and cried out: "That is execrable! It reminds me of a couple of cats squabbling on the tiles! . . ."

The performance of Schira's opera, although successful in many respects, did not perhaps meet with the approbation and enthusiasm the music should or would have commanded had it been produced in any other country prior to its performance in England.

I have always declared that unless a musical work bears a *cachet* of excellence from abroad it will probably be received in this country with reserve and even coldness at the outset. Absolutely unknown compositions, such as " Nicolo de Lapi," for instance, have stood, and always do stand, but faint chances of creating a favourable impression in London, the reason of which curious fact I have never been quite able to explain satisfactorily to myself.

And this brings me once more to that all-important subject, namely, the first production of " Faust " in London, on June 12th, 1863. As I said before, the rehearsals in their early stages had filled me with apprehension, all the more so since Gounod had not kept his promise of coming to superintend the production.

Towards the first night of performance, notwithstanding the deepening interest the orchestra had evinced, I felt that I greatly needed the master's approval and co-operation in the grave task that lay before me.

Gounod had failed me at the eleventh hour, and when I entered the orchestra to take my seat on that memorable night I own that I felt somewhat nervous.

Just as I was about to raise my bâton I looked round, and, to my intense surprise and pleasure, caught sight of Gounod, who was seated in the stage-box.

Unbeknown to everybody, he had travelled all day, accompanied by Choudens, his publisher, determined to witness " Faust's " triumph or defeat, since unavoidable engagements had prevented his coming to London sooner.

A great feeling of gratification rose within me, and the orchestra — each man had his eye upon me — seemed to understand exactly what I felt at that moment. They mustered all their energy, a half appealing, half commanding look from me reached their hearts, and all determined, *coûte que coûte*, to do honour to Gounod's great masterpiece.

The music went admirably. There was no flaw or hitch, and Gounod himself was so delighted with the rendering of both orchestra and artists that ere the first act was concluded it was reported to me that he turned enthusiastically to Choudens and exclaimed: "*Que Dieu soit béni; voilà mon 'Faust'! . . .*"

But what about the audience? Of course the house rose to enthusiasm and heartily cheered the singers and composer, who were called to the front; but, frankly, "Faust" did not immediately force its way into the hearts of the people. The work had many enemies, and encountered a great deal of opposition and unmerited abuse; and, although the opera was constantly repeated, it was not a financial success during the first year.

The cast was a strong one, the chief characters being sustained by Titiens (Marguerite), Trebelli (Siebel), Giuglini (Faust), Gassier (Mephistopheles), and Santley (Valentine), all of whom rose to a pitch of perfection that has rarely been excelled.

Although the physique of Thérèse Titiens was hardly suited to the part of Marguerite, her artistic temperament and inborn German sentiment admirably sustained the character. Her singing of the passionate music in the church scene and final trio has never, in my hearing, been surpassed.

Giuglini's sweetly mellow voice and exquisite style was heard to the greatest advantage in the "Salve dimora," the violin obligato being played by Viotti Collins.

Trebelli's Siebel was a happy combination of excellent singing and refined artistic acting. Santley sang with pure intonation and fluent delivery; his part, however, was very small as Valentine, and Gounod consequently adapted the melody from the introduction as a song — "Dio possente" — expressly for him.

It has always been a source of delight to me to conduct " Faust," for the beauties of the orchestration appealed to me from the very first.

The revivals of " Oberon " and " Le Nozze di Figaro " were the next important events of the season. Fräulein Louise Liebhardt made her first appearance in " Le Nozze di Figaro." She was a most artistic singer, and brought with her an excellent reputation from Vienna. Her impersonation of the sprightly Susanna added greatly to the strength of the cast, which was composed *entre autres* of Titiens, Santley, Trebelli, Bossi, Bettini.

Titiens, as the Countess, gave a performance of great excellence, while Trebelli had rarely been seen to greater advantage than as Cherubino the page, who found in her a spirited and engaging representative. At this time her voice and executive powers were almost at their best, her mezzo-soprano voice being possessed of great flexibility and brilliancy. Her figure was eminently suited to boys' parts, and, to my mind, she never looked better on the stage than when she was clad in male attire.

In 1864, Mdlle. Désirée Artôt created a favourable impression as Violetta, in " La Traviata," at Her Majesty's. She studied regularly with me during her sojourn in London, her principal *rôles* being " La Figlia del Reggimento," " Il Barbiere," " Faust," and " Le Nozze di Figaro," all of which suited her capitally.

Mdlle. Artôt's attractions lay in her vivacious manner and dramatic powers. As an actress she was most effective, and as a singer she was excellent. Her voice was a high mezzo-soprano of considerable volume, and she managed it with great ability.

Her Majesty's Theatre was rarely closed. On the off-nights — that is to say, upon the evenings on which opera was not given — Madame Ristori, the great tragic actress, appeared in a succession of plays. The season, which had been a very successful one, was finally brought to a close with " Faust " (for the twentieth time), and with Mr. Mapleson's benefit on the following night.

For our autumn provincial tour, commencing with Dublin, the company included Messrs. Sims Reeves and Santley, and a new *prima donna*, Mdlle. Volpini.

This tour was not signalised by any particular novelty, and after "starring" in Ireland and the provinces, Mapleson organised a few performances of " Faust," the cast being the same as before, with the exception of Sims Reeves, who proved himself to be a desirable acquisition.

Mr. Julius Benedict's concert, given at St. James' Hall, is, I think, the last feature of interest connected with my musical career during the year 1863. A new cantata, entitled " Richard Cœur de Lion," by the concert giver, was performed on November 6th. The principal singers were Titiens, Trebelli, Wilbye Cooper, and Mr. Santley, names which were always hailed with delight by the public, while the majority of the chorus, members of the Vocal Association, and the orchestra acquitted themselves admirably of their task.

The selections before and after the cantata were conducted by myself, and two new compositions of mine were introduced, — " The Stirrup Cup," admirably delivered by Mr. Santley, and a *Bolero*, " Leggero Invisibile," which Thérèse Titiens sang for the first time ; the latter song was afterwards, so to speak, appropriated by Madame Sinico, who invariably achieved a great success when singing it. Of this clever and charming artist I shall presently have more to relate.

The winter season of 1864 brings me to my first

conductorship of English opera in London. My power over the language of the country in which so many years of my life have been passed is not, I am ashamed to say, one jot easier or more fluent now than it was when first I directed opera in a tongue that is not my own. Nevertheless, I managed to make myself understood (Italians generally do) in the orchestra by means of vivid gesticulation and a fluent conglomeration of several languages, and being extremely fortunate in the able musicians who constituted the orchestra, I had no great difficulty in obtaining what I required at their hands.

" Faust " (the English adaptation by Chorley) brought Gounod's opera nearer to the hearts of the public than it had as yet been, and indeed, so much more interest did the frequenters of Her Majesty's Theatre exhibit when this opera was produced in their native tongue, that the early winter season, which was short, was exclusively confined to the one work.

It is with the greatest pleasure that I recall the sympathetic and sweet-voiced Madame Lemmens-Sherrington. Her impersonation of Margaret was neither so statuesquely cold as that of Madame Miolan-Carvalho, nor so impassioned and dramatic as that of Titiens, but she united freshness and purity of intonation to a happy technique and a most correct and tuneful delivery. Her method was conspicuously artistic and musician-like: in such passages as demanded light and facile delivery, Madame Lemmens-Sherrington proved herself a charming artist, and her capabilities were highly appreciated.

Of Mr. Sims Reeves' Faust I must speak in conjunction with the Margaret of Madame Lemmens-Sherrington, for one vied with the other in point of excellence.

The garden-scene, which perhaps offers the principal opportunity for the display of the singer's art, gave us Mr. Sims Reeves at his very best, which in those days meant a good deal. His expressive and excellent rendering of the " Salve dimora " was worthy of very high praise. Signor Marchesi was a very zealous, anxious-to-please sort of Mephistopheles, and Miss Florence Lancia was an engaging and pleasing Siebel.

There is not much more to say, I think, about " Faust " in English. The chorus was excellent, and the whole performance gave great satisfaction to the public, and to Gounod himself.

8

CHAPTER VIII.

IN the spring of 1864 Garibaldi paid a visit to London, where he was the honoured guest of the Duke and Duchess of Sutherland, at Stafford House.

He was received by the general public, as well as in the upper circles of society, with the greatest enthusiasm, in recognition of the remarkable feats by which he had delivered Southern Italy from the Bourbon yoke, and added an enormous province to the kingdom ruled by the house of Savoy.

General Garibaldi was nobly entertained by public bodies as well as by private hospitality, and every endeavour was made to render his sojourn in London agreeable. Among the many entertainments that were provided in his honour was a gala night at Her Majesty's Theatre, upon which occasion the General, accompanied by his two sons and by Signor Mordini, Colonel Missori, Colonel Chiosso, Colonel Chambers, etc., was present at the performance of "Lucrezia Borgia."

The General's appearance was the signal for a tremendous burst of acclamation on the part of the audience, and after the orchestra had played "Garibaldi's Hymn," in conjunction with the chorus and military band, the curtain rose upon "Lucrezia," which was performed for the first time that season.

Mdlle. Titiens, Signor Giuglini, Mdlle. Bettelheim (a charming Viennese singer possessed of a superb contralto voice), and Signor Gassier sang the principal *rôles* with all the fervour and enthusiasm that the occasion demanded.

As I mentioned in a previous chapter, Giuglini was very fond of introducing the Romanza from my opera "La Spia," "Colli nativi," in the last act of "Lucrezia Borgia," and he did so on this particular night. The words of the last bars, "O Santa Libertà," were particularly appropriate to the occasion; and when Giuglini poured forth his grand notes, stimulated by the exciting occasion, all the Italians in the house rose in a body and applauded, with shouts and waving of handkerchiefs.

Between the first and second acts of the opera my *canto nazionale*, "La Garibaldina," — the words (by Signor Semenza) of which run as follows:

> "Madre Italia vendetta, vendetta!
> Siamo uniti per l'ultima guerra;
> Accoriamo dell' Alpi alla vetta
> Che l'odiato straniero ancor serra," —

was also performed under my direction by the chorus and orchestra.

Garibaldi was delighted, and sent for me during the

The wives and daughters of the members of the Italian Committee, as well as the wives of the artists and musicians, occupied a large double *loge* on this occasion, and were all dressed in white, with ribbons composed of the Italian colours, — red, green, and white. — EDITOR.

entr'acte to compliment me on the music in flattering
terms.

How picturesque he looked in the grey *capote*, which
he wore over a red silk shirt!—a costume which had
grown so familiar to us that it would have seemed
strange to everybody had he appeared before us otherwise attired.

His manner was reserved, almost shy, in its sensitiveness; and when he came forward in his box (he had
carefully concealed himself during the performance so
as not to disturb the artists by exciting recognition) to
salute the house, a fresh burst of enthusiasm was the
result, to which he bowed his head with a mute, yet
eloquent mien, betokening his heartfelt appreciation of
the honour that was being conferred upon him by the
British public.

Previous to his departure from England, my wife and
I met General Garibaldi at a luncheon party given at
the house of Signor Semenza, one of the most hospitable
and generous Italians who ever resided in London. The
General, I remember, picked up in his arms a little
dark-eyed girl who stood shyly gazing at him, and after
kissing her affectionately, he laid his hands upon her
head and blessed her. That little maid was my only
daughter, Giulietta, who was then about three years old.

For all the kindness that was shown to this gallant
and patriotic hero during his sojourn in London he was
deeply sensible and grateful.

As an example of this I here insert a facsimile of the
affectionate letter I received from him in acknowledgment of the musical entertainments that were organised
in his honour at Her Majesty's Theatre under my care,
and in which he thanks all the artists warmly for their
share in the performances:—

Caprera 3 Maggio 1865

Mio caro Pozzi

Accettate una parola d'affetto e di gratitudi-
ne per vostre gentilese — Voi siate per
un caro Valente a tutti quegli ottimi amici
che ti compiangeno di ricorda in Londra — e
ch'io giammai dimenticherò —
Ricordatemi pur all'amabili Vostra Sig.ra
e Prendetemi pur per Vostro
e Prendetemi

G. Garibaldi

GIBRALTAR, May 3rd, 1864.

MY DEAR ARDITI, — Accept a word of affection and gratitude for your signal kindness. Be so good as to convey a cordial greeting to all those distinguished artists who were so good as to do me honour in London, which I shall never forget.

Remember me also to your amiable consort, and believe me always yours,

G. GARIBALDI.

A few nights later Nicolai's opera, " The Merry Wives of Windsor," was successfully produced. That " The Merry Wives " managed to hit off the public taste was undeniable, and the scenery by Telbin, which was admirable in every respect (especially the moon-lit scene in Windsor Forest), elicited much commendation from the critics.

Titiens, as Mistress Ford, was as perfect as though she had been trained in the part by Shakespeare himself, and seemed to have conceived her *rôle* in the highest spirit of comedy; she introduced a *Rondo Finale*, which I specially composed for her, and which was most brilliantly rendered. Mdlle. Bettelheim was an ideal

An address and sword were presented to General Garibaldi at the Crystal Palace on April 16th by the Italian Reception Committee, followed by a concert of Italian music. The Crystal Palace was on that occasion full to overflowing, and the crowd most enthusiastic, joining lustily in the chorus of Signor Arditi's war song, " O Garibaldi! nostro salvator! . . ."

Almost all the great singers were present on that occasion, and a funny incident occurred during the concert. Signor Arditi became very much excited while conducting the music, and when turning to the chorus and wielding his bâton he had the misfortune to bring the latter down rather sharply on Mario's head. " Mario," says Signor Arditi, " behaved most admirably, and, without even uttering a murmur, laughed the matter off as though nothing had happened! " — EDITOR.

A brilliant musical reception was also given at the Reform Club in honour of General Garibaldi's visit to London. Signor Arditi conducted the music, which was performed by the band of Her Majesty's Theatre. — EDITOR.

Mistress Page, both from the vocal and dramatic standpoint; while Santley as Ford, Giuglini as Fenton, and Junca as Falstaff completed an excellent *ensemble*.

Gounod's "Mireille" during March of that year was to be produced in Paris, whither I again went to be present at the first performance. As soon as the necessary formalities connected with the English rights of production had been obtained, this opera was put into rehearsal in London.

It is with pleasure that I here recall my first public concert. All the principal artists of Her Majesty's were kind enough to come forward and give their services; and the concert, which took place in the theatre, was really an extremely interesting one. Arabella Goddard, Titiens, Lemmens-Sherrington, Bettelheim, Sinico, Volpini, Grossi, and Trebelli, and Giuglini, Santley, Gardoni, Junca, Gassier, and Bettini were among those who contributed so generously to the success of the afternoon. On looking over an old programme I find that we played a selection from Rossini's "Stabat Mater," and the overture to "Leonora" (No. 3 in C); the due from "Roberto" (Bettini and Junca), "Salve dimora" (Giuglini), and "Le Parlate d'Amor" (Bettelheim); also selections from "Faust," "Don Giovanni," and "Falstaff" (Titiens, Lemmens-Sherrington, Bettelheim, Junca, Gassier, and Santley). That excellent pianist, Madame Arabella Goddard, played Mendels-

---

A pretty story is told about Madame Arditi's little daughter. Mdlle. Titiens, who had been rehearsing nearly all day and had then returned home with Signor Arditi to study the difficult *rôle* of Leonora in "Fidelio," was considerably overwrought, and suddenly burst into a torrent of tears.

Little Giulietta, who had witnessed the scene, crept out of the room and ran to call her mother. "Poor Resa is crying, Mummy," she said sympathetically; "won't you go up and kiss her?" — EDITOR.

sohn's concerto in G minor with great *verve* and fire, for her execution was then at its best. "La Garibaldina" was performed by the full chorus with orchestra and military band, and a *Grand Duo*,[1] which I wrote in conjunction with Benedict for violin and pianoforte, was played to perfection by Madame Goddard and Carrodus. It was a suitable occasion upon which to place before the public my songs, "Il Bacio," "L'Ardita," "Colli nativi," "The Stirrup Cup," and "Leggero Invisibile," and so excellently were they delivered by their able interpreters that they did honour to their composer.

I cannot remember a more striking performance than that of "Leonora," by Titiens, Beethoven's opera being given several times to positively crowded houses. I do not hesitate to say that the part was, in my opinion, her grandest creation.

She never failed to draw tears to the eyes of her hearers in her great duet with Rocco; and her singing was of such perfection and pathos that her rendering of the music allotted to "Leonora" became rooted in my mind as quite ideal.

I remember that on the night of the production of "Fidelio" I was extremely gratified and pleased when Jenny Lind's husband, Otto Goldschmidt, took the trouble to come over and introduce himself to me, complimenting me on the efficiency and completeness of the orchestra.

Looking back to the remarkable career of Titiens, I cannot recall to mind an artist who worked more arduously than she did. Hardly had she appeared in "Fidelio," in which she created a sensation, than

---

[1] The *Grand Duo* was dedicated to the Queen of Spain, by her permission, and dispatched to Madrid, beautifully bound in velvet. Neither Signor Arditi nor Mr. Benedict ever heard whether the music reached Her Majesty safely, as they did not receive any acknowledgment of it. — EDITOR.

My Dear Virginia,

Augusta I did not arrive therefore if you have not changed your mind I call at you ½ 1 o'clock and take you to the dear children. How nasty it is again to day not favourable for my cold I will rest till 12 in bed it will do me good

My love to Luigi

yours

Therese

FACSIMILE OF A LETTER FROM TITIENS.

"Mireille" was produced, her vocal and dramatic resources again calling forth unanimous praise.

The first success of Gounod's "Mireille" was never for one moment doubtful in London. Unanimous approval was accorded to the music, which is descriptive and lyric rather than dramatic, and the opera (the overture of which has since become a great favourite in concert rooms) added another to the list of Gounod's successful works.

The following letter, which I received from Gounod after the production of "Mireille," will, in some sort, convey the *maestro's* own entire satisfaction with the way in which the opera was performed in London in 1864:—

Saint - Cloud - mardi 12 juillet / '64 -

Mon cher Arditi,

J'apprends, par une lettre de Choudens, toute l'ardeur, tout le zèle et toute l'intelligence que vous avez déployés dans la direction de Mireilla : rien ne m'étonne en cela de votre part, et vous savez que je n'avais pas l'ombre d'un doute à ce sujet ; mais je tiens à vous dire de suite combien je vous en remercie - un de mes principes en fait d'exécution musicale est celui - ci : « le premier Sujet d'une troupe est le Chef - d'orchestre . Il se figure - t - on une

victoire facile ou même possible avec de bons
soldats et un mauvais général ? assurément non -
si la tête est mauvaise, tout va de travers -
— Maintenant, vous qui avez été à même de
juger le mérite de chacun de mes interprètes,
veuillez, de ma part, leur transmettre la part
d'éloges et de remercîments qui revient à tous =
veuillez dire à M. Mme les artistes de l' Orchestre et
des Chœurs combien je regrette qu'une captivité qui
dure encore, m'ait privé de l' honneur et du plaisir
de me rendre auprès d'eux, et de leur exprimer
personnellement et directement toute ma reconnaissante
satisfaction -

Je vous charge, enfin, de mes meilleurs souvenirs pour
M. M. mes Tietjens, Trebelli, Reboux, et pour M. M. rs
Gunglim, Santley, Junca, et Gassier que je remercie
de son obligeante et si modeste coopération

Recevez, mon cher Arditi, la nouvelle
assurance de mon sincère et affectueux dévouement

Ch. Gounod

39, Route Impériale, Saint - Cloud -
Seine et oise

TRANSLATION.

MY DEAR ARDITI, — I have heard from Choudens of the ardour, zeal, and intelligence you have devoted to "Mireille." I am not in the least surprised at this, and you know that I never entertained the shadow of a doubt on that score; but I wish to tell you how much I thank you, notwithstanding.

One of my principles in musical execution is the following : First and foremost in a company stands the conductor. Can one picture to one's self an easy or even possible victory with good soldiers, supposing them to have an inadequate general at their head ? Of course not. If the leader is bad, all goes wrong. Will you, who have been able to judge the merits of the many interpreters of my work, kindly convey to them my congratulations and thanks ? Please tell the members of the orchestra and the chorus how much I regret that my prolonged captivity has prevented my being able to personally express to them all my grateful satisfaction.

My best remembrances to Mesdames Titiens, Trebelli, Reboux, and Messrs. Giuglini, Santley, Junca, and Gassier, whom I thank for their obliging and modest co-operation.

Accept, my dear Arditi, the reiterated assurances of my sincere and affectionate devotion.

(Signed) CH. GOUNOD.

39 Route Impériale, Saint Cloud,
Seine et Oise.

After the close of the season, Giuglini invited Virginia and myself to accompany him on a flying visit to his country seat in Italy, which was situate on a picturesque incline at Fano, in Ancona, near Bologna.

Joyously we packed up a few necessaries, and departed for our "Sunny South," with Giuglini, two other friends of his, Madame Puzzi, and her daughter Fanny. To say that we behaved like a lot of schoolchildren returning home after lessons would give but a faint idea of the wild spirits that possessed us.

Having for a few brief days set our work aside, and determined to devote our time exclusively to pleasure, we were not to be balked; and it still makes me smile, even after a lapse of so many years, to think of the fun we had on that journey. Giuglini, when free of the worries and cares of singing, abandoned himself absolutely to any and every kind of amusement; and his good-natured, even sometimes childish, humours were very entertaining to witness.

His love for kites and fireworks was extraordinary, and I remember that he insisted upon letting off squibs out of the railway carriage windows during our journey, in spite of the risk he ran of being arrested for unlawful procedure in the train.

Giuglini's house was situate on so precipitous a spot that we had to be drawn by means of four oxen up the hill-side that led to the chief entrance.

We made several excursions to Ancona and environs, the weather being lovely, and we enjoyed our delightful but brief week immensely. Music, fireworks, and good Italian dinners were the order of the day.

At the conclusion of our visit we all started north with Madame Puzzi, to spend a few days at her villa at Piedmont.

Madame Arditi tells me of another funny experience in connection with Giuglini.

Giuglini invited Signor and Madame Arditi, Madame Puzzi, and several other artists, to accompany him to the Derby in an open barouche, with four horses and postilions. The party discovered, when they wanted to return to town, that the two postilions were seriously intoxicated, and all the Italians of the company were so alarmed that they wanted to go back by train. Madame Arditi, however, exclaimed, "I came by road, and by road I mean to return. . . ." Her pluck encouraged the others to follow suit, and accordingly Madame Puzzi and her guests drove back by the road at a terrific speed. All went well until the coach arrived at Madame Puzzi's house in Cork Street, where, fortunately, every one alighted. A moment later the coach started off again, the horses gave a sudden lurch and turned the vehicle over. Had the accident occurred five minutes sooner the occupants of the coach must have been very seriously injured.

— Editor.

The villa was grandly situated, and afforded a splendid view of the surrounding country. On the roof of the house stood the emblem of Signor Puzzi's past triumphs in the shape of a huge horn, he having been one of the most celebrated horn-players of the century.

Of course Giuglini treated us to his inevitable fireworks, and considerably astonished the inhabitants of the neighbouring villages with his displays.

We left Italy with Giuglini for Paris, *en route* for London, where I was due for the conducting of the autumn operatic season. Little did we think when we bade Giuglini good-bye at the station on the day he started for St. Petersburg, that we should never see him light-hearted and in good health again.

In 1865 an early season of English opera was given by Harrison, for which I was engaged to conduct "Faust," and an English version of "Lara," an opera by Aimé Maillart. The subject of the opera was taken from one of Lord Byron's poems, and the action of the plot takes place in the region of the Spanish coast.

Maillart, who was the author of "Les Dragons de Villars," achieved a great success with his music, which was never dull, and which, if it did not exhibit unmistakable originality, was fluent and tuneful from beginning to end.

Of Miss Louisa Pyne, whose florid and tasteful style has been particularly sympathetic to the British public, and whose delicate and flexible voice, pure in quality and great in compass, won her many admirers, I can only say that her great talent and engaging personality were undeniable. Her acting was picturesque, her singing invariably tuneful; she had studied under Sir George Smart, who had given her an admirable training, and to this excellent foundation she added genuine love of her art, so that her success was not surprising.

As Kaled, in "Lara," Miss Pyne presented an engaging embodiment of the character of the disguised Gulnare, while her singing was musically and dramatically expressive and interesting. The other *rôles* were filled by Mesdames Romer and Cotterell, Messrs. Swift (a sweet-voiced tenor), Renwick, Honey, and Terrott.

Maillart was delighted with the success "Lara" had obtained in London, and with the manner in which the orchestra as well as the artists performed the work. The following is a letter he wrote to me from Paris in March, 1865: —

MY DEAR CONFRÈRE, — I beg your acceptance of the accompanying score of "Lara" as a souvenir of all you have done for its success. I hope some day to have the pleasure of shaking hands with you in London or in Paris, and expressing to you personally my gratitude.

In the mean time, my dear and esteemed *confrère*, accept the assurance of my most affectionate and devoted sentiments.

(Signed)   A. MAILLART.

CHAPTER IX.

THE season proper of 1865 was a very successful one. Several new singers were introduced by Mapleson, among them Miss Laura Harris — later known as Madame Zagury — and Mdlle. Ilma de Murska, a vocalist of almost phenomenal voice compass.

Mdlle. de Murska's voice was a soprano of nearly three octaves, with great executive powers. Although her dramatic talent sometimes bordered on the extravagant, she was a remarkable actress as well as a brilliant singer. She would, however, with the greatest *sangfroid* introduce all sorts of cadenzas of her own while rehearsing, and even during the actual performance of her parts, and it was often said of her that when she reached a high note she was with difficulty induced to let it go again.

I remember, too, that she was rather eccentric and fond of ostentation, and that her dresses were invariably showy.

One day she called upon us when we were living in Albany Street, and we were really amazed at her appearance.

To begin with, she was accompanied by a huge black Swiss mountain dog (her constant companion), and gave one the impression of being clad in a dress similar to the Hungarian hussar costume. She wore her blond hair reaching to her waist, while on her head was an imitation of the hussar busby, slightly on one side. Her jacket was decidedly military-looking. She was not possessed of a beautiful face, by any means, but she looked very striking on the stage, and was extremely graceful in her movements.

Mdlle. de Murska was never seen on or off the stage without a golden belt, which she invariably wore, and for which she entertained a strange predilection.

There is an old saying in French to the effect that " *bonne renommée vaut mieux que ceinture dorée*," and I remember hearing an angry *prima donna* once exclaim, when speaking of Mdlle. de Murska, "*On vois bien que c'est la ceinture dorée qu'elle préfère, celle-là ! . . .*"

One of Mdlle. de Murska's greatest parts was that of Dinorah; besides which, she achieved an enormous success in the *rôles* of Astrifiammante, Amina, Lucia, Marta, Senta, etc.

At about the period of Mdlle. de Murska's *début* at Her Majesty's Theatre as Lucia, we first became aware of Giuglini's approaching illness. We were in Dublin awaiting his arrival to join the company after his return from St. Petersburg, where he had gone to fulfil an engagment, and having heard continually that his frequent absence from the theatre was only due to slight indisposition, the truth, which reached us suddenly and which brought with it the terrible facts connected with his condition, convinced us at last that we were about to lose one of our most brilliant musical stars.

9

Giuglini was confined in Dr. Tuke's private asylum at Chiswick, where he was treated like one of the family, since his madness only made itself apparent at times.

He became terribly sad as the end drew near, but was never averse to singing, which he would do quite willingly when requested, the voice having lost none of its former charm. His eyes sometimes filled with tears when he said, with a melancholy shake of the head, in Italian, " Who would believe that poor Giuglini was to sing to a lot of mad people ? . . ."

Giuglini was sent, in charge of an attendant, to Fano, where he died, curiously enough, in the room once occupied by his father, who had also died raving mad.

I shall never forget seeing him for the last time just before he was sent away ; it made a deep and terrible impression upon me. His mouth was distorted with the agonised twitching peculiar to madness, and his eyes, once so bright and full of merriment, were dull and roving, bearing no sign of intelligence or recognition.

The full details of that awful interview are too sad to relate here; suffice it to say that on the day I bade Giuglini an eternal farewell, I felt as though I had lost a brother.

His curious and childish mania for fireworks and kite-flying seemed a foreboding of his final break-down. I distinctly recollect that at a *matinée* of " Don Giovanni " he behaved in a very wild manner, gesticulating to me from behind the scenes by making a violent pretence of flying a kite, in order to get me to hasten the *tempi*, so as to finish the opera as soon as possible.

Antonio Giuglini died on the 12th October, 1865. Such a result of his attack at St. Petersburg was not unexpected, hopes of his recovery having long since been abandoned by his doctors. The loss of Giuglini to the operatic world was irreparable. He died in his fortieth year, beloved by all who knew him. — EDITOR.

Gent.ᵐᵃ Sig.ᵃ

Dovendo fare acquisto di una cosa, mi sarebbe necessaria la di Lei presenza. Potendomi favorire verrei circa il mezzogiorno a prenderla e in mezz'ora tutto sarà fatto. Si compiaccia dirmi con una linea se puol aderire, e con mille complimenti offeribili anche per il Profilo mi dico

Suo obbl. Giuglini

FACSIMILE OF A LETTER FROM GIUGLINI.

Another brilliant success was achieved in the production of Cherubini's "Medea."

This opera, as well as several other classical works of a similar character, of which I shall speak later, was produced through the advice and counsel of Henry Jarrett, the manager and right hand of Mr. Mapleson.

Jarrett was originally a very excellent horn-player in the orchestra at Her Majesty's (from which position he was advanced to that of confidential adviser to our Impresario). He was not only a clever musician, but was also very useful in his capacity of agent and acting manager, being a shrewd and far-seeing man; his suggestions as to producing the works of such great masters as Cherubini, Mozart, Gluck, etc., some of which were practically unknown at that time in England, showed his great wisdom and perspicacity.

If Mdlle. Titiens had needed yet another link to connect her name with those of the most famous singers of the century, the part of Medea, the tragic heroine, more than supplied it; for never, since her *début* in 1858, except perhaps in "Leonora," had her magnificent acting and vocal powers been more severely put to the test than in this great classical work.

The opera, the score of which contains some of the finest passages in operatic music, was admirably put on the stage by Mapleson, and was considered by musical amateurs one of the noblest dramatic compositions ever written.

Mario was engaged in lieu of Giuglini to take the place of principal tenor for the autumnal provincial tour. We started in Manchester, whence we proceeded to Dublin, Belfast, and Liverpool, giving performances of "Don Giovanni," "Faust" "Rigoletto," etc. Mario

Signor Arditi composed all the recitatives for "Medea." — EDITOR.

was, of course, a great draw, and phenomenal successes were achieved during that tour.

A laughable incident occurs to me when I recall to mind one of many of Mario's inimitable performances in the "Trovatore." The orchestra on tour was not of course to be compared with that of Her Majesty's Theatre, and we had on that occasion, as on many others, been obliged to engage a "scratch" lot of musicians.

On the night in question we had reached the last act, in which Manrico upbraids Leonora for her infidelity, when Mario suddenly smiled at the men in the orchestra, and sang the words, "*Ah! quest' infame*,"

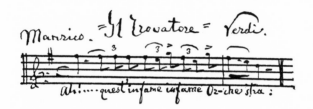

etc. (substituting the word "*orchestra*" for "*donna*"), in his most passionate style. It was amusing to see how good-naturedly the orchestra took Mario's joke, which instead of annoying them produced the opposite effect, and induced them to do better next time.

On the 18th of November I began my first series of Vocal and Instrumental Concerts at Her Majesty's Theatre for four weeks. My endeavour to introduce a serious class of music, rather than a light entertainment to which the public "walked and talked," was gladly accepted, and the "promenade concerts" offered me an excellent opportunity for bringing before the public such music as should be novel and welcome. On the next pages I venture to reproduce my original prospectus.

HER MAJESTY'S

𝕾ignor 𝕬rditi's 𝕲rand 𝖁ocal

SIGNOR ARDITI has the honour to announce that

SATURDAY,

AND CONTINUE FOR

IN selecting this period of the year for entering upon his undertaking, Signor ARDITI has acted upon the belief that these Concerts will in some degree fill the void which annually occurs in the musical world during the cessation of the performances of the Philharmonic Societies, the Musical Society, and the Monday Popular Concerts.

The time chosen has also enabled Signor ARDITI to make arrangements with the Lessee and Director, Mr. Mapleson, for Her Majesty's Theatre, and the Bijou Theatre, which are admirably adapted for Concerts appealing no less to the general public than to the musical amateur.

Guided by the great successes achieved by the revivals at Her Majesty's Theatre of "Fidelio," "Medea," "Il Flauto Magico," and "Der Freischütz," Signor ARDITI has determined to include in his programmes, which will be varied nightly, a large number of the compositions of the Great Masters, and among others many that have been seldom heard, or are entire novelties to English audiences.

Signor ARDITI believes the brief outline he has given of the main features of his programmes will be received with satisfaction; at the same time he thinks it right to make the announcement that "Popular Music" will also be fairly represented at every Concert.

With the view of rendering vocal as well as instrumental music a feature of interest in the Concerts, Signor ARDITI has the satisfaction to announce that, by the kind permission of Mr. Mapleson, he has made engagements with the following celebrated Artists: Mdlle. LAURA HARRIS, Mdlle. SAROLTA, and Mdlle. SINICO, Signor STAGNO, Signor FOLI, and Mr. SANTLEY.

The Orchestra will be composed of the Instrumentalists of Her Majesty's Theatre, and Signor ARDITI hopes he may be excused for recalling with some degree of pride the manner in which they have recently executed the difficult music of Cherubini, Beethoven, Mozart, and Weber, for which they received so much praise.

The first part of the programme will, on several occasions, be exclusively devoted to Classical Works, and on the Miscellaneous nights Instrumental and Vocal Selections from the most popular Operas will be introduced.

SYMPHONIES.

BEETHOVEN. — Eroica. The Battle Symphony: No. 4 in B flat; No. 5 in C minor; The Pastoral.
MENDELSSOHN. — A minor (Scotch); A major (Italian); C minor (No. 1).
SCHUMANN. — Symphony: No. 4 in E flat (first time of performance in England).
MOZART. — Jupiter Symphony; Symphony in E flat; Symphony in G minor.
HAYDN. — E flat (No. 10); G major (No.   ); E flat (No. 12).
SPOHR. — 1st Symphony, in E flat; 3rd Symphony, in C minor; The Power of Sound.
MEHUL. — Symphony in G minor.
GOUNOD. — Symphony in G (No. 1).

OVERTURES.

MEYERBEER. — Margherita D'Anjou; Il Crociato in Egitto; Emma di Resburgo (first time in England).
CHERUBINI. — L'Hôtellerie Portugaise; Elise; Lodoiska; Les Abencerrages; Ali Baba.
LINDPAINTER. — Faust; Der Vampyr; Joko.
SPONTINI. — Olympie; La Vestale; Fernand Cortez.
MARSCHNER. — Hans Heiling (first time of performance in England), and Der Vampyr
BALFE. — The Bondman (first time for eighteen years).
STERNDALE BENNETT. — The Wood Nymphs.
MACFARREN. — Chevy Chase.
BISHOP. — Aladdin (first time of performance since 1825), and the Doom Kiss (first time of performance since 1834).
SCHUBERT. — Fierabras.
VINCENT WALLACE. — Lurline.
HOWARD GLOVER. — Hero and Leander.
AUBER. — Le Macon; La Neige (first time of performance in England); Le Serment; La Fiancée; Gustave; Lestocq; Le Philtre; Fra Diavolo; La Bergère Chatelaine; Masaniello, and La Bayadere.
WAGNER. — Der Fliegende Holländer.
HEROLD. — Marie (first time of performance in England); Le Pré aux Clercs; Zampa.
ROSSINI. — Overture in B flat, originally written for Il Barbiere di Siviglia (first time of performance in England); Siege of Corinth; La Gazza Ladra; Semiramide; Italiana in Algeri; Corradino (first time of performance in England).
PICCINI. — Alessandro nell' Indie.
HUMMEL. — Matilda of Guise (first time of performance in England).
ONSLOW. — Le Colporteur.
PAESIELLO. — Il Re Teodoro.
CIMAROSA. — Il Matrimonio Segreto.
SALIERI. — Axur.
BELLINI. — Il Pirata.
GENERALI. — Bacchante (first time in England).
VERDI. — Luisa Miller.
DONIZETTI. — La Favorita; Maria di Rohan; Linda di Chamouni.

THEATRE.
and Instrumental Concerts.

his First Series of Concerts will commence on
NOVEMBER 18, 1865.
FOUR WEEKS ONLY.

WEBER. — Turandot (first time in England); Peter Schmoll (first time in England); Silvana (first time in England); Der Freischütz; Ruler of the Spirits; Oberon; Euryanthe; and Rubezahl (first time in England).
SCHUMANN. — Hermann and Dorothea; Bride of Messina.
BEETHOVEN. — Fidelio; 1, 2, 3 (Leonora), and 4 (Fidelio); Egmont.
BOILDIEU. — Les Deux Nuits (first time of performance in England); Le Petit Chaperon Rouge (first time of performance in England); La Dame Blanche.
MOSCHELES. — The Portrait.
SPOHR. — Jessonda; The Alchemyst; Bergeist Zweikampf (first time of performance in England); Kreuz-fahrer (first time of performance in England); Pietro von Abano (first time of performance in England); Alruna (first time of performance in England).
MEHUL. — Stratonice (first time for many years); Les Deux Aveugles de Toledo Adrien (first time of performance in England); La Chasse du Jeune Henri.
BERLIOZ. — Waverley; Le Carnaval Romain.
MOZART. — Die Zauberflöte; Le Nozze di Figaro; Il Direttor della Commedia; Cosi fan Tutte; Idomeneo.
BENEDICT. — Festival Overture; Tempest; Minnesinger.
MENDELSSOHN. — Military Overture, in C; The Calm of the Sea; Melusine; The Hebrides; Heimkehr; and A Midsummer Night's Dream.

MARCHES.
MEYERBEER. — **The Fest March (first** time in England; composed for the Coronation of His Majesty the King of Prussia); **Le Prophète.**
MENDELSSOHN. — **The Wedding March and March from Athalie.**

ARDITI. — New Pieces composed expressly for these Concerts: Duo, "Una notte à Venezia;" Valse, "Ilma Valse;" and song, "Many a time and oft" (to be sung by Mr. Santley).

Mendelssohn's Overture and Incidental Music to **A Midsummer Night's Dream;** the Music of the Witches' Scene from Spohr's **Faust;** the Ballet Music from Auber's Grand Opera **Gustave,** and from Auber's Ballet Opera **La Bayadere.**

SELECTIONS.
Selection from WAGNER's Grand Opera, **Tannhäuser.** Arranged expressly for these Concerts by Signor ARDITI.
Selection from GOUNOD's Opera, **Mirella.**
Selection from MAILLART's Grand Opera, **Roland a Roncevaux** (first time in England).
Selection from VERDI's Grand Opera, **La Forza del Destino,** arranged expressly for these Concerts by Signor ARDITI.
Selection from a MS. Opera (never performed) by **Donizetti.** Arranged by Signor ARDITI.

CANTATAS.
Le Desert. (The complete Work. First time of performance for twenty years.) Composed by FELICIEN DAVID.
Jubel Cantate. Poem by FRIEDERICH KIND. Composed by CARL MARIA VON WEBER (first time of performance in England).

VOCALISTS: Mdlle. LAURA HARRIS, Mdlle. SINICO, Mdlle. SAROLTA, Signor STAGNO, Signor FOLI, and Mr. SANTLEY.
SOLO INSTRUMENTALISTS: Principal Violin, Mr VIOTTI COLLINS; Viola, Mr. SCHREURS; Violoncello, Mr. PEZZE; Flute, Mr. SVENDSEN; Piccolo, Mr. JENSEN; Oboe, Mr. CROZIER; Clarionet, Mr. POLLARD; Fagotto, Mr. HUTCHINS; Horn, Mr. PAQUIS; Trumpet, Mr. ZEISS; Cornet-à-Piston, Mr. McGRATH; Trombone, Mr. HEALY; Euphonium, Mr PHASEY.
SOLO VIOLIN: Mdlle. EMILIA ARDITI, who has recently played with distinguished success at La Scala, Milan.

Conductor of the Dance Music, Mr. D. GODFREY.

CONDUCTOR   -   -   -   SIGNOR ARDITI.

The Programmes, published by Messrs. DAVIDSON & Co., may be obtained each evening at the Theatre.
The Bijou Theatre will be opened to the public as a refreshment and reading room, and will be supplied with all the principal Foreign and British journals.
The decorations will be executed by Messrs. UNIT, of Paddington. The lighting of the Theatre will be under the direction of Mr. DIMES.
The Refreshments will be supplied by Mdme. EPITAUX, of the Opera Colonnade
PRICES OF ADMISSION. — Private Boxes from 10s. 6d.; Dress Circle, from 4s.; Upper Boxes, from 2s.; Admission, 1s.
The Box Office, under the direction of Mr. NUGENT, will be open on Monday, and continue open daily from ten until six o'clock; also at MITCHELL's, LEADER's, Opera Colonnade, and the principal music-sellers.

On one of the miscellaneous evenings (we had German, French, and Italian nights) I gave a new selection from Wagner's "Tannhäuser," arranged by myself, for which performance the orchestra was composed of sixteen first violins, fourteen second violins, ten violas, ten violoncellos, ten contra-bassi, three flutes, two oboes, two clarionets, two bassoons, twelve horns, six trumpets, six trombones, two harps, two euphoniums, two bonbardons, drums, etc., and full chorus.

This selection met with unanimous approval when it was performed; but a funny story occurs to me with regard to Wagner's opera "Tannhäuser," which, by the way, was not, on the whole, favourably criticised at its production in London.

I had been reading over the score at the piano one day previous to arranging the selection, when my little girl Giulietta, who was sitting with her mother in the next room, suddenly looked up and said, "Who is playing the piano, mother?" My wife replied, "Your father, dear, of course; why did you ask?" Giulietta thought for a moment, and then said shortly, "Because *I thought it must be the tuner!*"

This little anecdote somehow reached the columns of a French newspaper, and after telling the story the paragraph concluded with the following little piece of sarcasm: "*Peut-on faire une plus spirituelle critique de la musique de Tannhäuser?*"

My sister, Mdlle. Emilia Arditi, who for some months past had met with considerable success at the Carcano and La Scala, Milan, contributed many violin solos during my series of promenade concerts, and I was well supported by the best artists that were to be obtained.

Pecuniarily, this venture proved eminently satisfactory, and the public was good enough to say that I had kept all my promises with regard to the " special nights" mentioned in my list of announcements, and that the concerts had been fully up to the expected mark.

The Grisi-Mario tour began early in January, Nottingham being the first town we visited. Madame Demeric Lablache, Signor Foli, and my sister (violin soloist) were also of the company, while Mr. Jarrett accompanied us as manager.

Of my old friend, and godmother to my son, Madame Demeric Lablache, I think with much affection. I shall speak of her in later pages. Every one knew her to be an artist to her finger-tips, besides being a woman of extraordinary charm, intelligence, and ability.

In spite of Madame Grisi's previous retirement from the stage, it was evident that her heart was still wrapped up in the work which had won her so much glory. That her voice had, perhaps, lost some of its brilliancy I will not deny, but she still held an undiminished power over her English audiences, while even to the last she exhibited much of her old marvellous fire and genius. Her *roulades* and rapid passages were given with great precision and aplomb, and her *ensembles* with Mario were a delight which can never be forgotten to all who heard them.

She was terribly loath to give up her public career, and I fear that towards the end of her operatic performances she herself knew and felt that the throne which she had so long occupied *alone* was being usurped by younger and more brilliant artists. The great triumphs which Mdlle. Adelina Patti was at that time achieving were keenly felt by her, and it is doing the great artist no injustice to say that the woman in her resented them, and that she was naturally enough jealous of Patti's success.

Her friends, prompted by judicious interest in what

was best for her welfare, induced Grisi to retire during the season of 1866, and her final appearance, which took place in " Lucrezia Borgia," was a very painful one to all who had known, loved, and respected that kind-hearted lady and brilliant artist.

My wife and I cherish the memory of countless happy days spent at her lovely house at Fulham, where Mario indulged in a mania for photography, and Caldesi was

invariably present with his camera, taking photographs and groups, of which we still possess many; one of Grisi and Mario in the Trovatore attitude is here given.

How few are left of the friends and *habitués* of that hospitable home, where such men as the late lamented Lord Leighton, John Woodford, Pinsuti, and Ciabatta, were constant visitors.

A few weeks ago I met the artist Baccani (who painted the two best portraits of Grisi and Mario extant). In the course of conversation he remarked that he and I were the only two men left of that charming coterie.

The reception awarded to " Medea " was an additional inducement for Mapleson to produce another classic opera, namely, Gluck's " Iphigenia in Tauris," a work

the intrinsic merits of which were no less remarkable
than the fact that it had been the immediate cause of a
long and violent artistic controversy, which had lasted
until Gluck's departure from France.

Without Mdlle. Titiens' co-operation I doubt whether
"Iphigenia" could have been given; with her, it was
not only possible, but even advisable. The *rôle* was a
worthy pendant to her "Medea," and took the house
by storm. Santley, Gassier, and Gardoni filled the
three other principal parts.

It would be superfluous to criticise Gluck's work,
which, with the sanction of a century, has been pronounced to be a classic; suffice it to say that the great
master's music was excellently interpreted by orchestra
and singers alike.

The revival of "Il Seraglio," Mozart's delightful
comic opera, proved to be another lucky venture.
Since its production at Drury Lane Theatre under
Jarrett's management, in 1854, "Il Seraglio," which
had been given in its original form as "Die Entführung
aus dem Serail," had not been heard in England again.
Now it was given in Italian, with some judicious curtail-
ments and transposition of the airs, while the spoken
dialogue was put in the form of "*parlante*" recitatives,
which I supplied.

Mesdames Titiens and Sinico as Constanza and
Biondina were admirable, while Signors Rokitansky,
Gunz, Stagno, and Foli completed a remarkable cast.

A leading musical critic wrote of the performance of "Iphigenia":
"Signor Arditi has gone to work *con amore* in preparing for representation
the opera of the old Bohemian master. Never were orchestra and chorus
more completely under control. Although in Gluck's operas, and even in
this, little or nothing in the shape of elaborate concerted music is to be
found, both chorus and orchestra are called upon for constant effort and
unrelaxed attention. But from the storm in the first act, to the interrupted sacrifice in the last, all was entirely satisfactory." — EDITOR.

My second annual concert at Her Majesty's was given to a crowded and fashionable audience, Signor Mongini (a new tenor whose career was fast becoming an important one) and Mdlle. de Murska being the additional attractions. Mr. Tom Hohler, by this time achieving a good reputation as a tenor singer, was the son of the Rev. T. W. Hohler, rector of Winstone, who became famous for the composition of the song called, "Follow, follow over mountain." It was said of the young artist at that time that he was destined to follow in the footsteps of poor Giuglini. Tom Hohler for some years held an appointment in the Civil Service, which he however resigned on becoming private secretary to the Earl of Dudley, the well-known musical amateur and patron of art.

In July, 1866, a second domestic event occurred to us, namely, the birth of my son. And that reminds me of a curious coincidence which is, perhaps, à propos of the subject.

There had been much comment in the Italian coterie of our friends in London on the fact that so many girls had been born to them and so few boys. Of course I desired dearly to have a son, and my wife heartily indorsed my wish.

One day Virginia said to me, — it was at the time when a certain event had become a matter of daily expectancy, — "If a son is born to us, Luigi, will you give me that chain with the snake's head in diamonds which you received as a souvenir from Grisi and Mario? I have always longed to possess it so as to wear it in the form of a bracelet. . . ."

I promised my wife that if she should present me with a son she should have the chain.

A very few days afterwards "Gigi," as he has always since been familiarly called, was born, and when Virginia said to me, shortly afterwards, " Where is the chain ? you see it has brought us luck," I at once had it made into a bracelet, and my wife still wears it in affectionate remembrance of Grisi, Mario — and Gigi.

While on one of our yearly visits to Mr. R. Garrard, who was a loyal patron of the opera and of singers alike, and at whose house musical gatherings were constantly being held, we first met the Marchioness of Downshire. This lady was also an ardent musician, and one whose efforts in the cause of charity were untiring.

In those days my wife sang very well *en amateur*, and Lady Downshire, whose pianoforte playing was excellent, often accompanied her in her songs. Lady Downshire was contemplating the arranging of a charity concert on the occasion above mentioned, and begged me to assist her. This I gladly consented to do, and asked her to let me know the date she had fixed upon for the entertainment.

After that we went on tour as usual for the autumn season, my wife accompanying me. I shall never forget Virginia's astonishment when, one morning, I laid a programme in her hands, on which her name had been placed for a song (Gounod's Serenade), which Lady Downshire had arranged, without consulting us, after hearing my wife sing.

At first Virginia demurred, for she had never yet appeared in a public capacity on any platform; but I persuaded her to consent, although she was very nervous at the prospect.

On the occasion of the concert, a few weeks later, Lady Downshire presided at the piano, Virginia sang the Serenade, and I accompanied with the violin obligato.

The trio went splendidly, and the *soirée* wound up with a big ball, at which we all danced until the small hours of the morning.

CHAPTER X.

FOR various reasons I did not go on tour with Mapleson's operatic company during the spring season
of 1867. Our boxes were packed, and we were in perfect readiness to start; but at the eleventh hour Mr.
Jarrett was so emphatic in his advice to me to give
up the project that I yielded, and the arrangement fell
through, Signor E. Bevignani (who had married a niece
of Mdlle. Titiens) departing in my stead.

I do not hesitate, however, to add that Jarrett particularly impressed upon me the desirability of my
keeping disengaged for the season proper, saying that
unless my name appeared on the announcement bills
and programmes of Her Majesty's Theatre there would
be a considerable falling off in the application for seats
from the libraries and ticket offices, and that Mapleson
would undoubtedly want to secure my services as usual.[1]

---

[1] It should be remembered that in the days of which the author writes,
the names of such men as Costa at Covent Garden, or Arditi at Her
Majesty's Theatre, were considerable attractions to the librarians and ticket-
sellers. Without the announcement of the name of a well-known conductor
to an operatic company the public were chary of purchasing tickets for the
season. — EDITOR.

My wife and I were in Paris with Titiens and Mapleson for a few days prior to the opening of the season in London, when we heard Christine Nilsson sing at the Théâtre Lyrique for the first time. Needless to say that Mapleson, always to the fore when talent was available, immediately secured the new Swedish singer for the following London season.

Mdlle. Christine Nilsson had been creating a great *furore* in Paris as Ophelia in Ambroise Thomas' opera, "Hamlet," and I recall with pleasure how delighted we were with her fresh, rich voice and attractive appearance.

My services were secured by Mapleson for the direction of Her Majesty's Theatre, as foretold by Jarrett, and the season opened with Mozart's "Nozze di Figaro."

The first appearance of Mdlle. Christine Nilsson on the boards of "The Old House" was a memorable one, while the success of the newcomer was never for one instant doubtful.

CHRISTINE NILSSON AS OPHELIA.

She made her *début* in "La Traviata," and even at the end of the first act her success was assured, and that all the more legitimately because she presented herself to a critical English audience in a perfectly unostentatious manner.

Nilsson's singing reminded me greatly of Angiolina

Bosio, her brilliant *fioriture* being delivered with the same exquisite grace and refinement that characterised the style of the Italian artist. Everything was in favour of the young Swedish artist, — her youthful freshness (in itself a priceless charm); a definite individuality; her slight, supple figure, which lent itself to the draping of any classical robe; and, above all, the voice, of extensive compass, mellow, sweet, and rich.

On the 17th of July an extraordinary musical festival was given at the Crystal Palace in honour of His Majesty the Sultan, who was at that time paying a visit to London. An act of munificence on the part of His Imperial Majesty, who, having been informed of the disaster which befell the building during the previous winter, hastened to present £1,000 towards its restoration, enhanced the interest of the occasion.

The orchestra was that of the Crystal Palace, but it was strengthened by the performers of Her Majesty's Theatre, thus producing an imposing instrumental force. Mr. Manns and I shared the duties of conducting the music, the programme of which comprised the following selections: —

OVERTURE, "La Gazza Ladra" . . . . *Rossini.*
DUETTO, "Suoni la Tromba" (Puritani) — Signor
    Pandolfini and Signor Foli . . . . *Bellini.*
RATAPLAN, "Al suon del Tamburo" (Forza del Destino) — Madame Trebelli-Bettini and Chorus of
    Her Majesty's Theatre . . . . *Verdi.*
ARIA, "Loving smile of sister kind" (Faust) — Mr.
    Santley . . . . *Gounod.*
PART SONG, "O Hills! O Vales!" — Chorus . . . *Mendelssohn.*
ARIA, "Ocean, thou mighty monster!" (Oberon) —
    Mdlle. Titiens . . . . *Weber.*
ARIA, "Una furtiva lagrima" (Elisire d'Amore) —
    Signor Gardoni . . . . *Donizetti.*
ARIA, "Ernani involami" (Ernani) — Mdlle. Nilsson *Verdi.*

CANZONE, "La donna è Mobile" (Rigoletto) —
Signor Mongini . . . . *Verdi.*
SOLO AND CHORUS, "Calm as the glassy ocean"
(Idomeneo) — Mdlle. Sinico and Chorus . . *Mozart.*
BALLAD, "My guiding star" (Robin Hood) — Mr.
Hohler . . . . *Macfarren.*
"Soldier's Chorus" (Faust) — The Chorus of Her
Majesty's Theatre . . . . *Gounod.*
POLACCA, "Vien un Giovin" (Freyschutz) — Mdlle.
Sinico . . . . *Weber.*
FIRST FINALE OF DON GIOVANNI — Mdlles. Titiens,
Nilsson, Sinico, and Baumeister; Mesdames
Trebelli-Bettini and Demeric Lablache; Signors
Mongini, Gardoni, Gassier, Pandolfini, Bossi,
Foli, and Agretti; Herr Rokitansky, Messrs.
Lyall, Hohler, and Santley, with full Band and
Chorus from Her Majesty's Theatre . . . . *Mozart.*
OVERTURE, "Zampa" . . . . *Herold.*

I composed a complimentary "Ode to the Sultan," the spirited words of which came from the pen of Zafiraki Effendi. I was fortunately able to introduce some characteristic Turkish melodies. The Ode was sung to the illustrious visitor by several of our artists and chorus, and met with a most flattering reception from the Sultan.

I remember that while traversing one of the lobbies, I came face to face with His Royal Highness the Prince of Wales. The heat was intense, and the Prince, who was evidently in search of a breath of fresh air, asked me whether he would have time to smoke a cigar during the pause following the first part of the programme. I informed His Royal Highness that he would have plenty of time for a smoke, whereupon he took out his cigar case, and said, with his genial smile, "Take a weed, too, Arditi; I'm sure you want it after your hard work."

The crush on that occasion was such as I rarely saw

equalled. My wife and little girl barely escaped injury, and had it not been for the kindness of Foli, who carried Giulietta on his shoulders (and owing to his unusual height held her above the heads of the people), the child must, without a doubt, have been seriously hurt.

The appearance of Miss Clara Louise Kellogg, who had previously earned honours in the States, and occupied an exceptional rank as an interpreter of the lyric drama of sentiment, was an interesting event in the history of Her Majesty's Theatre.

Her singing had many charms, among which the perfect enunciation of her words was a great point. Her phrasing was highly finished, and her cadences were so exquisitely rounded that they delighted the most exacting and critical of ears.

She appeared in " Faust," and later during the season made a great impression in " La Traviata."

Looking back to the musical criticisms of years gone by, it is curious to notice the manner in which the libretto of " La Traviata " was invariably and bitterly condemned. Why, I wonder, was " La Traviata " singled out to be the recipient of so much violent censure, when " Don Giovanni," " Lucrezia," and countless other operas were tolerated ?

The following comic letter was received by Signor Arditi at this period with regard to his popular song, " Il Bacio." — EDITOR.

CARO LUIGI, — Cheer up, old boy! Here's glorious news for you! Read and rejoice! I hear from New York that Madame Anna Bishop has been singing your tuneful and merry "Bacio" at Hong Kong with such tremendous success that her Celestial auditors in the greatest excitement embraced and kissed each other all round in the most frantic manner! The Emperor, viz., the cousin of the Sun, was himself so delighted with your tune that he encored it no less than ten times, at the end of which he insisted upon kissing the siren herself, creating her, on the spot, " Singer to His Celestial Majesty's Private Chapel!" Do write another " Bacio " soon, and oblige your sincere admirer,

J. E. S. ROMPIECOLLI.

"La Traviata" is, after all, still to the fore, in spite of the hard usage to which it has been subjected; whereas a host of problem plays of later years have found their way to the stage, possessed of far more unsavoury plots and objectionable situations, and unredeemed, moreover, by the accompaniment of tuneful music, which covers a multitude of sins.

We were rehearsing "Fidelio" on the 7th of December, a week prior to the proposed end of the season, when I left the theatre about six o'clock, in order to fetch my wife and little daughter to take them to a performance at Covent Garden.

On our return from the theatre we noticed that the sky was very red and angry-looking; whereupon Virginia remarked, —

"There's a terrible fire somewhere to-night. . . ."

We took no further notice of the incident, and drove to Albany Street, where, at Lumley's suggestion, we had taken a house, and had set up housekeeping for the first time in real earnest, a step which the advent of a son had rendered almost a necessity.

At breakfast the next morning I opened my newspaper as usual, only to receive an awful shock, for my eyes lighted on the following alarming heading: —

TOTAL DESTRUCTION OF HER MAJESTY'S THEATRE
BY FIRE.

For the moment it was hard to realise the meaning of those words; and hoping that it was all a mistake I rushed into the street, hailed a cab, and was, alas, soon informed that the news was only too true! A pitiful sight awaited me on my arrival at the Haymarket.

All the employees, chorus, orchestra, and artists, met beside the ruins to bemoan the fate of their professional home. There was literally nothing left of the theatre save the smouldering ashes. The cause of the fire never really transpired; enough that in a few hours the building and all its contents were absolutely destroyed. Here and there were the charred remains of stage properties and costumes, for of course nothing could be saved. I picked up the part of an operatic score partially burnt, and it was indeed a sorry sight to see the magnificent building I had only quitted a few hours previously burnt to the ground. When the flames reached the huge chandelier the noise produced by the cracking of glass was simply deafening. The flames, too, are said to have soared upwards to the heavens in all the colours of a rainbow, owing to the quantity of Bengal fire that had been stored on the premises. It must have been a magnificent spectacle, — one, however, which filled the hearts of many hard-working people with consternation, for it meant a total loss of livelihood to them for the time being. Mapleson, who was a man of many resources, lost no time in looking about for another theatre, and ultimately secured Drury Lane for the following season.

Prior to the opening of Her Majesty's Opera I went to Paris, where I had interviews with Rossini and Auber with reference to the productions of " La Gazza Ladra " and " Gustave III." Auber was working very hard at

Verdi's " La Forza del Destino " was produced for the first time in London during the season of 1867. Its success was, however, by no means conspicuous. — EDITOR.

In March of the year 1868 the principal members of the orchestra of Her Majesty's Theatre presented to Signor Arditi an illuminated address, in which they begged to testify their appreciation of his unremitting exertions on their behalf after the late fire, and of his having been one of the foremost to promote the movement set afoot to compensate them for their losses. The address concluded by stating that the disinterested kindness manifested by Signor Arditi in managing and conducting the concert for their benefit on the 9th of January would always be gratefully remembered by them, accompanied by a wish that the time might not be far distant when they would meet once more under his able direction. — EDITOR.

that time on a new work, and wrote me that the only time he could see me would be at six o'clock in the morning. Accordingly I called upon him at that hour, and found him busy with his MSS.

"I can only spare you a minute," cried Auber, when he greeted me, "so we shall have to be as brief as possible. But stay, I *must* play you a few bars of my new opera; just listen to this. . . ." And then he turned to his music and played snatches here and there, keeping me by his side for at least two hours!

Auber presented me with the score of "Le Premier jour de Bonheur," a charming work, in which I heard Mdlle. Marie Roze. She was at that time very beautiful, and her voice, a pure and melodious soprano, already gave promise of the successful career that lay before her.

We opened — I say *we*, for I was, as usual, director of the orchestra — with "Lucrezia Borgia," and I need hardly say that the reception accorded to all the survivors of the disaster of Her Majesty's Theatre was a hearty and prolonged one. Signor Foli, to whom I have up to the present only alluded cursorily, had at this time become a permanent member of the company. He used to be described as "Foli, the Gubetta with a voice," since he had made his *début* in that unimportant character. Of his charm as a singer it would be superfluous to speak, since he soon became, and has remained, a great favourite in England; of his personality, however, I, who count myself among his many faithful friends, may add that a more delightful or sterling good fellow never lived.

My annual concert of 1868, given at Drury Lane Theatre, was the most successful one I ever gave.

It was conspicuous by the fact that Christine Nilsson had promised to sing "the mad scene" from Ambroise

Thomas' "Hamlet" for the first time in London, and the announcement caused a rush for tickets which was extraordinary.

Without the advantages of stage, costume, scenery, orchestra, and chorus (the orchestral parts of "Hamlet" not having arrived from Paris in time), we had to give the famous scene (fourth act) "at the piano," without the necessary stage accessories, to a crowded and enthusiastic house. Nilsson was glorious, acting and singing to such absolute perfection that she riveted the attention of the audience from the first to the last note.

All the chief artists connected with Mr. Mapleson's theatre took part in the entertainment, and "Old Drury" was rarely seen more densely thronged. During this season Christine Nilsson used to study most of her parts with me at my house from about ten o'clock in the morning until two, and most faithfully and conscientiously did she work. She appeared in "Faust," "Lucia," "Marta," and "La Traviata," and I still entertain the liveliest recollections of her engaging personality and persevering industry. An associate of the brilliant Nilsson nights was Mongini, a dear friend and excellent artist, whose early death we have never ceased to mourn. He was possessed of a phenomenal Italian voice, and one of which Tamagno reminds me more strikingly than any other singer of the present day. In temperament he was a thorough enthusiast of his art, excitable and noisy to a degree. Campbell Clarke, an honoured representative of "The Daily Telegraph," used to say: "Nothing amuses me more than to sit at a table between Mongini and Arditi. When those two fellows begin arguing and gesticulating over politics it is great fun to be present, if only to see the excitement they are able to work up between them about the most trivial matter. . . ." We constantly met at the house of Signor and Madame

Semenza, which was, as I said before, a most hospitable rendezvous for all Italian artists in London.

Mongini was full of contradictions. He would sing his very best, in fact divinely, and rouse the house to such a pitch of enthusiasm that they insisted upon an encore; then he would come forward and interpolate some new and most ordinary commonplace cadenza, utterly spoiling the good effect he had previously made by his refined singing. On such occasions I used to hiss out at him, in Italian, every invective that I could lay my tongue to; but that had no effect whatever, and if a similar occasion presented itself on the following night, he would do the same thing again and again.

I remember we were dining together one day in Dublin; he was to appear the same evening, and as usual he was talking so loud and so fast that I feared he would be hoarse and unable to sing if he continued to use his voice so recklessly. I warned him several times without avail, and said finally: " I will make a compact with you. . . . You shall stand me two bottles of champagne at supper to-night if you don't reach your high note and sustain it properly, without making a *scrog*. . . ." Mongini agreed to this at once, so sure was he that he would not be called upon to pay the penalty.

That evening all went splendidly until we reached the passage in question. Our eyes met. Mongini was choking with laughter, and — I won the bet ! He scrambled over the note, made a hideous *scrog*, such as sent the blood like fire to my head, and after the performance he laughingly swore that I had made him lose his note ! !

On the 5th of August, 1868, I received the following note from the Imperial Ottoman Embassy : —

SIR, — I have the honour to inform you that His Imperial Majesty the Sultan has been graciously pleased to promote you to the Fourth Class of the Imperial Order of the Medjidie in token of his satisfaction with the music of the hymn composed by you and performed at the Crystal Palace last year.

In transmitting you herewith enclosed the insignia of the Fourth Class and the diploma conferring it upon you, I beg to offer you my sincere congratulations on your receiving this mark of the Imperial favour.   I have the honour to be

Your obedient servant,

(Signed)   MUSURUS.

Mr. Michael Costa was decorated with the same order that I had been honoured with in Constantinople in 1859. This reminds me that there was evidently a scarcity of "stars" at the Imperial Palace at that time, for I was requested to send my former star of the Medjidie back to the Embassy, in order that the identical decoration might be forwarded to Costa.

Our autumnal tour to Dublin and the provinces in 1868 was followed by a short season of Italian opera at Covent Garden, which house Mapleson leased of Mr. Gye for the purpose.

It was during this time that Mdlle. Minnie Hauk, the afterwards celebrated and ideal "Carmen," made her *début*, at the age of eighteen, on the English stage.

In her Mapleson had another most promising discovery. Her voice was a very high soprano, neither very powerful nor very rich, but clear and light, with a *mezza-voce* of peculiar charm. There was no trace of vibrato to be detected in her notes (a very prevalent

The following paragraph appeared in "The Morning Post" of August 24th, 1867 : —

"It must be satisfactory to Italian artists visiting and residing in England to find that they are not forgotten in their own country. A striking proof has just been given to Signor Arditi of the esteem in which he is held in Italy, in the shape of a decoration forwarded to him by King Victor Emmanuel. Signor Arditi has received from His Majesty the Cross and Insignia of the Honourable Order of San Maurizio and San Lazzaro."

— EDITOR.

and rising evil among the singers at that time), and altogether Mdlle. Hauk, who was an American by birth, and a pupil of Maurice Strakosch, was at once declared to be a most finished singer and competent actress.

Mdlle. Hauk's bright face and laughing eyes won the hearts of the people at once in her impersonation of Amina in Bellini's " Sonnambula," and her appearance was not only considered a matter of great interest, but as one of actual importance.

There is only one more event to record in 1868, and that is the death of the genial old master Rossini. In the thoughts of those who were privileged to know him personally he will ever live, exerting an active influence over their minds by his bright, sparkling music. Rossini's life verged almost upon the ideal. He encountered no obstacles during his great career, and he lived in the keenest enjoyment of the pleasures which fame brought him.

Rossini was the lode-star of Literature and Art. Very many celebrated personages thronged the master's fireside to bask in the sunshine of his wit. His happiness was infectious; it was impossible to know Rossini without seeing much that is joyous and mirth-moving in life, and his music reflects a corresponding joviality.

CHAPTER XI.

THE year 1869 was conspicuous by the extraordinary fact that Messrs. Gye and Mapleson amalgamated their forces, and, abandoning rivalry, clasped hands over a joint enterprise.

So much has been written elsewhere about the Mapleson-Gye alliance that it is unnecessary to dilate on the subject here. Suffice it to say that Mr. Costa's resignation of his conductorship at Covent Garden (by reason of his inability to come to favourable terms with the management) was followed by my being engaged in his stead, and after many discussions and negotiations we commenced the opera season with " Norma."

On the opening night, upon reaching my desk in the orchestra, I was heartily greeted by a large portion of the audience ; the members of the orchestra themselves, however, maintained a dogged silence, refraining from exhibiting any kind of demonstration. It should be mentioned that Mr. Costa's resignation had been followed by that of several of his principal musicians, Mr. Sainton among them, and I quite felt that this coolness was only natural for the orchestra, considering that the absence of their own particular conductor had, naturally enough, caused much discontent and irritation among them.

I admired them for the *esprit de corps* they maintained towards their leader, — all the more so, as it was the attitude I myself should have expected *my* orchestra to assume had the case been reversed.

In lieu of Sainton I placed that excellent musician Carrodus as leader at Covent Garden, and when he joined I told him that at last he was in his proper place, and that he would do well never to vacate it. Strange to say, Carrodus *did* remain at that very post until the day of his death.

The principal attraction of that season was Ambroise Thomas' "Hamlet."

A curious fact in connection with the dress rehearsal of "Hamlet" was that my own annual concert had been fixed to take place on the same date, the 13th of June. (My wife entertained a curious liking for Fridays and the 13th of the month, always selecting either of these days for any auspicious event in connection with ourselves, and I must admit that the days invariably proved to be lucky ones.) I shall never forget Gye's astonishment when he learnt that, despite the fact that my own concert was taking place, I elected to stop at my post so as to see the rehearsal through to the very end, arriving as I did at the Hanover Square rooms just in time to appear on the platform as the concert was over, the audience having been informed of the reason of my absence. I had, however, left my interests in very good hands, namely, in those of my wife, whose indefatigable energy in such matters has always been of invaluable assistance to me.

The day following, "Hamlet" was produced in London for the first time, achieving, unquestionably, a most legitimate triumph. With such admirable artists as Nilsson, Sinico, and Santley in the principal *rôles*, worthy associates of one another, and worthy interpreters of Ambroise Thomas' beautiful melodies, any further remarks on the production would at this date be superfluous.

The success of the performance of " Hamlet " was celebrated on the next day by a breakfast given to Ambroise Thomas by Jarrett, at which the principal artists, ourselves, and many members of the dear old Press of those days assisted.

My birthday, which we fêted the following evening, gave us the opportunity of entertaining the genial composer in our own home; and I cannot attempt to repeat all the congratulatory and gracious things he said to me about the production of his favourite work.

We started for Paris, *en route* for Homburg, with Madame Sinico and her husband. We stayed there a week, and were entertained *entre autres* by Christine Nilsson, at whose hospitable table we met the celebrated M. Wartel, who was her singing-master, the Trebelli-Bettinis, and other friends. We arrived at Homburg on August the 16th, just in time to witness the illuminations organised in honour of the late Emperor William, who was quietly walking about among the people in his sociable and pleasant manner, apparently greatly enjoying the fête.

I remember our visit to the gaming-rooms, and my wife's reluctance at first to try her luck at the tables! The Duke of Newcastle, who was of our party, at last induced her to make a venture, and just as the wheel was turning, and " *Rien ne va plus !* " was being cried out by the croupier, Virginia turned to me for a coin. In my haste the first piece of money I took from my pocket was a florin, which she promptly threw down on her favourite No. 13. Oddly enough 13 turned up, and Virginia's first plunge was signalised by her being paid thirty-six times the amount of her original stake.

From Homburg we proceeded to Baden-Baden, that most healthful and lovely resort, to hear Ambroise Thomas' "Mignon" (in which opera Christine Nilsson was appearing in the title *rôle*), and to negotiate for its production in London during the season.

M. Hengel, the publisher of "Hamlet" and "Mignon," gave a magnificent luncheon-party, under a tent situated at one of the prettiest spots in Baden, in honour of the great *prima donna* and heroine of the hour, at which we were present, together with Bevignani, Franchi (at that time the agent of Madame Adelina Patti, and a dear friend of mine), and several other well-known artists and musical people.

Mdlle. Nilsson was in the zenith of her beauty, and the cynosure of all admirers.

Like all artists, Christine Nilsson suffered from "nerves," and I recollect when she came to my house to go over her parts with me, she used, while singing, to tear the trimmings and laces off her skirts by continually fingering them. Her lady companion, Madame Richardson, was in despair about her dresses, and used to say how she wished it were fashionable for ladies to wear perfectly plain skirts, devoid of any kind of trimmings, so that Nilsson could not have the chance of spoiling all her *passementeries!*

In spite of all the admiration that was lavished upon Christine Nilsson in those early days, she was absolutely unspoilt and uninfluenced by flattery. At that luncheon given by M. Hengel (one of the most courteous and charming men of my acquaintance, by the way), a pretty incident occurred which is *à propos* of the subject. A gentleman, who happened to make a complimentary remark on the shapely form and whiteness of her hands, was rather taken aback when Mdlle. Nilsson answered in her pleasant, outspoken way, " Those hands, which you are good enough to admire, have done a lot of work in their time; for remember that they are peasant's hands, and were made to handle the plough! . . ."

Several of Nilsson's sister-artists were present at her first performance of " Mignon " in Baden-Baden, and testified their admiration for her in their own way. Madame Viardot sent round her card, "*Avec toute son admiration pour la délicieuse ' Mignon.'* " Pauline Lucca wrote: " It is not possible to be more dramatic, or to sing better. You were sublime, and it gives me the greatest pleasure to tell you so. . . ." And assuredly not the least gratifying among the many tributes she received were these encouraging words from her sisters in art.

A funny incident occurred to us on our homeward journey from Baden. Bevignani (who travelled with us) and I had both invested in " cuckoo " clocks (one of which stands in my hall at the present moment), and when our luggage was examined at the custom house, Bevignani, whose portmanteau was opened first, was asked to give his name, and to pay a heavy duty on the clock. When it came to my turn, and I informed the custom-house officer who I was, he threw up his hands and exclaimed, " Mein Gott, are you the Signor who composed ' Il Bacio' ? " (It must be remembered that at the time of which I write the song had reached the zenith of its popularity, and was a familiar tune of barrel organs and street bands.) When I nodded in acquiescence, the good man seemed to be so pleased that he waived the question of our paying any duty on the clock, much to the surprise of Bevignani, whom we chaffed unmercifully during the journey because he had not been similarly spared.

The season of 1869 at Covent Garden was a good one on the whole, and included such operas as "Fidelio," "Medea," "Hamlet," "Robert le Diable," "Le Prophète," and "Don Giovanni," while the Dublin tour, later, offered very much the same repertoire.

Jarrett, to whom the combination scheme of Gye and Mapleson had appeared anything but propitious, was meanwhile working hard to find an *entrepreneur* hazardous enough to start a company of Italian opera at Drury Lane Theatre, and having prevailed upon Mr. Wood, of the firm of Cramer & Co., to undertake the enterprise, he immediately began to engage artists for the following season.

Among those whom he induced to leave Covent Garden were Nilsson, Santley, Foli, Faure, Mongini, Ilma de Murska, Trebelli, myself, and others.

I had no wish at that time to leave Messrs. Mapleson & Gye, the latter gentleman having always shown a kindly appreciation of my efforts; but Jarrett's inducements were many, and plausible in the extreme. Firstly, he assured me that I should occupy the position of sole conductor at Drury Lane; secondly, that several of the best artists were in favour of the scheme, and that they greatly desired my co-operation; and, lastly, Jarrett boasted of his great influence with the gentlemen of the press as likely to insure a complete success to the enterprise. That I had reason to bitterly regret the step I took will be proved later; in fact, as Mr. Gye's son, Ernest, once remarked, had I not rashly quitted Covent Garden at that time I should no doubt have remained at the post as long as Gye *père's* management lasted.

There is only one more matter of importance to record during 1869, and that is the demise of Grisi.

We were informed of her death in December, during one of the winter season performances at Covent Garden.

A sharp attack of inflammation of the lungs had seized her in Berlin, where she died, after a few days' illness. Poor Mario was in St. Petersburg at the time, and Grisi was on her way to join him in Russia, when this fatal illness overtook her ere she had time to see him again. Her sister and brother artists one and all felt acutely the loss of a loyal and kind-hearted comrade. Although Madame Grisi had, for a good many years, ceased to be a prominent figure in the operatic world, she held a position in this country such as it has been the lot of only a very favoured few to hold. It will always be remembered of her that she worked valiantly in the cause of her art, and that of all the artists of her time she was perhaps *the* one who most seldom disappointed the public under any pretext whatsoever. Her artistic supremacy and personal popularity, moreover, impressed themselves for ever on those who were fortunate enough to hear her, and who knew the Grisi who, for so many years, was the delight of the operatic world.

. . . .

Great excitement prevailed in musical circles when Mr. Wood's prospectus, full of the promise of good things, was published early in 1870,—the novelties that were announced being Mozart's "L' Oca del Cairo," Weber's "Abu Hassan," Rossini's "Othello," Ambroise Thomas' "Mignon," and Wagner's "Flying Dutchman." The two last-named works were, of course, the great events of the season.

On the whole, Drury Lane was extremely active during its brief reign. To say nothing of Nilsson's artistic assumption of the Countess in "Le Nozze di Figaro," she was the means of permanently restoring Rossini's long-lost "Othello" to the lyric stage in England, and manifested, moreover, her ripened powers in "Mignon." The two quasi-classical novelties were

"L'Oca del Cairo," the production of which was perhaps better in intention than in result, and "Abu Hassan," a little gem, as full of light, life, and colour as any of Weber's more ambitious and important works. In "Mignon," Christine Nilsson's voice, singing, acting, appearance, and depth of pathos went straight to the hearts of her audience. The dresses suited her slender figure admirably; and although realism was not carried so far in those days as it is now (in the case of "Trilby," for instance, when the heroine appears *quite* barefooted on the stage), Nilsson's shapely feet were, nevertheless, seen to great advantage in her flesh-coloured stockings.

Faure, who sang the part of "Lothario" perfectly, was picturesque and dramatic as ever; and, indeed, all the artists were proportionately successful. After each act, which was followed by cheers and applause, Nilsson almost dragged Ambroise Thomas on to the stage, in order that he should share the honours with her; but Thomas appeared very reluctantly at the wings, and was with difficulty persuaded to come forward.

The production of "Mignon" was altogether a great event. Ambroise Thomas was delighted with the orchestra, and I recollect his saying to me, on hearing that "The Flying Dutchman" was to be produced in close proximity to "Mignon," "Good heavens! Arditi, you don't mean to say that you are going to do 'The Flying Dutchman' so soon after 'Mignon'? How will you manage it in such an incredibly short time?"

My players numbered between seventy and eighty, among whom were several first-class instrumentalists, new-comers: from La Scala, at Milan; the Teatro Reggio, at Turin; and the Lycée, at Barcelona. There was also no less a personage and virtuoso than Ludwig Strauss, whose playing at the Monday Popular Concerts and the Philharmonic Society's Concerts had placed

him in the foremost rank of the classical executants of
the day. With such excellent men it was not difficult
to accomplish a huge amount of work in a comparatively
short space of time.

The first performance in England of an opera by
Wagner, a composer who had so long been the object
of much angry discussion and misconception in artistic
circles, was an event of special interest. For twenty
years past Wagner had been agitating the world of
music by strong denunciations of operatic precedents,
and by his endeavours to practically illustrate his
theories by his works; hence a composition of the great
German musician was anxiously looked forward to
by all.

" L' Olandese Dannato " took the English public by
surprise, and the surprise was a pleasant one. The
work was produced just a week prior to the closing of
the Drury Lane season, and we all looked upon the feat as
being rather a remarkable one, considering that we were
allowed very few rehearsals. The house was well filled,
the musical connoisseurs and professors of the metrop-
olis being in noteworthy preponderance, and, despite
the terrific heat, those who came at the beginning to
scoff, remained to the end to applaud with enthusiasm.
I remember the surprise of myself, and of my leader,
Ludwig Strauss, when the overture was vociferously
encored.

Some of the critics were as bitter in their condemna-
tion of the opera as others were strong in their defence
of it; but, generally speaking, " The Dutchman " produced a much better effect than was anticipated.

The opera, of which parts are extremely difficult, was
admirably given on the whole. No one who heard that
weird, storm-tossed music for the first time will forget
the impression made upon him by the passionate

singing of Mdlle. de Murska, Signor Perotti, Mr. Santley, and Signor Foli.

A grave reason for the bad attendance at the subsequent performances was the declaration of war between France and Germany, which recalled thousands of German residents in London to their native soil, and cast a general gloom over every shape of amusement.

The Drury Lane season being over, we went in August to stay with our good friends the Garrards, and I remember how one morning before breakfast old Mr. Garrard surprised us by coming to our bedroom door with the exciting news of Napoleon's surrender, after the battle of Sedan.

Mapleson's autumn season of cheap nights at Covent Garden, at which Bevignani and I shared the duties of conductorship, brought 1870 to a close.

CHAPTER XII.

THE year 1871 did not dawn auspiciously for me,
for at the beginning there was a void in the busy
life I had hitherto led, and I found myself for the first
time minus an engagement for the London season.

Mapleson had naturally deeply resented my alliance
with the Wood enterprise, and Costa, having quitted
Mr. Gye, was only too happy to avail himself of
Mapleson's offer that he should conduct at Drury
Lane.

Thus matters appeared for the moment to be singularly infelicitous for me. I found, however, that " when
one door closed, there were others that opened wide,"
and a very short time elapsed ere Eugenio Merelli, the
well-known Impresario, made me a flattering and lucrative offer to conduct opera at St. Petersburg during the
following winter season, which proposal, I need scarcely
say, I accepted with pleasurable anticipation.

It now occurs to me that in May of that year we
gave one of our *matinées d'invitation* at the hospitable
home of Major Carpenter, a house at which all artists
were treated with the warmest kindness and consideration. It would be impossible to record the innumerable
acts of generosity of Major Carpenter towards struggling
musicians; everybody has heard of the good actions of

this valiant patron of art, and there are few artists living at the present moment who will not gladly corroborate what I say.

To My dear Maestro Luigi Arditi —
Alvina Valleria

Major Carpenter kindly lent us his house for our musical matinée, and on this occasion I had great pleasure in bringing before our friends a young pupil of mine, Miss Alvina Lohmann, in whose promising voice I was taking a very deep interest. This talented

lady, better known at the present moment as Madame
Valleria, made a decidedly favourable impression, and
on the occasion of my annual concert in Hanover
Square Rooms, a few weeks later, her voice was put to
a severe test in her delivery of " Gli angui d' inferno,"
which she sang in the orignal keys, D minor and F,
earning for herself such applause as is rarely evoked on
a first public appearance.

I must, in speaking of Madame Valleria's *début*, say
a few words appreciative of the gratitude she has always
shown me during our subsequent friendship, in return
for my efforts to help her when her career was only
just budding. Gratitude is not, as a rule, a trait which
is largely developed among musicians, and therefore it
has in this particular instance appealed to me all the
more warmly. Madame Valleria — she was of course
Mdlle. at the time of which I write — made so favourable an impression by her agreeable range of voice and
executive skill, that the Impresario Merelli came to my
house to supper on the night of the concert (it was, as
usual, on a Friday, and Merelli was leaving town early
on the following Saturday) to propose an engagement
for the lady for St. Petersburg, the particulars of which
we chatted over and decided upon between the hours of
of 12 and 1; for, curiously enough, Merelli did not
believe in there being any luck in Friday, and preferred
to wait until Saturday had dawned ere we closed the
contract.

During the season — an idle one for me — I was able
to accept the many invitations we received, and I see
by my diary that the year 1871 was one of our gayest
on record.

I am not, however, going to weary my readers with
a recapitulation of our countless *soirées*, etc., at the
house of Lord this and Lady that; the meetings and

gatherings which chiefly impressed themselves upon my memory were spent in the company of such artistic and, to us, intensely sympathetic people as the Dion Boucicaults, Virginia Gabriel (Mrs. G. March), Charles Mathews, Sergeant Ballantine, and many others.

Sergeant Ballantine's name recalls innumerable dinners at the "Star and Garter," Richmond, and elsewhere, which he was in the habit of giving to his enormously wide circle of friends, — for there never lived a more generous man, or one who entertained more widely or lavishly.

My wife met him one day in Piccadilly, and they stopped and chatted. The Sergeant, whose gallantry towards the fair sex was proverbial, rather alarmed her by suddenly exclaiming in his bluff, hearty way, "Do you know that I have put you in the book?" (It was at the time that he was publishing his reminiscences.) Virginia's look of alarm and "Oh! good gracious!" made him laugh heartily. "But your husband is in, too," he rejoined quickly, "so you need not be afraid, . . ." and Virginia gave a sigh of relief, about which he often chaffed her later on.

The Dion Boucicaults were living near Regent Street at the time of which I write, and I have many pleasant remembrances of the charming host and hostess, and of the attractions around them. It was at one of their delightful reunions that we first met William Terriss, then one of the handsomest young fellows I have ever seen, and even now, to my mind, one of the most pre-possessing actors on the English stage. Salvini, too, we met there; he was particularly taken with Virginia, because she spoke Italian so fluently.

Mr. and Mrs. Charles Mathews gave delightful parties, of which our host was the life and soul. He revelled in gathering Italians and foreigners around him, and one night at one of our supper parties Virginia, having retired with the ladies, was surprised to find that the men remained so long in the smoking-room. She came downstairs after a while to see the cause of the delay, and found Charles Mathews surrounded by Italians, who were listening amid roars of laughter to anecdotes which he was telling in the Neapolitan dialect. He was a great linguist, and spoke several languages fluently. His wife, I am happy to say, is just as bright, vivacious, and brilliant a hostess now as she was in the days of her husband's fame, while the friendship which has existed between us is as firm now as it was twenty-five years ago.

The Franco-German war drove many artists from Paris to London in 1871, and among these were Prince Poniatowski, Alberto Visetti, a clever musician; Madame Conneau, the wife of Dr. Conneau, Napoleon's medical adviser, and a distinguished vocalist; De Soria, whose singing, once heard, could never be forgotten; Pietro Mazzoni, who was not only a musician but a poet, whose charming words have served as texts to many of my compositions; and many others who have since become well-known personages. Opportunity, through lack of work, was afforded me to make the acquaintance of many of these artists, all charming people, and, as I said before, we were plunged in gayeties, races, luncheons, dinners, suppers, from morning till night.

We were very intimate at this period with Mrs. George March, better known as Virginia Gabriel, a lady whose talent for musical composition was much appreciated in those days. She composed several operettas, the principal soprano parts of which used to be charmingly impersonated by Miss Harriet Young.

I remember also going to Mrs. Weldon's house one

day to meet Gounod, in order to go over " Romeo e Giulietta " prior to its production in St. Petersburg.

Gounod insisted upon cutting out the Prologue, which had been given in its entirety in Paris, and of course his wishes were carried out. And that reminds me that on the night of the production of this opera in St. Petersburg, the Grand Duke Constantine (to whom, as well as to the Grand Duchess, I took letters of introduction, and by whom I was cordially received) came down on the stage after the first act, and wanted to know why the Prologue had been suppressed. I explained that I had carefully gone into the matter with Gounod in London, and that it had been done by his express desire. The Grand Duke was still vexed, and persisted that in Paris, where he had heard the music, the Prologue had particularly delighted him. I argued that in London it had been left out; but he seemed to look upon London as a very unimportant place, and would listen to no argument in favour of the omission. During the fourth act a march was played, and the Grand Duke, still chafing under the vexation of the missing Prologue, came subsequently to me and exclaimed, " If you had cut out the march, now, and left the Prologue, you would have pleased *me* better. . . ."

But to return. In August we went to Homburg for four weeks prior to my departure for St. Petersburg. I felt the parting from my wife acutely, but left her in charge of a good friend, Madame Schuster, at Frankfurt, at whose lovely house Virginia was hospitably entertained for over three weeks.

Madame Adelina Patti (then Marquise de Caux) entertained us several times at her charming villa at Homburg, and since she also was bound for St. Petersburg we had many opportunities of becoming very intimate with her. Together we went over her wonderful répertoire, preparatory to our joint engagements at the Imperial Opera House in the Russian capital.

On the 30th of September I left for St. Petersburg, where, I am glad to say, I found an excellent orchestra, composed of eminent men, which lent to my efforts an additional zest.

The critics and papers accorded me very high praise on the occasion of my first professional visit to Russia, and the following extracts from " Le Journal de St. Pétersbourg " will serve to show the esteem in which they held me : —

" M. Arditi jouit dans l'Europe Occidentale d'une grande réputation ; Londres surtout en fait le plus grand cas, et si nous avons attendu d'en parler avec éloges, c'est parceque nous avons voulu le voir à l'œuvre dans une des productions de Meyerbeer, où l'orchestre a un rôle presqu'aussi important que celui des chanteurs. Dans ' Les Huguenots ' par exemple, l'orchestre c'est la palette du peintre. Il donne le coloris nécessaire aux différents groupes tracés au crayon. Il assombrit la situation à un moment donné, ou bien projette un éclat extraordinaire sur le tissu mélodique, quand les passions grondent et se déchâinent. Malheur au peintre qui entasse trop de couleurs. Gare au chef d'orchestre qui ne nuance pas suffisamment les effets. Maintenant que nous avons entendu les Huguenots nous pouvons affirmer hardiment que M. Arditi est parfaitement à la hauteur de sa réputation. On n'accompagne pas avec plus de douceur, le chant mélodieux — et l'on n'éclata pas avec plus de force quand il le faut. En un mot, M. Arditi manie admirablement *la palette* — nous voulons dire l'orchestre qui se trouve à sa disposition.

" M. Arditi, qui aura certainement entendu parler du goût très prononcé d'une grande partie de notre public pour la musique instrumentale en général, et la musique Allemande de cette espèce en particulier, aura voulu probablement se faire valoir en faisant exécuter sous sa direction la magnifique ouverture du ' Freischütz.' Effectivement cette exécution a été parfaite.

" On ne saurait y mettre plus de nuances, plus de coloris, et

plus d'ensemble. Aussi le public a-t-il acclamé si chaleureuse-
ment et si longtemps cette ouverture, que le chef d'orchestre
s'est vu finalement obligé de faire face au public pour le
remercier de l'ovation dont il était l'objet.

"M. Arditi a salué à plusieurs reprises les artistes de l'orchestre, comme pour dire qu'il voulait leur attribuer une large
part des applaudissements qui venaient d'être prodigués. . . ."

The orchestra of the Imperial Opera House at St.
Petersburg comprised several well-known musicians,
such as Maurer (first violin), Davidoff (violoncello),
Ferrero (double bass), and others of equal eminence;
while the operatic company was a brilliant one, the
names of Patti, Lucca, Sinico, Artôt, Valleria, Trebelli,
Nicolini, Graziani, Bagagiolo, etc., proving an enormous
attraction to the music-loving Russians.

The life in St. Petersburg was a totally new one to
me, and one fraught with stirring interest and striking incident. Merelli entertained very largely, and the
hospitality that was shown to us during our sojourn
there was enormous. Alas that my memory for names
has always been execrable, and in trying to recall those
of the many Russian families who added to the pleasure
of our visit I find myself quite unequal to the task.

I do remember, however, that I saw a good deal of
Ernesto Nicolini, whose voice was really magnificent at
the time, and whose impersonations of " Raoul " in " Les
Huguenots " and " Romeo " in Gounod's opera were my
ideals of perfection.

The season lasted throughout the winter, during
which time we gave " Faust," " Il Barbiere," La

Signor Arditi composed two Romanze, which he dedicated to the
Empress of Russia during his sojourn in St. Petersburg. The Czarina
appears to have been much gratified by the thoughful act, since she presented Signor Arditi with two magnificent rings, — one composed of
diamonds, the other of diamonds and rubies. — EDITOR.

Juive," " Les Huguenots," " Nozze di Figaro," with several other well-known operas, " Romeo e Giulietta " being the novelty which was most triumphantly received.

Madame Valleria made her *début* on the operatic stage at St. Petersburg as " Linda " on the 4th of November of that year, and came before her audience with so many natural advantages that she was obviously destined to become a general favourite.

At this time Merelli offered me a good engagement to accompany him to Vienna for a Patti season exclusively.

Adelina Patti caused an absolute *furore* in Vienna; indeed, the Viennese were perfectly wild about her.

Of those kind, genial Austrians I shall have more to say when touching upon the eight seasons I spent consecutively in Vienna while conducting Italian opera. The Viennese love Italian music, and are among the most appreciative audiences it has been my good fortune to come into contact with.

I stayed on each occasion at the Hôtel Munsch, in the Neuer Markt, where Adelina Patti has always taken her suite of apartments, and it was at her table that I met the famous critic, composer, and author, Dr. Hanslick.

To all who know the great man, his charm of manner and brilliant conversation are familiar. We used to spend most exhilarating hours together over the piano; and when he wanted to particularly delight me he let his fingers wander dreamily over the keys while playing one or two of my compositions from memory. Then there was that dear kind family Fishoff, by whom I was

Madame Valleria made a great hit in Signor Arditi's song, " L· Incontro," which she introduced in " Linda," and which was written expressly for her. — EDITOR.

received with open arms during my many visits to
Vienna. I have known all the boys intimately, and
have seen them grow up to manhood; one of them
married Miss Sigrid Arnoldson, the distinguished *prima
donna.*

Of the orchestra at the Theater an der Wien I
cannot, however, speak with great enthusiasm. It
required a great deal of drilling and manipulation to
bring it into working order; but the men were earnest,
and amenable to discipline, and very soon matters became more satisfactory than they were at the outset.

I returned to London in May, 1872, and my wife, I
remember, took the occasion of my birthday to celebrate
my home-coming. We gave a big party, at which
Adelina Patti, Mdlle. Sessi (the *prima donna* with the
beautiful hair, who afterwards married Baron Erlanger),
and many other cordial friends assisted.

In July His Royal Highness the Prince of Wales did
me the honour to invite me to his annual garden party
at Chiswick, an invitation which the Prince was good
enough to repeat for several subsequent years, and in
August my wife and I paid our usual summer visit to
Homburg, where Madame Patti was singing in Italian
opera. The Diva introduced a composition of mine,
" Forosetta: tempo di Tarantella," in the lesson scene
of " Il Barbiere," which was very successful.

In October we returned to town for the winter, and I
then signed a contract to conduct opera at Vienna for
the following spring season, accepting at the same time
another offer to direct the orchestra in St. Petersburg
for the winter of 1873.

CHAPTER XIII.

EARLY in February, 1873, I went to Milan (*en route* for Vienna), where I assisted at the *début* of Mdlle. Valleria at La Scala. The interest I had always taken in my pupil drew me thither, and I was very glad to witness her triumphs in Italy, which proved to be as great as they had been in England and Russia.

A curious fact, by the way, in connection with the dress rehearsal of "Un Ballo in Maschera" (the opera in which Mdlle. Valleria made her *début*) was the absence from the theatre of a stage-manager. Mr. Augustus Harris, father of the present Sir Augustus, happened to be in the house at the time, so Faccio, the well-known Italian conductor, and I begged him to help us all out of an awkward predicament, which he did with his usual amiability, undertaking the direction of the final rehearsal, and greatly helping to insure the success of the production by his valuable advice. Mdlle. Valleria appeared in "Roberto il Diavolo" and other operas with equal popularity at Milan, where she was at once installed as a favourite, and voted a great artist.

My stay in Milan was very brief, and I hastened on to Vienna, where, as I mentioned before, I was engaged to conduct for the Italian opera season.

With what pleasure did I return to that bright and sympathetic country! The cordial receptions accorded to me, in fact to us all, went straight to our hearts, and, for my part, the happy memories of past sojourns in Vienna caused me to look forward to my visit with most pleasant anticipations.

À propos of happy memories, I recollect that on my arrival in the orchestra at the Ring Theatre for the first rehearsal, on the occasion of my second visit, I was, much to my astonishment, treated to a lusty fanfaronade (roll of the drums) as a mark of respect from my musicians.

A good story occurs to me while speaking of Vienna. One evening, at a party given by Baron Sina (the Rothschild of Vienna, and a man of princely hospitality), I was carelessly seated at the piano, looking over some music, when a gentleman who was unknown to me came up and began chatting in a friendly manner about divers musical matters.

He asked my opinion on the subject of Wagner as compared with the operas of the Italian school, and wanted to know whether I thought Wagner's music would outlive and supersede the works of the old masters. I told him that, although I greatly admired Wagner, I felt confident that Italian works would continue to hold their own as long as the world lasted ; and for some time we discussed the topic of the *new* music, which was at that period causing a universal sensation.

During our chat I had remained seated, with my legs crossed, maintaining a perfectly indifferent demeanour, until a casual remark from me elicited the following answer from the stranger: " Bravo, Signor Arditi," he said, smiling; "*c'est aussi l'avis de mon frère l'Empereur!*"

I started to my feet, deeply embarrassed at the discovery that I had been talking to the Arch-Duke in this extremely unceremonious fashion, and forthwith offered him all my apologies for the awkward mistake I had made. The Arch-Duke was highly amused at my confusion, and on looking round me I perceived that Adelina Patti and the Marquis de Caux had been watching the little incident amid suppressed merriment, while making wild signs to me to apprise me of my mistake.

The Diva has often reminded me of that occasion, and delights in telling the joke against me.

Speaking of Madame Patti recalls the intense, almost frantic, *furore* she created in Vienna at that time. It was Patti, Patti, Patti, and nothing but Patti. All the enthusiasm, all the excitement, was concentrated on her. People followed her carriage for miles just to catch a glimpse of her, and I have heard tell that some of her admirers took rooms in the Hotel Munsch (where she invariably stayed) in the hope of being privileged to meet her on the stairs, or to see her coming from or going to her room.

I had, in my leisure hours during the preceding winter, written an Ode to the text of Walter Maynard, in commemoration of the late Prince Consort, which was given at the Crystal Palace on the 10th of June (shortly after my return to London), to signalise the twentieth birthday of that popular building.

I conducted my music with the valuable aid of my good friend Mr. Manns, the orchestra and chorus being composed of the Crystal Palace musicians, all excellent artists, and the whole performance being accepted with enthusiasm by the public, no doubt because of its devotional and patriotic nature.

The Ode was played a second time at my subsequent morning concert with the identical cast, orchestra, and chorus of three hundred and fifty musicians who had assisted me at the Crystal Palace. I remember, by the way, that on the day we performed the Ode at the Crystal Palace I was strolling through one of the lobbies between the parts, when a lady-like person, clad in black, suddenly confronted us and curtsied very low. I had no idea who she was, but, thinking that I must have met her *somewhere*, I held out my hand, which she cordially grasped.

Her manner, moreover, was exceedingly effusive, and she so overpowered me with compliments with regard to the music that, while shaking hands, I turned to Virginia with the suppressed inquiry, " *Che cos' è ?* " (Who is it?) My wife was convulsed with laughter at my air of perplexity, and answered in a whisper, " Good gracious, Luigi, *how distrait* you are, to be sure ; *can't you see that it's our cook ? "* The old dame bustled off, highly content with herself, while it suddenly occurred to me that I had never, till that moment, set eyes on the good soul to whom I was indebted for my many luscious dishes of macaroni at home.

. . . .

I had for some time past been desirous of visiting my birthplace, the little town of Crescentino, Piedmont, which I had not seen for seventeen years, and was glad of the opportunity afforded me in July of that year to take the trip to Italy with Bevignani and my dear friend Franchi. In my diary I find that I signalised the date of my arrival there as *the happiest day in my life*, and, indeed, the occasion, simple enough in itself, drew forth a manifestation of public feeling that I can never forget.

On our arrival at Saluggia we were met by a deputation, which was headed by the mayor, while most of the school-children, dressed in white, who had been treated to a half-holiday, presented me with flowers at the railway station.

As we proceeded along the picturesque little town, I noticed that many of the old familiar windows and balconies were bright with laughing, eager faces, and Mass being just concluded, the people all came running out of the church to see the sight, followed by the priest himself. Never had Crescentino looked more resplendent or joyous than when doing honour to the return of one of its people.

My friend Signor Galimberti had arranged for a huge dinner, which was given with great *éclat* in a pavilion ; we sat down sixty to table.

With touching *naïveté* my portrait, around which a garland of flowers had been twined, stood in a place of honour, while the pavilion itself had been most lavishly decorated with flowers. At the end of the repast the Secretary of the Municipality, Signor Giuseppe Buffa, read aloud some complimentary verses, which were deeply gratifying and touching to me.

When returning my heartfelt thanks for their hearty welcome, I was glad of the opportunity of assuring my friends, one and all, that I am ever proud to remember that I am an Italian, when far away in distant lands, and that I always retain a grateful recollection of my native place.

A band of *dilettanti* played " Il Bacio," the inevitable, and other compositions of mine, during the repast, while a duet by Professor Rossaro, which he had composed for piano and violin, and had dedicated to me, and which bore the touching inscription, " Oh ! T' e ti qui' l me car Luisin," in Piedmontese dialect, was played at Signor Galimberti's house later in the evening, by my sister and the composer.

There is, after all, nothing more gratifying in the world than the assurance that one is beloved in one's own home and among one's own people. The warm-hearted demonstrations, so simple and kindly, manifested by the good and faithful Crescentinese, were indeed a revelation to me; and I cannot call to mind any subsequent ovation or distinction bestowed upon me during my career that has affected me so much as the reception which was afforded to me by my own country people on the occasion of my visit to Italy in 1873.

It was during my winter season of that year at St. Petersburg that I first made the acquaintance of Mdlle. Emma Albani. She was then already spoken about in glowing terms in Russia, Germany, and France, besides England and the States, where she had achieved great success with her effective and brilliant singing.

What particularly appealed to me in the matter of her voice in those early days was its rare evenness, and her power and art in the use of the crescendo. Another quality in which she excelled was the union of the registers; her style was graceful and pathetic, while she infused an earnestness and industry into her studies which were never lessened, in spite of her many subsequent triumphs.

I was told that Mdlle. Albani was anxious to sing under my bâton, an honour I was deeply sensible of, and I remember I called at her hotel in St. Petersburg with Merelli, who was kind enough to introduce me to the charming *prima donna*.

We chatted for a long time, and I was quite fascinated by her amiability and gentle manner. One thing struck me in the early days of our friendship, and I have not had the slightest reason to alter my opinion; namely, that Madame Albani is one of the few *prime donne* whom I have never heard utter an unkind or uncharitable word concerning any of her sister artists.

On the occasion of the Duke of Edinburgh's wedding to Princess Marie of Russia I composed and conducted a Cantata, which was performed at the State Concert given in honour of the auspicious occasion at the Winter Palace. The artists were Madame Patti, Mdlle. Albani, Mdlle. Scalchi (in those days already a magnificent vocalist), Nicolini, and Graziani, whose singing drew forth great enthusiasm from the Imperial and Royal assembly. I remember being elaborately " got up " during the festivities, appearing, by order of the Emperor, in court costume, at the banquet as well as at the State performance.

The *coup d'œil* from the gallery, where the orchestra had been placed, was a magnificent one. The reception rooms in the Winter Palace, which are of stupendous proportions, were illuminated by hundreds of thousands of white wax candles, heightening the brilliancy, dazzling effect and splendour of the jewellery worn by the illustrious guests. St. Petersburg is renowned for its lavish display of precious stones at royal and other distinguished functions, and is considered to be the town *par excellence* for general gorgeousness of array.

The ladies were clad in rich robes of cloth of silver or cloth of gold, the bodices of which were shrouded in priceless Valenciennes or Brussels lace, while diaphanous veils floated from their jewelled Russian caps on to the costly trains beneath. The English Duke's distinguished air and pleasant manner entirely won the hearts of those who were present to wish him God-speed, and the illustrious hero of the evening, together with his lovely bride, were the admired of all admirers.

I shall never forget the extraordinary effect produced by the huge roaring furnaces which had been built outside in the courtyards of the palace for the benefit and comfort of the coachmen, who cowered round them, endeavouring to keep warm while they awaited their royal masters. Without these they must, one and all, inevitably have been frozen to death, since the cold that year was more horribly intense than I ever remember it to have been on my previous visits to the Russian capital.

While in Vienna for the usual spring season, in 1874, I received a letter from the mayor of Reggio d'Emilia, asking me to go and conduct a short season of opera at that town. I replied in the affirmative, and received the following telegram in answer to my letter : —

" Municipality of Reggio enthusiastic to have you here. Name your own terms, which we shall be happy to accept. . . "

The unheard-of salary, for Italy, of 4,000 francs was paid to me for conducting one month at Reggio, and Verdi's " Don Carlos " was practically the feature of the season. The company on that occasion was a fine one, the orchestra and chorus proving themselves to be entirely satisfactory.

A short concert tour with Madame Patti and company, in September of 1874, brings us to another important event of that year, namely, a tour with Madame Désirée Artôt, Cristino, Padilla, etc., in Germany.

We visited many of the principal towns, and Mdlle. Artôt, who was a great favourite with the Germans, added enormously to the success of the enterprise. To her I owe my thanks for having introduced several of my songs into Germany, " Il Bacio " in particular, which became almost always associated with her name.

At Berlin we gave a concert at the Emperor's palace, Unter den Linden, and that reminds me of the extreme kindness of both the Emperor William and Empress Augusta to the artists on that occasion.

Although the Emperor had only just obtained leave to quit his room (he had been very ill), he insisted upon walking round the supper table that had been spread for the artists, so as to see that every one was well looked after.   He had a pleasant word and smile for everybody, and although he walked with apparent difficulty, and used a stick, his lameness did not deter him from seeing personally after his guests.   The Empress, too, graciously expressed her entire approval of the concert, at the end of which she came up and spoke to me.   On inquiring where I had been born, I informed Her Majesty that I was a Piedmontese.   The Empress seemed interested on hearing this, and rejoined with a smile : " *Tiens ; vous venez donc du pays de notre bon ami Victor Emmanuel ?* . . ."

From Berlin I went to Vienna for the early season, returning thence to London in May.

Major Carpenter was getting up an amateur perform-ance of " Ruy Blas," which was to be given at the Bijou Theatre in the Albert Hall.   He came to me in great consternation to ask me to undertake the con-ducting of the whole, since Mr. Vandeleur Lee, who was an able singing-master, did not seem to be quite capable of directing the music.   Of course I was only too happy to do anything for a man whose friendship was so dear to me, and I readily consented to help him.

Sir (then Mr.) Augustus Harris assisted us in the capacity of stage-manager, Alberto Visetti was at the harmonium, Mr. William Shakespeare (now an eminent singing-master, possessed of an exquisite tenor voice) was at the piano, and the performance was a great success.

I still prize a very handsome souvenir, in the shape of a silver jug, which Major Carpenter sent me in recogni-tion of my services ; and I value the following letter I received from him as much, if not more, than his graceful idea of the " Roba Fresca."

MY DEAR ARDITI, — Having once heard you express a wish to drink " Roba Fresca," I hope you will do me the honour to accept the silver jug that the bearer brings you as a souvenir from me, and let me hope that when I am away you will not think of me as " Don Pedro," the third-rate tenor, but as your sincere friend.

I do not know how to thank you for your great kindness in conducting us in " Ruy Blas."

Every one knows that without you the whole thing would have been a failure, and that you are the only man who could have organised and kept such undisciplined troops together.

In the name of my guests and myself I thank you, and with kindest regards to you and your wife, I am,

Cordially yours,

(Signed)   GEORGE W. WALLACE CARPENTER.

·   ·   ·   ·   ·   ·   ·   ·   ·

In August, 1874, I was engaged by Messrs. A. and S. Gatti to conduct the promenade concerts at Covent Garden. This was my first appointment under their management, and one which was repeated three years in succession.

From 1874 to 1877 my duties were divided by the seasons in Vienna and the Covent Garden concerts, and I may add that during that time I worked extremely hard.

My principal exertions were devoted to the arranging of selections from the operas of " Lohengrin," " Tann-häuser," " The Flying Dutchman," " Aïda," " Mosé in Egitto," " Cinq Mars," " Un Ballo in Maschera," and other grand works, performed at the concerts by the full orchestra and band of the Coldstream Guards (Bandmaster, Frederick Godfrey).

The orchestra consisted of such eminent men as Messrs. Burnett, Viotti Collins (first violins), Val Nicholson (second ditto), Messrs. Hann, Ould, Howell, Lazarus, Wotton, and many others who have achieved considerable distinction; while some of the principal artists who took part in the first year of the series (it were impossible to particularise them all) were Mesdames Bianchi, Cristino, Edith Wynne, Heilbron, Orfa, Marie Roze, José Sherrington, Norman Neruda, Blanche Cole, and Messrs. Fabrini, Snazelle, Wilhemj, and Tito Mattei.

The artists of 1876 were Madame Fernandez-Bentham, Rose Hersee, Agnes Larkcom, Anna Williams, Mary Davies, Mr. Maybrick, and Mr. Henry Ketten, a most delightful pianist and charming man, whose playing created quite a *furore*. The third year of the series introduced Miss Giulia Warwick (who assumed that surname professionally, giving the rather quaint explanation that she was prompted to do so from having made her first public appearance in the town of that name), Frank Celli (brother of the well-known actor), Herbert Standing, and Victor Maurel. Mesdames Lucia Raymondi, and Giuditta Celega, and Lisa Walters were likewise agreeable vocalists, whose co-operation added greatly to the success of the concerts.

The Wagner nights, even at that date, invariably brought particularly large and select audiences, and created much more enthusiasm than the ordinary programmes. I remember that on one of these occasions my wife was seated in her box when one of the brothers Gatti rushed in in a highly elated state, and whispered: —

" *There are actually fourteen footmen in the hall; what do you think of that? . . .*"

During my eight years of conductorship in Vienna,

Adelina Patti was the object of almost idolatrous admiration at the hands of the Viennese. Other stars, too, such as Nilsson, Lucca, Trebelli, Faure, were immensely attractive, and a great source of prosperity during those successive seasons.

It was at Vienna that I first was introduced to Wagner. I delighted in his music, and used to attend the performances regularly, score in hand, on our own off-nights.

A curious fact, and one I delight in recalling, is that Hans Richter often came to our theatre during rehearsals, and used to say: "Is there a corner for me in the orchestra? if so, I want to hear that divine Italian music. . . ." He was particularly partial to the " Barbiere," an opera which, I regret to say, some of the English up-to-date critics are bold enough to describe as being *hackneyed* and *trivial*.

I shall never forget seeing Wagner conduct. His carriage was erect and imposing, and made the impression of his being somewhat taller than he really was. His manner was sharp and hasty, and at times intensely nervous; but his rich voice gave effect to his words, and all who came in contact with him were bound to be subdued by his commanding personality. He was always unconventional, and his appearance betokened great refinement.

After the concert was over I went round to the artists' room in order to pay my respects to the great man. I was informed at the door (by a zealous attendant, evidently burning for promotion) that the *maestro* could not, on any account, see me, and that he never

The Society of the Concordia in Vienna, at whose concerts Signor Arditi often conducted, presented him with a handsome bâton, and a pin consisting of a lyre studded with precious stones, in the Hungarian colours.
— EDITOR.

received after the concert. I gently but firmly insisted upon my name being taken to him, whereupon the attendant came back and told me to pass through the private door leading to the artists' room.

Wagner was waiting for me with outstretched hands, and as soon as I approached him he embraced me affectionately, and exclaimed: " Yes, come in by all means, Arditi; *voi siete dei nostri*. . . ." I had some talk with Madame Wagner, who, together with her husband, was full of pleasant and interesting chat, and ere I left them they complimented me in the kindest possible manner on the success I had achieved in Vienna.

CHAPTER XIV.

Death of Titiens — I conduct Opera at Madrid — A Pleasant
Recollection of Emilio Castelar — Our Visits to Hungary —
Dublin en route for America — I go to the States with
Mapleson and Company — We are enthusiastically received —
Début of Gerster — Two Good Stories about Madame Lablache
— Our Répertoire — Ole Bull's Concert d'Adieux — I return
to Her Majesty's Theatre and conduct at the Saturday
Morning Performances — Our Second American Tour — Mdlle.
Marimon is a Great Success in America.

THE month of October, 1877, was fatefully signalised by the lamentable death of Mdlle. Thérèse
Titiens. She had for a long time been suffering from
an internal complaint, and I believe that she realised,
some time prior to her death, that her illness was
drawing to a fatal close. The last time the *prima
donna* sang was on the 19th of May, in the title *rôle*
of " Lucrezia Borgia;" but her sufferings were already
then so acute that she hardly managed to get through her
part, and left the theatre after a painful performance,
never to return thither again.

The death of that brilliant artist and estimable
woman was universally deplored. Words fail me to
describe the loss her demise proved to the operatic
world in general, and to Mapleson in particular; for
her unflagging energy and assiduity had proved the
mainstay of so many of his enterprises. A curious
circumstance in connection with the deaths of three
of the most celebrated *prime donne*, Sontag, Grisi,
and Titiens, is that their last appearances all took place
in " Lucrezia Borgia."

Rovira, the Spanish Impresario, offered me a good engagement to conduct opera for two months in Madrid at the Teatro Principe Alfonso in January, 1878, which I accepted. The company there was a very good one, with Donadio (a *prima donna* who was possessed of a rich, fresh soprano voice, and who sang like a musician) at its head. I discovered, on closer intimacy, that the orchestra was composed of artists (each hailing from different Spanish towns) who were far from being in touch with one another regarding the music; thus I had considerable difficulty in securing a satisfactory *ensemble.* I was at first far from being satisfied with my instrumentalists, but after a series of careful rehearsals I found that my little doses of advice and censure had wrought wonders, and that both the style of their playing and their spirit and animation for the work had greatly improved. Rovira was anxious to secure the Grand Theatre for his seasons in Madrid, and had only taken the Teatro Principe Alfonso provisionally. He also counted on my services, which he was in hopes of securing for some years to come; and I certainly did entertain the idea seriously until I communicated with my wife, who, however, was dead against the plan. Virginia's argument was a very plausible and sensible one. She contended that if I should take up my abode in Madrid for a specified number of years, it would necessitate our giving up our home in London and taking the children to Spain. Our Giulietta was then growing up, and I believe my wife was afraid that she would fall in love with and marry some fiery Spaniard; besides, the notion of leaving London, where we had settled down permanently, to go abroad and live in a "revolutionary country," as Virginia called Spain, was one which filled her with no little apprehension and disquietude.

Mapleson was, at that time, making overtures to me with regard to the conductorship of an operatic company he proposed to take to America during the autumn of that same year; thus the offer of a post as conductor in Madrid appeared less propitious, and eventually fell through.

My sojourn in Madrid was a very pleasant one. First and foremost occurs the recollection of my acquaintance with Emilio Castelar, a republican propagandist and public favourite, whose kindness to me all through my stay in Spain was remarkable.

Castelar, whose appearance was singularly prepossessing, belonged to a people among whom natural and oratorical gifts are the rule rather than the exception. He owed the success of his career to a fervent and figurative delivery, which probably had not then its equal in the utterances of any other European speaker; he was, moreover, a perfectly sincere and honest politician, perhaps the rarest variety of the species in Spain.

Castelar enjoyed almost unique popularity, — only equalled, in fact, by that of Don Juan Prim, then the idol of his countrymen, who, more is the shame, subsequently murdered him in cold blood.

It was Castelar who brought me the decoration of the " Carlos III.," and when delivering it remarked, with a knowing smile, " This, Arditi, is an order you *can* wear. . . ."

I left Madrid on the 6th of March for the Vienna opera season, which proved to be my last one in Austria. I had half promised Kuhe to conduct his annual concert at Brighton, and should have come to London direct for that purpose had I not been compelled, at the last moment, to put off my departure for a day, since a special concert had been arranged in honour of the press, at which Rovira insisted that I should conduct. It was a big and successful affair, at which all the artists from the opera were present, as indeed they were at every concert of the sort. Among these I remember Tamberlik, who was then singing his best and causing a great sensation among the Spaniards.

At the conclusion of the concert Castelar presented me with a diploma and a handsome silver bâton, on which occasion he also made a (to me) very gratifying and impressive speech, subsequently sending me his book, " Recuerdos de Italia," with the following inscription: " *To the illustrious Maestro Arditi, from his affectionate friend and enthusiastic admirer. — E. C.*"

The next morning I lunched quietly with him, and left for Vienna that afternoon.

Lucca, Nilsson, Trebelli, Faure, Campanini, Masini, Salla, and Padilla were the chief attractions of my final season in 1878.

Speaking of my several visits to Vienna, I forgot to mention that we invariably visited Buda-Pesth during the Holy Week, for the purpose of giving operatic recitals in that town. Those charming trips to the music-loving and enthusiastic Hungarians are among my bright particular memories of days gone by.

Nobody who has ever heard the wild, passionate Magyar music, the " Csardas," for instance (with its two movements, " lassu," or slow movement, first, after which follows the " friss," or *allegro vivace*), can forget the impression it first makes upon him. The gypsy bands are the recognised musicians of the country, and only play in restaurants and hotels in Buda-Pesth ; if, however, one penetrates into the interior of Hungary, one finds that there the gypsies ply their art with far greater freedom than they do in town, loitering from Csarda to Csarda, and finally accompanying their most liberal patron homewards, preceding him while playing the Hunyadi or Racocsy March. Thus these weird sons of the plains make a capital living, since the natural generosity of the people is strongly appealed to when they hear their national music played.

I remember, on one of our visits, making the acquaintance of the celebrated *primàs*, Ratz Pal, who was the most famous leader of all the Czigane orchestras. He was a wonderfully able violinist; and although he had never learnt a note of music in his life, he conducted and played, entirely by ear, with a fire and pathos which has rarely been equalled, excepting, perhaps, in the case of Farkás Mor, the present leader of the Grand Duke Joseph's private band.

During the summer of 1878 Virginia and I went to Paris on behalf of Mapleson, to arrange some business with Choudens, the publisher of Gounod's "Faust," at the same time seizing the opportunity of seeing the French exhibition in all its glory. There we spent a happy week of quiet recreation, preparatory to my departure for Ireland *en route* for America.

Although I was about to revisit the country of my early triumphs, it was not without a feeling akin to desolation that I left my home and family in England to travel thither alone.

To be more lucid, I must explain that while we were mere wanderers, without any fixed abode, my wife went with me everywhere. Our house and children now of course stood in the way of Virginia's accompanying me to America until many years later; and this fact is deplorable to me in more than one respect, since my memory often fails me in matters respecting which my wife's recollections would be invaluable. I am, however, happy to say that my daughter Giulietta has since her marriage kept many of her mother's letters, written to

her from Mexico and other countries, and I hope some
of these may prove interesting to my readers in later
pages of this book, inasmuch as they give a very fair
description of our life and artistic *entourage* while
touring in the States.

After an absence of several years from Dublin, I met
once more with the most cordial reception from my
Irish friends, whose warm-heartedness towards me since
my name was identified, so far back as the year 1857,
with the famous Piccolomini and Grisi days, has ever
been most genial.

At the head of these kind people, whose hospitality
I shall always have reason to remember, stand Mr. and
Mrs. Michael Gunn, of whom I shall have many pleasant
things to say later on.

On the 25th of September, 1878, we left Queenstown
for New York, with a strong company, comprising
Mesdames Minnie Hauk, Etelka Gerster, Marie Roze,
Sinico, Lablache, and Signori Campanini, Del Puente,
Foli, Frapolli, Galassi, and other artists. The journey
was a splendid one ; but in spite of the tolerably calm
attitude of the sea, Mapleson and I were the only two
people who maintained steady sea legs and never
missed a meal by any chance, nearly all the artists,
and especially the ladies, having exhibited a rooted
objection to being sociable during the first few days of
the voyage. Towards the end we organised a concert
for the benefit of a charity in aid of the Sailors' Home
in New Orleans, and the time sped merrily enough until
we found ourselves steaming up the North River, when
I once more beheld the familiar characteristics of the
great commercial port of New York. The well-known
low and peculiar architecture of Castle Garden, with its
vivid throng of arriving emigrants. and the busy, potent
life of this marvellous city, was as impressive a sight
as ever.

The lovely panorama stretched out grandly before us, Brooklyn to our left, with its many spires, and the great bridge connecting it with New York, enveloped in a hazy mist. The speedy little tugs and other various river craft, and the innumerable ferry boats continually crossing and recrossing the river, made us strikingly aware that we had left the repose and leisure of the old world behind us, and had at last arrived in the land of stir, blizzards, and general flurry.

It seemed to me that I had reached home once more, so heartily were we all received and fêted by the thousands of people who assembled to witness our arrival: but there was something wanting, an absent face, I thought, to have made the home-coming complete; and, sure enough, on looking about me, I realised that it was Virginia whom, in the midst of such a hearty welcome, I missed from my side.

A few evenings after our arrival in New York the whole company of the orchestra of the Academy of Music congregated outside my window at the hotel, under the direction of Mr. Botsford, and serenaded me. In my broken English I thanked my musicians, one and all, for their kindness and hearty welcome, and told them how surprised and flattered I was to have been the recipient of so high a favour at their hands.

Our first opera was "La Traviata," with Minnie Hauk as Violetta, in which *rôle* that charming singer gained a great success.

Madame Gerster had been announced to appear on the opening night, but she fell ill, and her life was for some days despaired of. Gerster recovered, however, and in November sang Amina in "La Sonnambula," for the first time to an American public, achieving a really extraordinary artistic triumph, and creating a *furore* which lasted unflaggingly during our tour.

In America Minnie Hauk's two great parts were
Carmen, and Elsa in " Lohengrin ; " she was a tremendous draw in both operas, and filled the houses
to overflowing whenever she appeared in either *rôle*.
The personality of this clever and attractive lady is an
interesting and winning one. Of course she was im-
petuous, and sometimes hasty when singing, and I am
bound to smile when I recall her little fiery outbursts of
temper if thwarted by any one, — outbursts which, however, resembling April showers, disappeared as quickly
as they came, leaving her smiling countenance sunnier
and more radiant than ever. Personally, Minnie Hauk
and I have always been the best and firmest of friends,
and she has never been otherwise than amiability and
serenity itself to me.

Madame Lablache, one of the most delightfully amusing women I have ever known, was a very important
acquisition to the company. Always ready to sing, she
never feigned indisposition for some trivial reason, or
squabble in connection with her fellow artists, as several
of the other singers were only too wont to do. In spite
of our great intimacy (she is godmother to my boy), I
feel that the opportunity of telling a good story about
her is so *àpropos* at this moment that I am irresistibly
tempted to draw a smile from my readers at her
expense.

Madame Lablache's great weakness was her desire
to spend money, and I must add that when she was
in funds her generosity and kindness were proverbial.
Her good-heartedness ran side by side with her
extravagance and fondness for dress, — which failings
often brought her into serious monetary scrapes. I
remember how, on one occasion, a famous dressmaker
sued her for the payment of a costly mantle she had
chosen, and how, when the case came into court, she

This clever caricature, which appeared at this time in " Puck," represents myself conducting the company, with Minnie Hauk as Carmen, Campanini as José, Foli as Mephistopheles, Del Puente as the "Toreador," Bizet the composer in the left-hand corner, and Madame Gerster as the poor invalid she then was.

appeared in the witness-box, smiling and self-possessed, and at once gained everybody's sympathy by her affable manner.

When asked to state her name, the judge, who had heard Madame Lablache sing in opera on the previous evening, of course recognised the eminent vocalist, and began to compliment her profusely on her voice and acting, telling her how much he had enjoyed the music, etc. Hereupon they entered into a lively conversation, which had nothing whatever to do with the case; and, to make a long story short, Madame Lablache so entirely fascinated the judge that she not only gained her case with costs, but sailed triumphantly out of the court, *wearing, by the way, the identical cloak that had been the cause of the law-suit!*

Here is another funny story illustrative of one of her *spirituelle* remarks, for which she is justly celebrated.

Madame Lablache was once, at the eleventh hour, asked to sing the *rôle* of Donna Anna in "Don Giovanni," in lieu of a lady who had been suddenly taken ill. Madame Lablache, being unable to wear the stage robe that had been provided for the part, elected to wear one of her own private dresses (a very handsome and costly one).

Brignoli, the tenor, who impersonated Don Ottavio, had a very bad habit of continually expectorating while singing, so much so as to cause Madame Lablache grave anxiety as to the possible fate of her beautiful gown.

During the famous trio Madame Lablache watched Brignoli very anxiously, and finally, unable to contain her fears any longer, she whispered to him in a voice full of appeal: "*Voyons, mon cher ami, ne pourriez vous pas, une foi par hasard, cracher sur la robe de Donna Elvira?*"

Our first season in the States was an eminently successful one. Mapleson had, at that time, everything in his favour. His energy and unflagging zeal, which had earned for him the title of " King of Impresari," bore him good fruit, and considering the vast amount of work we all got through during that season, I look back on those turbulent days almost incredulously, and wonder how we managed our productions with such completeness and efficiency. We gave a different opera every night, two performances on Saturdays, and on Sundays a concert of sacred music! Our répertoire numbered no less than twenty-six operas.

I am reminded here of a characteristic story about Henry Mapleson, the husband of that most kindly and amiable of *prime donne*, Marie Roze. His craze for advertising his wife on every available occasion amounted well-nigh to a mania. He so overdid what, had it been tempered with moderation, would have undoubtedly proved advantageous to the lady, that it became a popular saying among the members of the company: " *Allons donc ; voilà Mapleson qui nous plante encore une biographie de sa femme !* "

One day I was extremely pleased with a highly com-plimentary notice that had been written concerning me in a local American paper, and chancing to meet Henry Mapleson in the lobby of the theatre I handed it to him, asking him to read it. He seized the paper with avidity, only to drop it with a look of disgust when he discovered that the article did not contain anything of personal interest to him. " My dear fellow," he said, with a lame attempt at a smile, " what is the good of showing me that d—d thing? I thought it was some-thing about my wife." " No," I replied, highly amused, " I thought it would be a pleasant change for you to read something concerning me *once in a way*."

We visited Philadelphia, Boston, Chicago, St. Louis, Cincinnati, Baltimore, and Washington, returning to New York at the conclusion of the tour.

"Carmen" was performed twenty-six times in all, "Lucia" being second, and "Sonnambula" a third favourite; while "Ruy Blas," "Robert le Diable," and "Barbiere" were only played twice, — other operas, such as "Faust," "Puritani," "Don Giovanni," "Rigoletto," "Nozze di Figaro," "Lohengrin," "Huguenots," etc., being obviously preferred by the public of the States.

An interesting item in connection with our first American tour was Ole Bull's *concert d'adieux*, on the 14th December, at the Steinway Hall. Everybody who knew that delightful violinist will, at the mention of his name, recall his fervid nature, his strong individuality, and the grace and vigour with which he used to handle his superb Da Salo violin. He was undoubtedly the sole exponent of his own particular school of violin-playing, and was at times quite irresistible in regard to the pathos and almost human tone he drew from his instrument.

Miss Minnie Hauk, Signor Galassi, and I, together with the orchestra of our opera company, assisted him at his concert, at the conclusion of which he and I had a battle royal on the subject of a £20 note. Ole Bull would insist upon paying me for my services of conducting, — a fact I very much resented, since I should have been only too happy to render him that or any other favour. Ole Bull was obdurate, and so was I; our tussle lasted for some time, until Ole Bull triumphed. The kind old fellow was visibly pained at my persistent refusal; and so, to please him, I was finally and reluctantly bound to give way, with the promise to buy myself a souvenir of him.

After Ole Bull's retirement he went back to his native home in Scandinavia, where, so I learnt from my son Gigi, he lived in a fine old château, the rooms of which were nearly all built and decorated in carved oak of exquisite design.

A few days prior to our departure for England, and at the conclusion of the opera season, the musicians of my orchestra presented me with a wreath of silvered laurel leaves, and a case containing a handsome gold medal, as a souvenir of our first joint success. The inscription on the medal is as follows (inscribed in notes of music) : —

" SHOULD AULD ACQUAINTANCE BE FORGOT."

TOKEN

OF ADMIRATION AND ESTEEM

To

SIGNOR LUIGI ARDITI,

FROM THE MEMBERS OF HIS ORCHESTRA,

ACADEMY OF MUSIC, NEW YORK, U. S. A.

APRIL 4TH, 1879.

When the " City of Chester " was on the point of starting for London, carrying with it the " precious operatic freight," flowers, fruits, and gifts of every description were literally showered on the various members of the company, and it would be impossible for me to give an adequate description of the hospitality and kindness shown by the most generous people in the world to us on our departure. The following letter from Mr. Hassard, editor of the " New York Tribune," was sent to me on board just a moment before the final landing stage was removed : —

"TRIBUNE" OFFICE, U. S., April 5th, 1879.

MY DEAR SIR, — One of the pleasantest parts of the performance last night was the announcement by Mr. Mapleson that you would soon return to America. I cannot let you go away without expressing individually my gratification at this news, and my thanks for the great pleasure and profit I have derived from the representations given under the *bâton* of a *maestro* who shows the heart and the interest of a real artist. We are all your sincere friends and admirers, and shall all give you the warmest of welcomes when you come back. Please remember me among the most cordial of your admirers, and believe me, very truly and gratefully,   Your obedient servant,

JNO. R. G. HASSARD.

I must not forget to mention the handsome photographic album also presented to me by the members of the orchestra on that occasion, containing the photographs of each individual artist.

Before we quitted America, Mapleson, as already stated, had asked me to accompany him thither on his next tour, and the contract for that undertaking was signed and sealed before we reached the English shore.

During our sojourn in the States, Mapleson had been working London and New York opera concurrently. My great successes in the "New World" had not, unnaturally, been highly gratifying to him, and he forthwith began to give evidence of his desire to see me once more back at my post. *Entre nous*, I believe he was also becoming a little tired of Sir Michael, whose invaluable services were somewhat obscured by his autocratic ways, and the Impresario appeared to wish to make up for my nine years' absence from Her Majesty's company (during which time, frankly speaking, he had treated me just a little " cavalierly "); so he proposed that I should, to begin with, conduct the Saturday morning performances at Her Majesty's.

For divers reasons, I agreed to this arrangement, which was carried out through the season.

As long as Sir Michael was at the head of the orchestra, there was practically no chance of any other conductor being allowed to share the honours (considering the fact that poor Bottesini had been engaged during one season as assistant conductor to Sir Michael, and was, as a matter of fact, never for one night allowed the privilege of " wielding the wand "); consequently these morning performances were only the forerunners of the regular season throughout which I was requested to conduct after Sir Michael's resignation.

About this time our old friend Pelligrini made one of his clever caricatures of myself, and I am indebted to the courtesy of the proprietors of " Vanity Fair " for permission to reproduce it here.

In July, 1879, I took a hasty trip to Italy, being accompanied by my son, whom I left at Milan, where he intended commencing his studies at the Conservatoire. Virginia and I whiled away a pleasant week or so at Boulogne in August, and I started for America on our second tour, aboard the " City of Berlin," on the 25th of September, our season, however, not opening under such favourable auspices as had that of the foregoing year. To begin with, Gerster at the eleventh hour was too ill to leave Italy, and Mapleson, knowing that the American public would be more than dis-

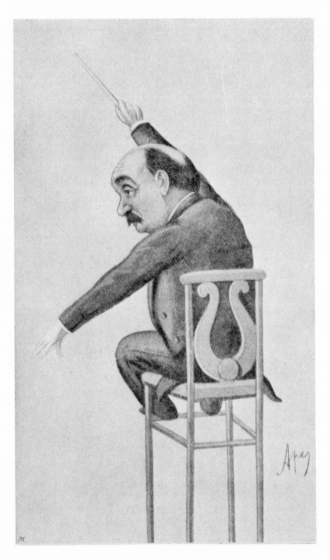

FROM "VANITY FAIR."

(*By special permission.*)

appointed at her absence, was telegraphing right and left to secure an equivalent attraction.

Our company comprised Mdlles. Valleria, Bellocca (a contralto of much ability, and possessed of great personal charm), Madame Ambré, a singer of Moorish extraction, for many years reputed to have been the King of Holland's favourite, Adini, Cary, a capital contralto and a good actress to boot, Lablache, and Signori Campanini, Galassi, Aramburo, and many other artists who had accompanied us thither on the previous tour. Mapleson had prevailed upon Mdlle. Marie Marimon to join the company in New York, and having narrowly escaped being shipwrecked on the voyage out, she insisted, on her arrival in the States, upon making for the first Roman Catholic church in order to offer up thanks for her safe arrival. Unfortunately the *prima donna*, while engaged in her devotions, caught a fearful chill, which almost killed her, and she was compelled to remain a prisoner in her room for many days after.

When at last she was well enough to appear, which she did in the *rôle* of Amina in "La Sonnambula," she took the public by storm, and created an enthusiasm which was only equalled by that aroused by Madame Gerster during the preceding season.

Mdlle. Valleria also became a great favourite, especially in "Faust," "Lucia," "Linda," "Aïda," and "Trovatore," in which operas she was rapturously applauded.

During the western trip we were most successful at Baltimore, owing to the personal popularity in that town of Mdlle. Valleria, who appeared there as Aïda; and that reminds me of the furious jealousy she succeeded in arousing in Madame Ambré on that occasion.

Madame Ambré, notwithstanding much puffing, was not by any means a draw. Her voice was a fine organ, and her appearance prepossessing, and yet — well, in spite of her having appeared in "La Traviata" one huge blaze of diamonds, — not paste, mark you, but *real* brilliants (and the gifts, so it is said, of the King of Holland, who was devoted to "Art"), — she failed to secure public sympathy, and became a decided drug in the market.

Some of the incidents of our journeys were very funny. I remember that one man walked twenty miles to St. Louis in the hopes of hearing *Queen Victoria sing in Her Majesty's troupe*, and when he was informed of his mistake, he became furious, and wanted his money returned to him. In Cleveland a large deputation of the foremost citizens called upon Colonel Mapleson at his hotel one morning and proposed that he should give " H. M. S. Pinafore " (instead of Italian opera, which they did n't understand), with Mdlle. Marimon as Buttercup, because, as they naïvely explained, " every one in Cleveland knew Sullivan's music." These two instances may serve as an example of the oddities with which we often had to contend.

Mapleson had some trouble, too, with the orchestra, which struck for an increase of pay on one or two occasions; but we always, in spite of innumerable difficulties, managed to give the public a first-rate performance, for which all who were concerned received unqualified praise.

On the whole, the second visit to the States, including Detroit, Philadelphia, and Chicago, besides the two other towns I have already mentioned, was not financially so great a success as the first; but Mapleson, whose pluck was indomitable, saw his way to repeating the tour at the end of the year, — for which all the principal arrangements were made ere we left America, — and the entire company returned to London on the 28th of April, 1880.

CHAPTER XV.

EARLY in May, 1880, I signed an engagement for the season at Her Majesty's Theatre, Dr. Hans Richter, who happened to be in London at the time, being asked to conduct "Lohengrin" for a few nights.

We opened with "Faust," — Nilsson, Joseph Maas, and Del Puente sustaining the principal characters.

Maas made his first appearance on that occasion at Her Majesty's, and to play Faust in company with such an ideal Marguerite would have proved a trying ordeal for any one whose voice had been less fine, or whose absence of effort less conspicuous. As it was, he scored a great success, and one which continued to increase steadily until the day of his death.

It is pleasurable to record the *début*, under my bâton, of Mdlle. Emma Nevada, a dainty little Californian lady, who, in "Sonnambula," in later years, rose to the ranks of our very first-class *prime donne*. The then new Amina's voice was a light soprano; it was heard at its best in her sleep-walking scenes, which she gave so softly, yet impressively, that, though every note was audible, it seemed like a thread of gossamer fineness. Her delicate delivery was the chief attraction of her voice in those days; but since then she has become too great and recognised a favourite all the world over to need further comment from me.

"Mephistophele" was now in active rehearsal, being superintended by the composer, Arrigo Boito, himself; and, in consequence, my orchestra was on its best behaviour. Christine Nilsson as Marguerite and Helen was an ideal type of classic grace and beauty; Madame Trebelli was Martha and Pantalis; Campanini, an old favourite, whom all knew and none can forget, was Faust, Mephisto being played by Signor Nanetti, a very excellent artist. With such a powerful combination it was not surprising that all the music should have gone as well as it did.

Boito, poet and composer *par excellence*, was more than delighted with the way in which the opera was mounted and produced, and I remember with much pride all the pleasant things he said about the efficiency of my orchestra.

Boito was unexpectedly obliged to leave London after the production of "Mephistophele;" otherwise he had promised to spend an evening with us. I never saw him from that time until two years ago, when my friend Alberto Visetti gave a party in his honour, on which occasion his wife, a charming American lady, decorated her house most lavishly with the costliest flowers, according to true American fashion.

Miss Lilli Lehmann made her *début* during that season. To people who know what a really great artist she has since become it will seem incredible that her success was not at once established at Her Majesty's Theatre. In my opinion the parts allotted to her were unsuited to her style. As far as personal beauty and elegance were concerned, Violetta in "La Traviata," and Filina in " Mignon," afforded her every opportunity for distinguishing herself; but her style was an intensely dramatic one, and she always impressed me with the idea that she sang these particular *rôles contre cœur*.

I always thought, somehow, that there was an undercurrent of unjust jealousy among the artists at Her Majesty's concerning Lilli Lehmann, and that the feelings against her were ill-natured and uncalled for. To me she was a very charming, talented artist, and a ladylike woman, whose greatest fault was, perhaps, that she was too refined to suit the tastes of some of those who surrounded her. Be that as it may, she was not encouraged to sing more than once or twice here, and departed without having had, I consider, a legitimate opportunity of giving her voice a thoroughly fair chance. At a later period I shall hope to speak of the triumphs she achieved in " Fidelio " under my bâton.

At this time Ravelli, the tenor, was engaged by Mapleson under circumstances worthy of recital.

Poor Maas, whose ill-health often incapacitated him from appearing when he was announced to sing, suddenly fell ill at the last moment; in fact, on the very day he was to have appeared in " Lucia."

Mapleson, whose fate it was to be ever on tenterhooks concerning the vagaries or indispositions of his artists, never lost heart, and was heard to exclaim boastingly, " Oh, I shall find another tenor to-day; never fear! "

It so happened that some one came into Mapleson's office at this moment, and said, " Joking apart, there *is* a tenor walking about under the portico of the theatre, only waiting to be engaged. His name is Ravelli, and if you go down at once you may still find him. . . ."

Mapleson was downstairs in a trice, and having spotted the tenor, who was strolling about with a huge cigar in his mouth, he assumed an indifferent air, managing, somehow, to enter into conversation with Ravelli. Both parties acted off-handedly with one another, as though each man was conferring an honour upon the other by conversing with him. When Mapleson casually observed that he was in want of a tenor for that night's performance, Ravelli replied by looking dubiously at his book of engagements, and saying that, oddly enough, he was free that evening, and would " not mind " singing in lieu of Maas.

Thus Ravelli first trod the boards of Her Majesty's Theatre, and there has been a standing joke ever since against Mapleson, to the effect that whenever he was in want of artists he would surely find as many as he required walking about under the portico, only waiting to be engaged.

During our absence in America, in the autumn of 1880, Her Majesty's Theatre was given over to the performances of a troupe of artists called the Haverly Minstrels, previous to which Moody and Sankey, the evangelists, had occupied the boards for the purpose of giving their lectures.

I cannot help thinking that this was a serious blow to the prestige of our professional home, and one which had a deteriorating effect in the direction of lowering its standard and tone ; the invasion of the Minstrels, in short, seemed to me to be the sad beginning of a sad end.

We arrived in New York on our third tour, with Mesdames Gerster, Minnie Hauk, Valleria, Bellocca, Ferni, Emma Juch, Dotti, Rossini, Cavalazzi (who had married Colonel Mapleson's son Charles, and who is as good and sincere a woman as she is handsome and amiable); also Signori Ravelli, Campanini, Prévost (a glorious tenor), and many others.

A funny story occurs to me in connection with one of our visits to the States.

I was in receipt of a check from Mapleson, and, being anxious to cash it, I drove one afternoon, just before closing time, to the bank at which it was made payable. When presenting the check the clerk asked me if I had not brought any one who could identify me. I laughed, and said: "Don't you know me? I am Signor Arditi." The man still appeared to be uncertain as to my identity, when a happy thought occurred to me. I asked, "Do you ever go to the opera?" The clerk replied, "Yes, often." Then I turned my back and raised my hat, disclosing my bald head. "Do you not know me now?" I urged. A grin spread all over his countenance, and he exclaimed: "Oh, yes; now I know that you are Signor Arditi; it's all right; here's the money!"

I do not propose to weary my readers with a strict recapitulation of each of our visits to America, which, although the companies varied greatly, were necessarily confined to more or less the same routine, — opera at the Academy of Music, the tours to the Western towns, and so on. The opera festivals at Cincinnati, of which two were organised in 1881 and 1882, are, however, an interesting reminiscence.

The festival in conjunction with the College of Music brought together the most eminent musicians imaginable, including Gerster, Minnie Hauk, Valleria, Del Puente, Campanini, etc., together with a powerful orchestra of one hundred and fifty, and a chorus consisting of four hundred voices. Madame Patti, who happened to have gone to the States with a company of her own, was persuaded by Mapleson to sing at the second grand festival in February, 1882.

This enterprise was undoubtedly organised on a very grand scale, the attraction of Patti's name, together with a generally fine company, gathering together every night over five thousand distinguished representatives of the city of Cincinnati. The operatic performances took place at the Music Hall, of which the acoustic properties are quite admirable.

Speaking of theatres gives me an opportunity of saying that in America they are built on a scale which, as far as comfort and acoustics are concerned, exceeds any English houses I have ever become acquainted with.

The theatres in the United States, the decorations of which are most elaborate, are constructed without a pit, so that the stalls extend to the back of the house, each row being raised behind the other, thus enabling every one in the house to see and to be seen. My favourite theatre of all is, I think, the Opera House in Philadelphia; although, of course, the handsomest and really most superb building in America at the present moment is the Auditorium in Chicago, which we opened in that city in 1889, and of which more anon.

A propos of Philadelphia, a funny incident occurs to me. I was walking through the "Quaker City" one afternoon, when I heard my poor "Il Bacio" valse

Extract from a letter, dated Cincinnati, with regard to the Opera Festival : —

" The orchestra is of equal importance with the voices, and it may be justly said their performance during the week was excellent. The amount of tone was ample ; the purity of intonation, for so large a body of instrumentalists, was admirable, and the perfection with which they accompanied the vocal music placed the band, as an opera orchestra, on the same pinnacle of efficiency as the Thomas Symphony Orchestra. Signor Arditi has a mastery over the complexity of opera music which is surpassed by no conductor, and equalled by few. His intelligence seems to be omnipresent, and every detail is infallibly watched by his quick eye, and followed by his sensitive ear. . . ." — EDITOR.

being played in such a drawling, funereal *tempo*, on a
decrepit hand-organ, that I made a rush for the wretch
who was massacring my music, and remonstrated
with him vehemently. He coolly told me that if I did
not approve of the *tempo* I could play it myself, with
which impertinent suggestion I immediately complied.
At that moment I espied one or two members of our
company, who were strolling in my direction, and
seizing the handle of the organ I began to grind out the
air to their intense astonishment, coupled with roars of
laughter.

By that time a crowd had collected round us, and I
was being looked upon as a harmless musical lunatic,
who had escaped from his keeper. I was not to be
thwarted, however, so I played the tune to the bitter
end, and then sauntered on, despite the shouts and
comments of the crowd.

After the success of the Cincinnati Festival, Mapleson
made overtures to Madame Patti, with the view of
obtaining her co-operation for the season of 1883, in
America, in which he was successful; he secured also
Madame Albani, Miss Minnie Hauk, Madame Fursch-
Madi, Mdlle. Valleria, Madame Scalchi, Mdlle. Rossini,
Nicolini, Campanini, Ravelli, Del Puente, Galassi,
Novara, etc.

Trouble was ahead between the Royal Italian Opera
Company, Limited (of which the Brothers Gye were
directors), and Mapleson's Company of the Academy of
Music. It was rumoured that as soon as the Metropolitan Opera House should be opened by Gye (which he
confidently hoped to do), the Academy Opera would be
crushed by the superior attractions of the opposition
forces, thus establishing in New York a monopoly
similar to that existing some years previously in
London.

The Americans, however, vehemently pooh-poohed the suggestion. They contended that, far from opposing the opera houses, they would be only too happy to support and encourage two companies, as long as they were both of first-class calibre.

The season of 1883 broke upon us with a great deal of trouble at first. Patti caught cold several times and was unable to sing, while many of the other artists were continually being seized with some ailment or other at the very last moment. It seems almost incredible to me how, with so many difficulties, Mapleson managed, on several memorable occasions, to produce an opera at all.

The nervous tension and agitation that beset us all (for we never knew from " rosy morn till dewy eve " what new perplexity was shaping itself) was trying in the extreme.

I remember one year (it was at the time when the Abbey and Grau Company was giving Italian opera in opposition to the Mapleson troupe, and had engaged several of our artists at higher salaries than Mapleson was in a position to pay) " La Favorita " had been announced by Abbey, but the *prima donna* fell ill, and Abbey, at the last moment, changed the opera to the " Prophète."

Madame Scalchi was called upon to sing the principal part; but she refused to comply with Abbey's request, stating the fact that she had just dined off, among other delicacies, a good dish of macaroni, and that it was an absolute impossibility to render the part of Fides.

Her refusal of course placed Abbey in an awkward predicament, and, indeed, one which was only dissolved in a law court.

He sued Scalchi for breach of contract, and, oddly enough, I was, *entre autres* subpœnaed on her behalf, my evidence winning the case for her. I contended that it would have been quite impossible for her to sing *immediately* after a heavy meal, and there the matter ended. Scalchi was so pleased to have had a " rise " out of Abbey that she sent me a ruby and diamond pin in memory of the occasion.

After the season at New York we went west, visiting, as usual, several big cities.

At Chicago the greatest excitement prevailed, for we met Abbey's Company, which had taken up its quarters at the same hotel (the Grand Pacific) as we had done. Mapleson had, I must not omit to mention, severed his former connection with the Royal Italian Opera Company by this time, through difficulties which are far too complicated for me to enter into here. Funny in the extreme were the airs and graces, the proud and disdainful looks launched at one another by the various ladies of both companies, while the tenors and baritones scowled at their rivals, and looked " daggers " at each other when they met on the stairs or in the lifts of the hotel.

During this year my friend Madame Murio Celli, the well-known teacher of singing in New York, asked me to conduct her annual concert, at which many of her distinguished pupils were to appear. The affair, which was most successful, terminated with a presentation to me of a handsome silver set, tastefully arranged in a box lined with red satin, and got up in that unique and lavish style characteristic of the Americans. The inscription it bore ran as follows: —

" *To Luigi Arditi. A token of gratitude from his friend Adelina Murio Celli. 14th April,* 1883."

We opened our season of 1884 with Gerster, achieving a splendid triumph ; but Abbey ran us very close, since he had engaged several of Mapleson's finest singers, and it cannot be denied that the season was an

anxious and harassing one, despite the co-operation of
Adelina Patti, the "Queen of Song."

The next notable event of that year was our visit to
San Francisco. Words fail me to give an adequate
description of the sensation caused there by Patti and
Gerster, or of the impression made upon those members
of the company who were visiting that lovely country
for the first time. Virginia, who went to California
later on, will come to my rescue in the matter of
reminiscences of " Frisco." Suffice it to say at present
that money was almost being coined by Mapleson ; so
great was the rush for tickets by the musically mad

" L' Incantatrice," the song which Madame Patti introduced with such
great success in several operas, was dedicated by Signor Arditi to Her
Majesty the Queen of Italy. Subjoined is a copy of the letter which was
sent to the composer in acceptance of the same. — EDITOR.

ROME, 28th Feb., 1884.

SIR, — Her Majesty the Queen has accepted with particular approbation
the copy of your vocal valse, " L' Incantatrice," which, with delicate attention, you dedicated to Her Majesty. Our Gracious Sovereign appreciates
the affectionate and devotional sentiment which your courteous act inspired,
and, desirous of manifesting in a special manner her sentiments towards you,
encloses as a souvenir the accompanying jewel, adorned with her royal
cipher. With the greatest pleasure I participate in being the sender of
this flattering recognition.

(Signed) MARQUIS DI VILLAMARINA.

Here is a funny description of Signor Arditi, which I have unearthed
from a San Francisco journal. — EDITOR.

" It was rather amusing the other day to watch Arditi at the Pavilion
Concert, sitting on a music stool on the platform, looking at the large
audience and scanning their faces. He is the pleasantest of men, frank,
genial, light-hearted, and happy as a boy; it is easy to understand that
his company all adore him. His face is wonderfully young and bright in
expression for a man who has been a conductor for thirty years, and I
doubt if he has changed very much.

" I possess a caricature of him done in New York by Mr. Butler, well-
known to all San Francisco grown-up musical people, and he has not a
hair less to-day, not a line more. It might have been done yesterday in
the Grand Opera House, so exactly is it like Arditi to-day. Yet it was
sketched somewhere in the fifties, and I dare say even Arditi himself has
begun to forget the occasion."

enthusiasts that they literally scattered it about, paying blindly any price merely to be accorded standing-room if nothing else. As a matter of fact, the money accumulated so quickly that each night it had to be placed in sacks and slung over the backs of trustworthy porters to be delivered to the bank.

Among the exciting events of the trip I remember that an earthquake took place which greatly alarmed everybody. It occurred one morning while most of our company were still at the Palace Hotel. The most curious fact in connection with it as regards myself was that I happened to be descending in a lift at the time, *and felt absolutely nothing whatever of the shock.*

When I came out of the lift, I found everybody rushing about in a great state of agitation, looking as though they were scared to death ; and on inquiring the reason of the alarm, I was informed that the vibration had been terribly intense, lasting for about eight to ten seconds, and that the earthquake had been an unusually severe one, even for San Francisco. Mapleson told us a good story *à propos* of the landlord, whom he met immediately afterwards.

" Nervous ? " inquired the latter, laconically (he was used to such panics).

" Rather," answered Mapleson, emphatically.

" Well, you need not be," pursued the landlord, cheerfully, "*for my hotel is earthquake-proof, as well as fireproof !* "

We ascertained later that the building practically lay in a gigantic swing, and that no amount of earthquaking could in any way affect the equanimity of " the Palace."

On our way to California we paid a visit to Salt Lake City. We, that is Franchi and I, were anxious to visit the Mormon Tabernacle, the " Temple of the Prophet," as it was called, and thither we adjourned on the day of our arrival. To our intense astonishment, the honours of the Temple were tendered to us by a *ci-devant suonatore di corno* (horn player), who had, *upwards of twenty years previously, played at the Italian opera under my bâton.*

With the greatest possible pride and delight the old fellow produced and showed us the contract for his engagement, which had been signed by Henry Jarrett on behalf of Mapleson, and which he had carefully preserved.

A domestic event in July, previous to our autumn tour, 1884, recalls itself to my mind at this moment; and being one which concerns me very nearly, I am induced to interrupt the chain of circumstances for a few moments, in order to mention the wedding of Giulietta, my daughter, who has figured once or twice in the preceding pages. A daily paper gave the following account of the event : —

" The marriage of Giulietta, daughter of Signor and Madame Arditi, to Mr. Romaine Walker, son of the esteemed vicar of St. Saviour's, took place on Thursday, July 10th, at St. Saviour's Church. The bride, attended by four bridesmaids, Miss Walker (sister of the bridegroom), Miss Wike, Miss Knox, and Miss Hasbuck, leaning on the arm of her father, who gave her away, was met at the church door by the Rev. John Walker, Canon Sanderson, Canon Duckworth, the Rev. Mr. Crochett, who, with the choir, proceeded up the aisle to the altar. The best man was Mr. Louis Fagan, with Luigi Arditi, junior, Mr. Ayrton Bankes, and Mr. Warburton. The service was choral, at the conclusion of which a wedding march, composed expressly by Signor Arditi, was played by Mr. Bending. The bride's dress was of the richest brocade, caught back by wreaths of myrtle over a petticoat embroidered in appliqué velvet, the design by the bridegroom, and worked by the bride. The bridesmaids wore cream net dresses with satin bodices, the skirts sprinkled with red flowers and green leaves, their bouquets tied with the same, being the Italian colours. The church was crowded, and about two hundred guests repaired afterwards to 41 Albany Street, the residence of the bride's parents, where, in a tent erected in the garden, the wedding breakfast was laid, during the progress of which the band of the Honourable Artillery Company repeated Signor Arditi's wedding march, together with many of his best-known compositions. The presents were over two hundred in number, amongst which were a diamond and ruby bracelet from Lord Ailesbury, a diamond and ruby brooch from Madame Adelina Patti, a dining-room suite from Madame Valleria, a quantity of silver plate from the bridegroom's relations, besides many valuable souvenirs from the numerous friends of the bride. Telegrams of congratulation poured in from all parts of the world, and from many friends unavoidably absent, amongst whom were Mesdames Minnie Hauk, Valleria, Gerster, Marie Roze, Bottesini, Franchi, etc."

Emma Nevada made her *début* in San Francisco in 1885. Being a Californian, the receipts on the occasion of her first appearance on the stage in her own country may be said to have reached the height of a " Patti night."

When first she was seen, the people roared and shouted so wildly, waving their hats and handkerchiefs, that the poor little lady was quite overpowered, and could hardly control her emotion.

I very much prize a letter she wrote to me on the evening of her *début* in California; it is so gracefully and charmingly expressed that I cannot do better than give it to my readers in its entirety: —

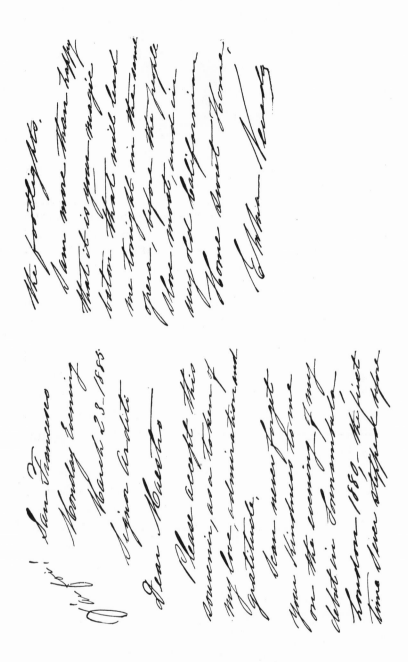

CHAPTER XVI.

ON our return from America, early in 1885, Mapleson
opened Covent Garden, with Patti and Scalchi as
his principal stars. There is no need to dwell upon the
oft-repeated tale of the financial and artistic success
invariably achieved by Patti ; but several times during
that season she failed to appear, and on these occasions
Mapleson was the recipient of many and bitter complaints in consequence of the serious disappointment
her absence caused to the public.

It was during this season that Patti celebrated her
" silver wedding," so to speak, with Covent Garden, in
memory of which a subscription was organised to present her with a diamond bracelet, Mapleson address-
ing to her a flattering speech after the performance of
" Il Trovatore."

A procession, headed by a brass band, accompanied
the Diva's carriage to her hotel, where she gave a
supper to the principal artists and several of her intimate friends. The din and uproar caused by this
unusual scene was extraordinary. Torch-lights flared

through the streets, fireworks were let off in front of the hotel, crowds of people followed the procession; in short, everybody along the route (for the artists and ourselves followed the procession in cabs) turned out to see the sight.

A funny fact in connection with this demonstration was that, having passed the house of Signor Mazzoni, we asked him the next day whether he had heard the band. He only answered, "Of course I did, but I thought it was the Salvation Army! . . ."

The autumn of 1885, our last and memorable American tour with Mapleson, was fraught with troubles of every description. Significant enough is the saying that "troubles never come singly;" and indeed, energetic as the Impresario had shown himself in forming an efficient company, the one name which never failed to draw crowded houses was absent, namely, that of Patti, and the subscriptions which should have poured in to us were very largely devoted by many of our former most ardent supporters to the promotion of German opera at the Metropolitan House. From that moment everything went wrong.

The constant worries and anxieties we were all subjected to made every one disagreeable and discontented; our hard-earned salaries were not paid; the orchestra refused to play (that reminds me of an occasion when we got through a whole opera with the aid of a piano and harmonium, the musicians having failed to turn up at the appointed hour); and the artists, of whom it is no injustice to say that they are never particularly amenable, even under the most auspicious circumstances, were in such a state of irritation and rage that the condition of things became quite unbearable.

Financially, the American season of 1885-86 was disastrous in the extreme; but it nevertheless showed its

This caricature from "Puck" represents the rivalry of the German and Italian companies, the two conductors, Seidl and myself, trying to oust each other.

humourous side, when I think of the woe-begone pictures which some of the artists and chorus presented, as, after the close of the tour at San Francisco, they, with their belongings, were detained, and compelled to sit on their luggage, unable to depart until the money for the hotel accommodation was forthcoming. I am bound to laugh now, as indeed we were obliged to do at the very time.

That season not only brought about Mapleson's downfall, and subsequent bankruptcy, but the serious illness of many members of the company, including my unfortunate self. I caught a severe chill on leaving the theatre one night, and was compelled to take to my bed, as my attack, suddenly developing into pneumonia, became extremely dangerous. The company was obliged to leave me behind at a hotel in Chicago, Mapleson being due at Minneapolis, and for some days I lay between life and death. Mapleson, with the grim humour which characterised some of his sayings, headed a chapter of his book with the title, " Arditi's Remains," which, if it was not conspicuous for good taste, at least proves the serious nature of my condition at that time. Virginia, who was not with me, knew nothing of my sudden illness, and it was only on her receipt of a telegram from Patti from Madrid, asking, "*How is Arditi? Grieved to hear of his dreadful attack*," that she knew something had happened to me. Bimboni, the assistant conductor, took my place during my temporary absence, and I was fortunately able to rejoin the company in a week or two.

Matters had not improved during my illness, and a good deal of trouble was brewing among the artists, who wanted their money, and refused to sing unless they were paid. Ravelli and De Anna were the most awkward customers whom Mapleson had to tackle, the former tenor simply behaving like a madman, and inciting many of the other artists to act in a similarly ferocious manner.

Everybody was anxious to receive his or her salary, and of course I wanted mine. Mapleson was then owing me a considerable sum of money, which he proposed to settle by paying me £300. Being anxious to take anything I could get, I agreed to that sum. I need scarcely say that I never received a penny of that money — but stay, to be quite accurate, when Mapleson was ultimately declared a bankrupt, I *did* get something towards what he owed me, namely, £3 6s. od.

That was the last tour I made with Mapleson, and one which, alas, does not recall any pleasurable reminiscences.

Mapleson, who had indisputably placed before the American world most of the principal artists of the century, broke down under the weight of his continued misfortunes, lost all his prestige, and, as subsequent events show, was never again in a position to return to America at the head of an operatic company, in spite of the many efforts he has since made in that direction.

On my return to London, in 1886, I signed a contract to accompany Henry Abbey's Operatic Troupe as conductor, while in August of that year Virginia and I paid our first visit to Craig-y-nos Castle, Adelina Patti's Welsh home.

This is how Virginia recorded our arrival and subsequent short stay there in her diary : —

" 25*th of August.* — Left Paddington Station at 10.30, and arrived at Craig-y-nos at 7.30. Adelina and Nicolini received us with open arms. We were too tired to dress, so we adjourned to a perfect dinner, served in a magnificent conservatory (a sort of hall of enchantment, illuminated by myriads of electric fairy lights).

" After dinner we played billiards, and heard the wonderful

organ which hails from Switzerland and gives a rendering of fifty or more operas, to say nothing of concerted pieces and other music. . . .

"I have no idea how many *parures* of brilliants, rubies, sapphires, pearls, emeralds, and turquoises, etc., the Diva possesses; for night after night she appears before us adorned by new splendours. . . . We pass our days in walking, driving, eating, and sleeping; no music save the organ, yet always the same charming manner of whiling away our time in this Paradise. . . . We went to the Hut yesterday in the hopes of seeing some salmon caught; but Nicolini was unsuccessful, and attributes his failure to the fact that it has not rained enough lately.

"Luigi and I are enchanted with the castle. It would take one quite a fortnight to visit each room and its treasures, for the Diva's store of mementos of celebrities is inexhaustible. We have, however, seen most of her decorations, gifts, and jewellery, and her collection is quite unique. . . ."

. . . .

The auspices under which the Abbey concert tour, beginning with Dublin, *en route* for New York, New Orleans, Mexico, etc., was started were strikingly free of worry and anxiety.

Henry Abbey treats his companies with every consideration; he is courteous, and ever thoughtful as to their wants and requirements. His charming wife (*née* Miss Florence Gerard), who at that time was little more than a bride (and a sweetly pretty one), proved the life and soul of that tour, devoting herself to everybody, and doing all in her power to make things pleasant all round.

Patti accompanied us, also Novara and his wife, Guille (a tenor possessed of a magnificent voice), Galassi, Scalchi and her husband, Count Lolli, — the tour commencing in Dublin, with the opening of that imposing building, Leinster Hall. My boy Gigi made his *début*, by the way, at a concert in Dublin, in the capacity of

pianist, at this time, and played Liszt's Rhapsodie No.
12, achieving therein much success.

Virginia and my son had come with us as far as
Ireland, intending to return to London on the day we
should start for America; and I must again refer to the
immense hospitality shown to us during our brief stay
by those kindly Dublinites. With such excellent and
big-hearted people as Henry Abbey and his wife, and
Mr. and Mrs. Michael Gunn, who positively vied with
one another as to who should entertain the most lavishly, there was indeed little fear that we should fare
otherwise than in the very best manner.

And now our departure, on the 7th of November,
from Queenstown for New York, once more brings
me to the States, where the first tour under Abbey's
management was conspicuously successful.

We discovered a daring piece of effrontery which
had been perpetrated prior to the company's arrival
at Mexico. An individual representing himself to be
Marcus Mayer, Abbey's agent, stole a march upon us,
and, proceeding to Mexico, stated that Abbey had
authorised him to sell the theatre tickets in advance
for the performances advertised. No one suspected
treachery, and the fellow carried out his nefarious
scheme to the tune of hundreds of pounds; after which
he promptly took his departure.

Needless to say that this shameful imposition did us
much harm in the outset, for the public was cold and
angry, and could not quite get over the fact that it had
been swindled; but after a while the *contretemps* was forgotten, and we played and sang to crowded houses.

Work was not only easy but extremely agreeable
under Abbey's management, and offered a remarkable
contrast to the continual toil of the foregoing tours.
We gave concerts, with one act of an opera, three times

a week, visiting New Orleans, San Francisco, and other towns.

On the journey to San Francisco, we came very near being killed, one and all. It must have been about twelve o'clock one morning, and Sapio, our accompanist, was busily preparing macaroni, while I was engaged in mixing a salad, when the train suddenly gave a lurch, and rushed down an incline at a terrific speed. The rapidity of the motion was too great to admit of speech; but when the train was finally stopped, and several of the company were discovered to be very much shaken and bruised, everybody's tongue found words to abuse the driver. He, however, stayed our fury by remarking, in an impressive tone: "Only be thankful to God that you were not all killed."

This is what had happened. The brake had, for some unaccountable reason, refused to act at the vital moment in descending the incline, and had the driver lost his presence of mind and omitted to resort to other means we should, without doubt, have been precipitated into space. As it was, we were saved by a miracle.

On our return to London, Abbey gave two Patti concerts with orchestra, which I conducted; at the latter my dear old friend and comrade of yore, Bottesini, assisted. Among the artists were Madame Trebelli, Guille, Del Puente, Novara, and others, while Sapio was the accompanist.

Mapleson had, during a short interim, not been idle, and had secured Her Majesty's once more for the purpose of giving a series of operatic performances.

The season was opened with " Fidelio," and Miss Lilli Lehmann's excellent impersonation of the title *rôle* is really deserving of especial mention.

Mapleson had arranged with Abbey that the latter should allow Madame Patti to appear for a succession of nights, but when payment was not forthcoming, Abbey refused to permit Patti to appear after the first night, and a great deal of trouble ensued.

I remember a good story in connection with Novara which occurs to me while speaking of the everlasting question of filthy lucre.

Novara had been engaged to sing the part of Rocco for the three " Fidelio " nights, on the understanding that he, like all of us, should be paid in advance. The first evening he had no difficulty in obtaining his money ; but the second performance was paid for with considerable trouble, in consequence of which he made up his mind not to sing on the third occasion unless he had his money safely in his pocket.

Novara arrived at the theatre in time to dress, and when he asked Levelly, Mapleson's agent, for his salary, Levelly said Mapleson was dining out, and had " forgotten to sign a check for him."

Novara, however, was determined not to sing unless he were paid, and so he told Levelly that Mapleson must be searched for until found.

" I don't know where he is," said Levelly, in despair. " Here, take my watch as a guarantee, Novara, and, for God's sake, get into your clothes."

" I don't require your watch, man," answered the obdurate baritone; " I want my money, and unless I get it before the curtain rises I shall take off this d—d wig, and the stage carpenter can sing the *rôle* of Rocco."

Levelly was rushing about like a madman by this time, and Novara, with his hand on his wig, calmly awaited eventualities in his dressing-room.

It will be remembered that when the curtain rises on the first act of " Fidelio," Rocco is heard singing behind the scenes, and I was filled with consternation at the strange voice that greeted my ears. Of course I knew nothing at that time of the *contretemps* between Levelly and Novara, and it was only on making inquiries that I learned that Novara had refused to sing Rocco's opening bars, and that Parry, the stage-manager, had been obliged to sing them instead, and had, to the best of his ability, imitated Novara's deep bass notes.

Levelly, seeing that Novara meant what he said, had taken a cab and gone, Heaven knows where, in search of the truant Impresario. Whether he found Mapleson or not, I never knew; but he obtained Novara's salary, and reached the theatre, dripping with perspiration, and thrust the cash into Rocco's hand, who, stuffing it in his pocket, rushed on to the stage just in the nick of time to save the performance.

At the conclusion of the opera season Mapleson arranged to give a series of promenade concerts in conjunction with Mr. G. Wood, of the firm of Cramer and Co.; but after some ten days the latter backed out of the enterprise, and payments being much in arrear, I had, on more than one occasion, to guarantee the salaries due to the orchestra, in order to induce the musicians to appear. Levelly behaved capitally to me on these occasions, and always saw to my getting my salary; he used to positively clutch it for me on Saturday nights at the box office.

These concerts came to an end in September, 1887.

The indefatigable Mapleson once more got together a company of artists for a tour in Ireland and the provinces, and having offered me the same conditions, namely, payment in advance, I accepted. I am sorry to say that things went badly, very badly, during that tour, and the only pleasant episode I can recall, as far as I am concerned, was the occasion upon which I was presented with a bâton at Dublin.

It was in October, on the night of the performance of

"Ernani," when Mrs. Michael Gunn, in whose box my wife occupied a seat, called Virginia's attention to a spot in the gallery where the Italian colours were suspended. Mrs. Gunn remarked, "There is something up there for your husband," to which Virginia, who was very much mystified, said, "Why, they are not going to *throw* it at him, are they?"

At the end of the act, by means of a well-devised plan, a long case tied up with red, green, and white ribbons, was slowly lowered in my direction, and was, much to my astonishment, presented to me amid great enthusiasm and applause. While with trembling fingers I undid the case, the gallery shouted vociferously, "Speech, Arditi; speech!"

All I could do at this overwhelming moment was to thank everybody with heartfelt gratitude for their kindness, and to recall, in a very few words, my great appreciation of the many favours invariably shown to me in Ireland; and I believe I was guilty of an Irishism, *entre autres*, in saying that my first appearance in *England* had taken place in *Dublin*.

I wielded the handsome bâton with enormous pride that night. It is an ebony stick, mounted in gold and studded with precious stones, and bears the following inscription : " *To Signor Luigi Arditi, from a few of his admirers in Dublin;* " and if I remember rightly, the last time I conducted with it was when Lago's company was honoured by a royal command to give a performance at Windsor of " The Cavalleria Rusticana."

After Dublin, the company proceeded to Cork ; and on our return my son Gigi, I grieve to say, fell ill with typhoid fever, and I was compelled to leave him in charge of my wife. For four weeks she was kept a prisoner, when the kindness of Mr. and Mrs. Gunn did much to alleviate her anxiety.

In July, 1888, our good friends, Mr. and Mrs. Binny-Smith, lent us their house, with its splendid music-room, for the purpose of giving a large reception; the occasion is particularly vivid in my recollection, since it was the last time we enjoyed the privilege of the late Madame Trebelli's company. I remember how she delighted every one with her expressive voice, and although she was sadly changed in appearance since her return from America, the old charm of manner and bewitching smile still clung to her as of yore.

My son had decided to go to Leipzig to study at the Conservatoire, and at last we made up our minds to leave our house, in which we had lived over twenty-one years. Virginia was now anxious to accompany me to America and on my wanderings abroad, although it was not without a heavy heart that we left the dear old home and our kind friend and neighbour, Mr. Fuller, whose ever watchful and solicitous attentions had so often and untiringly helped our little ones over their infantine ailments.

The late Sir Augustus Harris engaged me to conduct his autumnal provincial tour of that year. We had a monster company, among the artists being Mesdames Ella Russell, Mackintyre, Rolla, Alameda, Ponti, Baurmeister, Scalchi, Demeric Lablache, Jeanne Devignes, and Signori Ravelli, Runcio, Caprili, De Anna, D'Andrade, Rinaldini, Bialetto, De Vaschetti, Abramoff, Miranda, Ciampi, and others; and, in spite of the importance of the company, I learnt from the late Sir Augustus Harris' own lips that he lost £4,000 over the transaction.

I remember a funny incident in connection with one of Harris' provincial tours. It occurred in Liverpool, when I was the object of a burly policeman's persistent notice. I was conducting the Italian opera, and the previous evening we had been performing "Aïda." That morning I was about to pay Madame Valleria a visit, and when I left my hotel and crossed over by St. George's Hall, a big police-officer looked at me very hard, and then began to follow me. I went to the other side of the road, and the constable followed. I turned down a side street, and so did the policeman. I began to be alarmed. I was being shadowed, beyond a doubt. What had I done? I knew of nothing. I had not committed any crime, or perpetrated any grievous wrong. I stopped, determined to know the worst. The officer came up, saluted, and said, "Good morning, Signor Arditi; how did you like *our band* last night?" "Your band," I gasped. "Yes, sir, the police band played on the stage last night in 'Aïda' for you!" "Oh, yes," I ejaculated, as I began to understand; "the police band was excellent, magnificent, beautiful." "Thank you, Signor," said the delighted constable; "I'll go and tell my mates." And he left me with a heart as light as my own. But I trembled at one time; I thought he was going to take me to the — what you call it — the lock-up, — and I had not taken anything!

During the spring of 1889 a successful tour under Dr. Gardini's management took us to Berlin, where I brought out "Lakmé," in which Marie Van Zandt created a sensation. Among the artists who accompanied us were Rolla, Ravelli, D'Andrade, Vecchioni, and Pini Corsi, — Van Zandt being the principal star, and deservedly achieving a great artistic triumph in Germany. For the Covent Garden opera season of that year I was engaged by the late Sir Augustus Harris as conductor jointly with Signor Mancinelli. Of that season I find I have nothing pleasant to say, and prefer, under such circumstances, to dismiss the subject with a well-known Italian proverb: "*Un bel tacere non fu mai scritto.*"

I shall never forget the circumstances under which I conducted the overture of " Fidelio " on the occasion of the Shah's visit to Covent Garden that season. I was under strict orders to break off the music at the moment that the Royal guests should appear in their box, and launch into the Turkish March. I had, therefore, to keep one eye on the Royal box, while the other was engaged in directing the musicians ; but happily the Shah's proverbial unpunctuality served us a good turn, and we got to the end of the overture without any interruption.

In August I was engaged by Freeman Thomas to conduct his promenade concerts, which were most successful. A friend of mine reminds me of a good story in connection with them. We were disappointed at the eleventh hour one night by the absence of a soprano, and in my anxiety to fill the vacant place I glanced round the house to see if I could espy an artist who would fill her place.

Mdlle. de Lido, that charming Russian vocalist, was seated with her mother in a box, so I ran upstairs and begged her to help us out of our predicament. Womanlike, although she was willing to assist, she thought at once of her toilette, and said, " How can I sing ? I am not dressed."

I persuaded her to consent, however ; and in my pleasurable excitement at the good news, I hurried on to the platform to announce it to the public. Ere I bethought myself, the words were out of my mouth. This is what I said : —

"Ladies and gentlemen, I am happy to say that although Mdlle. de Lido has nothing on, she has kindly consented to sing in place of Miss X. . . ."

I feel sure Mdlle. de Lido will pardon my telling this story against myself, especially as she was afforded a tremendous ovation when she stepped on to the platform !

CHAPTER XVII.

EXTRACTS FROM MY WIFE'S LETTERS TO OUR DAUGHTER, WRITTEN DURING OUR TOUR WITH MESSRS. ABBEY AND GRAU IN THE UNITED STATES, MEXICO, AND SAN FRANCISCO, IN 1889-90.

VIRGINIA accompanied me to the States in 1889. I propose to extract some passages from her letters to our daughter, Mrs. Romaine Walker, which give a very fair idea of these interesting trips. To quote part of her first letter from Chicago, she described the journey by sea, which was a rather tempestuous one, and then goes on to say : —

We arrived at Leland's Hotel, Chicago, last night, and to-day it is just two weeks since we left London. Here we are, out in the far West, having passed through part of Canada on our journey from New York.

On first entering the train I was immensely struck by the elegance of the interiors of the state saloons, and the beautiful fittings of inlaid cedar wood; but when one came to inspect the sleeping accommodation, I longed for an English first-class carriage. We crossed the river, train and all, in huge ferry boats. Tamagno and Valda occupied the only two private compartments, and all the rest of us were expected to manage as best we could, and the *best* was very uncomfortable for everybody. It was curious to note during the journey that the most primitive towns and small villages were supplied with electric light, which gave the houses a ghostly and uncanny appearance. Added to that, the snow, which had robed everything in its mantle of pure white, produced a very remarkable effect.

The negroes who wait upon us at the hotel are such fun! They are most interested in the company, shake hands with

To Maestro Arditi
In Kind Remembrance
of 'Desdemona'
Em. Albani Gye
1892

everybody, and are extremely polite to us all. The man who brought up our coffee this morning said he was our attendant, and when I asked if there were no chambermaid as well, he answered, " Oh, yes; *there is a lady to fix the room !* "

Tamagno is an extremely pleasant man, and not a bit like the generality of tenors, frightened to hear himself speak, but of a cheerful and pleasant disposition. Every one predicts that he will make a great success in the States. . . .

Last night I went with Luigi to see the Auditorium, which is a magnificent building. It cost eight millions of dollars, and is built with a species of brown granite, while the hall is of marble, with marble pillars and staircases.

The opening night is to be devoted to the dedication and to the making of sundry speeches, while Patti will sing, "Home, Sweet Home" (the only musical item), *for which she will be paid £800!* . . .

Patti and Nordica arrive to-night. One of the papers said: " Patti is bringing her voice, and Nordica her wardrobe," which is a quaint way of putting it; but as it is rumoured that Nordica has spent £2,000 at Worth's on her new costumes, there is some justification for this somewhat sarcastic remark. . . .

Nordica was angry at not having a car to herself, and Abbey told her she could have an entire *train* by paying for it. . . .

I must tell you of the great success of " William Tell " with Tamagno. After his first grand air he fairly roused the public with his magnificent voice and splendid declamation, when the applause and shouting were almost deafening. There is no doubt that Tamagno has achieved a tremendous triumph, and one, moreover, which will leave its mark.

Madame Albani is as charming as ever, and Valda is a kind-hearted madcap, full of fun and spirit, but rather negligent of her voice, I fear.

We have just received an invitation to dine with Albani on Christmas Day. How nice it will be to be in the company of friends whose sympathies are so thoroughly English as theirs! Charles Wyndham has just arrived at this hotel; I met him in the elevator with Miss Mary Moore, to whom he introduced me. She looks *so* young and pretty off the stage. Mr. Wyndham says it is very bad business for him to be here while the Opera

Company reigns supreme, because we get all the big audiences; but he consoled himself with the thought that he will have a fortnight here after we leave. I am going to his theatre some night; it will be such a treat to hear English voices! . . .

January 3rd, 1890. — " Othello " came, saw, and conquered; and, considering that Tamagno rose from a sick bed to sing the part, he made a tremendous hit. Albani as Desdemona was simply *splendid*. The rendering of the " Ave Maria " was sublime in its touching simplicity. Del Puente's idea of Iago is more easily imagined than described; and I really must quote a remark his wife made the other day *à propos* of the subject. Some one told her that Del Puente ought to shave off his moustache for the part, to which she replied, with an air of dignity: " My husband is not in the habit of taking *buffo* parts! . . ."

As to Luigi, I cannot tell you how astonished and delighted I was to see the quiet, unostentatious way in which he conducted a really marvellous performance. Knowing and loving the music as he does, he has thoroughly imbued the orchestra with its sentiment, and they, as well as the chorus, did themselves full justice in response to the hopes and labours of their leader.

After the opera, as a souvenir of her first singing the part under his direction, Albani presented Luigi with a lovely ruby and diamond pin. She gave it to him in such a sweet manner that we felt it really came straight from her heart. . . .

Our journey to Mexico, dear Giulietta, was a very interesting one. Fortunately, Luigi and I had our private compartment, a favour not granted to everybody, and there was not an hour that some new scene or incident did not awaken us from any lethargy to which we might have been predisposed by the extraordinary heat we experienced.

After passing St. Louis we followed the banks of an immense river, the Mississippi, and soon found ourselves in a most perfect climate. The sun was so hot, and the vegetation so luxuriant, that, passing through the different settlements, I almost fancied we were witnessing scenes from a theatre. We get up very early in the cars, and are served with a delicious breakfast at 8.30 by the negroes. The life is very

TAMAGNO'S DEATH SCENE IN "OTHELLO."

entertaining, because the ever-changing scenes are rife with novelties.

As we approached Texas it seemed as though the roads were garnished with cactus plants; and all along the line the natives turn out of their huts to stare at Patti's car, which bears her name in large letters, and is, of course, *the* great attraction.

The air is divine. I cannot realise, with such a climate, that we are in the month of January. We seem to be enjoying life as a huge picnic, at which the chief attractions and alternations are cocktails and poker.

On our arrival at the frontier, a town called Eagles, an exciting scene took place. We found the entire population, headed by a brass band, awaiting us at the station. The Mexicans were clad in shirt and drawers, with draperies of striped blankets, and their picturesque sombreros, trimmed with silver cords, were very becoming to their handsome faces. The women wore roses in their dusky locks, many carrying in their arms their babes, covered only with little shirts, while the mothers complacently smoked their cigarettes.

This is the place *par excellence* to see really handsome men and women.

At night-time we halted at another station, and here the brilliant colouring of the people's dresses, upon which the bright moonshine cast its quiet spell, presented a scene which I shall never forget. Then we reached the sandy desert, and there it was curious to note the queer, inadequate huts, built of the branches of trees, in which several families reside together, — everything, of course, being covered with sand. We came suddenly to a stand-still on account of a bridge having broken down, and were obliged to wait until the following morning to proceed on our journey.

Our cars were surrounded by women and children, who were only half clothed; and, considering this is their winter, what must their summer be? Some of them carried large pitchers, and reminded me of the pictures we have seen of Ruth and Naomi. One little baby girl, I particularly noticed, had nothing on but a scanty chemise, and she was such a perfect little statue that I could not keep my eyes off her.

At a short stretch from this were the gold and silver mines,

while the blue mountains in the far distance formed a splendid
background to the long plain of sand, overgrown by cactus
plants.

We all got out of the cars, and tried to potter about in the
sand; but we soon burnt our feet, and were glad to scramble
back again.

To-night we are invited to dine with the Diva in her car,
which is most luxurious; it is, in fact, fit for any queen. Her
suite is decorated in the most artistic fashion, her monogram
being interspersed here and there on the walls with flowers and
musical instruments; the saloon is furnished with lounges and
chairs of pale-blue plush, and her bedroom is made of inlaid
satin wood, with a brass bedstead, a plush counterpane bearing
her monogram exquisitely embroidered, while she has every
luxury, such as a long glass, bath, electric light, piano, etc.

.   .   .   .

We have just experienced a terrible emotion, which no one
will forget for some time. I told you yesterday that we
were at a stand-still on account of a broken bridge; but we were
not informed that just before our arrival here an engine and
goods train had gone down with it. Fortunately the drivers
were able to save themselves by jumping off and clinging to the
railings, and, until we passed it just now, we had no idea of the
extent of the wreck. The accident occurred last Sunday, and
to-day is Thursday, but a temporary bridge has already been
erected in this wonderfully short space of time.

We crossed the new bridge in fear and trembling, and were
horrified to see the old one broken in the middle, with the
engine and wrecked cars lying at the bottom; it is terrible to
think this might have been *our* fate! Everybody is so thankful for the lucky escape that there has been no grumbling or
discontent all day! . . .

The nights are so lovely that we sit outside the cars and revel
in the exquisitely warm and balmy air. The moon is brilliant,
and throws into relief the native huts like silhouettes against
the dark-blue sky. As I told you, they are composed of the
branches of trees (somewhat inflammable material, I fear), and
the people, walking about wrapped in their white woollen
blankets, are most picturesque.

To-day we ran another risk of an accident which might have ended badly. Our car became detached from the rest of the train, and the other divided carriages came within an ace of running into us and smashing us up. All the nigger waiters (so much for their courage) made a rush for the fields, jumping from the car at the risk of their lives, but no accident occurred. You see these journeys are not uneventful, and there is always something unexpected happening.

The scenery has completely changed, and now we pass small towns with churches which are built in the Eastern style, while whole streets seem to be composed of mud hovels only.

The men on horseback look so picturesque with their saddle-bags, revolvers, and lassos, etc. Their type resembles that of the Neapolitans; they have such lovely eyes, white gleaming teeth, and blue-black hair in abundant masses.

We continually stop at small towns, where the women walk about half naked, a very *sans gêne* style, and are often to be seen washing their clothes in the streams.

Mexico at last! A perfect paradise of a place! A band of musicians to meet us at the station! Our hotel was formerly a convent, and is built around a garden of orange-trees, and palms fifteen feet in height, and trees which have not lost their leaves despite the time of year. A veranda runs round the building, and everybody is drinking in the exhilarating air. What a glorious sky! We are six thousand feet above the level of the sea, so you can imagine how pure the atmosphere is! . . .

The house for our first performance was magnificent. Such wealth, dresses, and diamonds; such a galaxy of beauty, and such appreciative though exacting audiences one does not often see combined. Money seems to be of no value to some people, and I heard of a lady who positively paid £30 for a box, and £14 for two seats in the gallery for her maid and her husband's valet! . . .

Before our arrival the best rooms in the hotel were denuded of some of their furniture so as to add to the elegance of Patti's apartments; and, as a special compliment to the company in general, every servant was *ordered to have a bath*, — an interesting event, that does not speak greatly in favour of Mexican cleanliness. . . .

Luigi and I have just visited the Cathedral, which, to do it justice, should be described by a far abler pen than mine. The old part, which gives one the impression of being composed of carved ivory, was erected on the ruins of the Aztec temple, and is a marvel. The newer part, dating from 1600, is immense, and contains no less than forty altars, each one of which is shut in separately with carved screens, each more exquisite in design than the other. The huge pillars are composed of malachite; everywhere the eye dwells on marvellous specimens of carvings or gilding, and as for pictures, the Cathedral is full of them, and I hear they are priceless.

It is a most delightful experience to go out in the streets here. All is life, gaiety, and colour. One meets such splendid-looking Mexicans, dressed in the tightest of trousers with large silver buttons up the sides (how they get into them is a mystery to me), and armed with silver-handled revolvers, which are slipped into their waist-belts. Then they wear *such* wonderful hats! These are their greatest pride, and I hear that Mexicans think nothing of paying as much as £16 for their head-gear.

Luigi is becoming more and more mixed every day as regards languages. Last night I wanted one of the servants to unstrap my trunk before bringing it upstairs, and called to Luigi, since he speaks Spanish, to explain. Imagine how I laughed when he came into the room and calmly addressed the Mexican in *English!* The Spaniards adore him; there are many in the orchestra who played with him when he was here before. . . .

Who do you think came to see us yesterday? The son of our old friend the late Lord Chesterfield, Chandos Stanhope. He has, in manner and expression, grown very like to Lady Chesterfield, and consequently very charming.

We went for a drive with him to Chepultepec, the Emperor Maximilian's palace, built on a lovely spot formed by rocks which, by some convulsion of nature, have been thrown up to a tremendous height. From the palace terrace the view of the glorious cypress and orange groves and the luxuriant verdure is beautiful beyond description; while in the far distance the mountain chains spread out endlessly, in the midst of which rose one huge snow-capped peak, supposed to be an extinct volcano.

The palace has an interest of melancholy importance, for many of the objects and rooms have been left exactly as Maximilian last used them. The President often stays there. . . .

We are sitting at our window, in front of which a huge palm is growing, at least twenty feet in height, and although every one suffers somewhat from the tremendous height of the situation, the beauty and grandeur of the spot reconcile one to any shortcoming.

The living here is vastly different from that in England. We take coffee in our rooms in the morning; from twelve to two o'clock we have "comida," which is supposed to be dinner; while supper is served between six and eight, late meals in Mexico being considered very injurious to the health.

Patti has just sent us in a delicious dish from her table; she has brought her own *chef* with her, so you may be sure she often surprises us agreeably with some sort of unexpected delicacy. . . .

I must not forget to mention that we spent a most charming day with the Hon. Chandos Stanhope. The party consisted of Madame Albani and her husband, Mr. and Mrs. Clark, Lady Cecilia Rose, Sir F. Dennis, young Mr. Goschen, and Prince Poniatowski (nephew of our old friend). Mr. Stanhope being Vice-President of the new line of railways, we had a special train which took us to Toluka, fifty miles from the city of Mexico, and passed through the most wonderful scenery and over perilous-looking bridges. We were received on our arrival by the Governor, and drove all over the town in carriages specially provided for us. The weather was perfect, and the city most interesting to view, and decidedly cleaner than Mexico.

After partaking of refreshments, and being introduced to the Governor's wife, we returned to our hotel, thankful at having reached home safely, and full of pleasant recollections of the courtesy of our kind host.

We shall not leave Mexico until the 3rd of February. I suppose Abbey wants to get as much money out of the Mexicans as possible. They are so crazy here about the opera that they positively pawn their jewellery to buy seats at the theatre.

We have only given fifteen performances, and have already taken over £40,000!

I believe I am the only one in the company who really enjoys the life here. Luigi, when he is at work, is too nervous and absorbed to think much of his surroundings, and every one of the artists has been indisposed. As to the public, no wonder the singers are frightened of it; it is more *exigeant* than an Italian audience, *et c'est tout dire !*

"Faust" was produced last night for the first time, and Ravelli, who is certainly not in good voice, was simply *hissed*.

Novara never had a hand the whole evening, and Albani was only applauded *when she sang alone*. This is decidedly a novel experience for the artists. The audience very soon lets them know when they sing out of tune. . . .

Some members of the company went to a bull fight yesterday; I could not summon courage enough to witness such wholesale butchery, but I am told the excitement of the scene is tremendous. One of the famous Toreadors fought most valiantly with a bull, and every time he struck the poor brute a deft blow the people screamed and roared, " Bravo, Tamagno !" This will, in some measure, give you an idea of the latter's success here.

Patti's benefit, which took place on the 29th of January, was a tremendous success. The house was a wonderful sight, and the gifts presented to her were extraordinary. . . . Mrs. Clark (the lady I told you about who gave £30 for a box on our opening night) was thinking of spending a fabulous sum of money on flowers for Patti, but I advised her to give Adelina something she could keep in remembrance of her; consequently she bought an exquisite little clock in the shape of a Sedan chair, which Luigi handed to her from the orchestra. Grau gave her a card-case inlaid with diamonds, the President's wife a filigree silver box containing precious coins, while many other souvenirs were presented to her. " La Traviata " was the opera, and Patti was in perfect voice.

Between the acts Luigi played his composition " L'Ingénue," which created a *furore* and was wildly encored; but poor Vicini, who sang in lieu of Ravelli, never had a hand, and would have been *hissed* had it not been Patti's benefit. . . .

February 4th. — Here we are in the train once more, and turning our back regretfully upon picturesque Mexico. We have had a lovely time financially as well as artistically, and above all I was intensely gratified to see what a favourite Luigi is with the Spaniards.

When we were passing Chiwawa this morning Adelina sent me a present of a charming little dog, measuring from head to tail a quarter of a yard. I shall call him Chiquito, which means "tiny." We are passing through desolate, sandy plains just now, with big, unfriendly looking mountains in the distance, and there is so little vegetation in this district that now and again dead cattle are discovered lying across our track. The sun is burning hot, and the sand so penetrating and blinding that, in spite of the double windows in the car, it manages to penetrate our food; the very air we breathe is gritty. . . .

. . . Last night we entered California, which is radiantly green and lovely. We saw a marvellous sunrise this morning when we stopped at Los Angeles, a little town of such beauty that it were almost impossible to describe it. People in England have no idea of the grandeur of the vegetation out here; it must be seen to be realised.

Before arriving at San Francisco we passed over mountains and perilous passes that were frightful to contemplate, although they were intensely grand. We descended 4,000 feet in fifty miles, while the plains we skirted were a huge mass of orange marigolds! . . .

. . . We are very comfortable at Baldwin's Hotel, and I feel sure we are going to have a lovely stay here.

Yesterday Mr. Heyman, a member of the Bohemian Club and a great friend of Luigi, took us to the Cliff House, the famous rock upon which seals congregate in shoals. Our trip thither was another new experience to me. We travelled on the cable car, a train which apparently goes by itself without the aid of steam, electricity, or horse power. The car is wound up, and the cable (which is laid *under* the road) is about ten miles long. The machinery is, however, quite invisible, and the "fairy" car, having seats inside and outside, traverses the most tremendous hills and inclines. In respect to hills, San Francisco quite surpasses Rome. These wonderful cars go all over the city in every direction, and have a most bewildering effect upon a stranger.

Neither Luigi or I will ever forget the kindness shown to us by the members of the Bohemian Club in San Francisco (Mr. Heyman in particular); Luigi is an honorary member of the club, and each time he has been to San Francisco a big supper has been given in his honour. A beautifully drawn certificate announcing his membership has been presented to us.[1]

The trip will figure among the pleasantest of my recollections, for the drive to the cliff was delicious, and the first sight of the vast expanse of the Pacific most striking.

A large restaurant, surrounded by balconies, is built upon the cliff, where people sit to watch the seals which play about on the huge slippery rocks, and have the appearance, from a distance, of being so many leeches.

The Golden Gate, which is the entrance to the magnificent harbour, is indeed appropriately named; a grander spectacle I have never seen.

Last night we visited the Chinese quarter, and there again I imagined myself in a new part of the world. The tea houses, barbers' and other shops, — in fact, everything and everybody is Chinese. They are very deft workmen, if one may judge their capabilities by the remarkable gilding and carving one sees in their shop decorations. We also went to a Chinese theatre, and were taken behind the scenes after the performance. The acting was too ludicrous for words, and the music (?) so deafening that we could not stand much of it. The theatre is open every afternoon and evening, and is invariably crowded with Chinese men and women, — for the latter of whom seats are always reserved. We are thinking, too, of visiting the opium dens, situated under-ground. They are so iniquitous that in order to visit them one must, for the sake of safety, be accompanied by an official or a detective.

To-night we open with "William Tell." Valda, who has been hoarse, has recovered, and will sing.

When I was about to take my seat in the stalls last night I overheard a remark made by one lady to another which greatly amused me. "I have not come to see 'William Tell,'" she whispered to a friend; "it is Arditi's *entrée* to the orchestra, which I would not miss for worlds!"

[1] The Address hangs now in his gallery of souvenirs. — EDITOR.

My little dog Chiquito goes with me to the theatre every night. Patti takes hers to her dressing-room, and Mdlle. Fabbri likewise; but my little pet sits on my lap in the wings, and never stirs, seemingly enjoying the music very much.

Another charming episode of San Francisco was a dinner given to us by Judge Boult and his wife. The judge is a most intellectual man, and the company consisted of lawyers and members of the Bo-hemian Club. On taking our places we found that a delicate compliment had been paid us in the shape of two decorative and beautifully painted satin squares bearing our names, above which were two bars of Luigi's Gavotte, "L'Ingénue," a most unexpected surprise.

That reminds me that at one of the *matinées* at Boston, when "Othello" was being performed, I was, as usual, sitting in my accustomed place in the wings. At the end of the performance Albani and Tamagno had been called and recalled many times, and Albani, catching sight of Chiquito, whisked him off my lap, and took him in her arms before the delighted audience, much to the astonishment of Luigi, who had remained at his post.

We left Chicago on Saturday morning, and as our car which took us to Mexico and back was not going on, I was afraid we might have a repetition of the same awful experience we had when first coming to New York. . . . Words, however, fail me to give you an adequate description of the luxurious car placed at our disposal for the journey. The compartments were almost as roomy as the staterooms on board steamers, and were panelled with brocaded silk of different colours. Lounges of brocaded velvet were placed about in abundance, and the decorations of the car consisted of handsomely carved walnut wood. The sleeping compartment was far more adequately fitted up than many a bedroom at a first-class hotel, and even furnished a hot and cold water supply by day and night, besides electric light, a cheval glass, and other luxuries.

I quite regretted our arrival at Boston, although the journey lasted longer than we first supposed it would, for we were timed to reach there at six o'clock on Monday morning, instead of which, owing to an accident on our line, we had to make a lengthy *détour*, and it was three o'clock in the afternoon ere we steamed into the station.

" Othello " was announced for the same evening, and poor Luigi only had time to barely rehearse one act with the extras of the orchestra. Mr. Abbey was a little nervous as to the result, but I told him it was just at such times that Luigi would show his coolness and *savoir faire*, and you can imagine *how* necessary it was, for " Othello " is not " Lucia."

The extra members of the orchestra did not know the opera at all; but the musicians, who are mostly Germans, have a thorough respect for Luigi, and follow his beat with implicit faith and intelligence, so that the whole opera went off splendidly, both Tamagno and Albani being in magnificent voice.

Back to New York again, dear Giulietta, and now every day brings us nearer our return to dear old England.

We are performing at the Metropolitan Opera House, which has just been vacated by the German company, and last night Luigi had a very enthusiastic reception on taking his seat, and was the recipient of a splendid horse-shoe of flowers, with ribbons upon which were painted in gold letters the words, " Welcome, Arditi." Everything is done in the best possible style, but I do think it is sinful to spend such fabulous sums of money as they do on flowers. Fifteen pounds for a large bunch of roses is nothing uncommon, and I have seen bouquets thrown on the stage amounting to the value of £40 to £50!

These are my last lines to you ere we shall be able to greet you all in person. We leave New York on the 26th in the "Etruria" (April, 1890), and hope to reach Liverpool on the following Sunday. What a lot we shall have to talk about! Till then, *au revoir*.

Your ever affectionate

MADRE.

CHAPTER XVIII.

ON our return to London, after the 1889-90 trip to
the States, I enjoyed the novel experience, for
reasons unnecessary to dwell upon here, of being paid
a salary for the whole season without having to work for
it. Later in that year, during the month of August,
we again visited Craig-y-nos Castle, where we enjoyed
four weeks of uninterrupted pleasure and hospitality.
Madame Patti's Bijou Theatre being then in active
preparation, every one was most interested to see the
clear-sightedness and precision with which the Diva
herself superintended the planning and arrangements
of the whole building.

Lago's autumn season at Covent Garden brings me
to the close of 1890. I conducted jointly with Bevignani, and it would be impossible to speak otherwise
than favourably of Lago's short season, since it was the
means of bringing those charming and cultivated
singers, the Sisters Ravogli, before the public.

During the season of 1891 I conducted two Patti
concerts at the Albert Hall, at one of which Madame

Patti sang, for the first time, a new vocal valse of mine called " Rosebuds," which was perfectly rendered and enthusiastically received.

On the 12th of August of the same year the Patti Theatre at Craig-y-nos was formally opened by an operatic performance given to a house full of distinguished guests.

The building is a handsome one, oblong in shape, and sufficiently spacious to accommodate three hundred persons. The side walls are decorated with arabesqued panels of pale blue and gold between fluted pillars with highly ornate pediments. Its principal entrance is approached by a passage leading from one of the billiard rooms, while the stage door is accessible through a shrubbery which faces the upper pheasantry. The drop-curtain is a very beautiful one, and was, I believe, painted by Hawes Craven. It represents the Diva in the costume of Semiramide, standing in a Roman chariot and driving two fiery steeds. When, prior to the performance, the heavy blue-plush curtains are drawn aside, this work of art produces a striking effect.

The theatre gives ample room for a band of twenty performers, located in an orchestral well sunk between the stage and the stalls. All the latest modern appliances for scene-shifting have been adopted, and scenery requisite for the mounting of six or more of the Diva's favourite operas is on the spot, so that when Patti's spirit is moved to give a performance in the evening, all she has to do is to send for her head scene-shifter and tell him what opera she proposes to appear in.

On the opening night a large party of friends assembled at the Castle to witness the initial performance, and the pretty house, filled to overflowing with visitors from Swansea, Brecon, and the intervening rural districts, echoed and re-echoed with the storms of applause which followed a unique performance.

The programme of the evening's entertainment was as follows: —

FIRST ACT OF "LA TRAVIATA."

Violetta Valery	MADAME PATTI NICOLINI.
Alfredo Germont	MR. DURWARD LELY.
Flora Bervoix	MISS FLYNN.
Gaston	M. R. BROPHY.
Marchese	MR. E. BALL.
Barone	MR. E. JONES.

CHORUS : St. David's Amateur Operatic Society.
Entr'acte, Morceau à la Gavotte, "*L'Ingénue*" (ARDITI).

THIRD ACT OF "FAUST" (GARDEN SCENE).

Faust	SIGNOR NICOLINI.
Mephistopheles	SIGNOR NOVARA.
Margherita	MADAME PATTI NICOLINI.
Siebel ⎫ Marta ⎭	MADAME GIULIA VALDA.

"GOD SAVE THE QUEEN."

The little orchestra, Mr. Hulley's from Swansea, which I conducted, acquitted itself with spirited energy and excellent discretion, while Mr. William Terriss, in the unavoidable absence of Sir (then Mr.) Henry Irving, declared the theatre open, in a graceful address to the audience, which had been expressly written for the occasion by my valued friend, Mr. Beatty-Kingston, of "Daily Telegraph" fame.

It was a great night. Madame Patti, singing her favourite *rôles* of Violetta and Margherita on her own stage in her beautiful home to an audience composed of appreciative and intimate friends, rose to a height of executive skill which I have rarely known

CRAIG-Y-NOS.

excelled. The matchless voice — as rich and mellow as it was thirty years ago — held us all spell-bound, going straight to the hearts of her hearers, and calling forth enthusiastic applause. In "Faust," too, she was inimitably fine, and being assisted by Nicolini, who for so many years had filled the title *rôle* with much power and grace, the performance was, if possible, even more remarkable than that which preceded it.

A magnificent supper was afterwards served for the guests in the large glass conservatory (where, by-the-bye, 450 bottles of champagne were consumed), a vote of thanks was proposed by Sir Hussey Vivian in enthusiastic and feeling terms, and so ended a performance which should always hold a place of distinction in the annals of musical events.

The festivities did not, however, end here: many who witnessed the performance were guests at the Castle, and for three days and nights the little theatre was kept at work with burlesque and pantomime impromptus rendered by the younger generation of visitors, and operatic selections, etc., given by the Diva and the artists who had so ably assisted her on the opening night. The amusement never once lagged, nor grew less interesting.

Previous to the departure of many of the guests, the Second Act of Flotow's "Marta," and the Third Act of Gounod's "Romeo and Juliet" were admirably rendered at a *matinée* on Saturday, August the 16th; by two o'clock every place in the theatre was occupied by an audience quite as numerous as that which had gathered together on the previous Wednesday night.

The notables of "the Valley" and the *élite* of Swansea and Brecon — the two county towns from which Craig-y-nos is equidistant — had been arriving at the Castle by road and rail for more than an hour before the doors of the theatre were opened, and formed a *queue* of such length and breadth as would have gladdened the heart and raised the hopes of many a theatrical manager in town during the season.

Among the visitors who were present at the opening of the theatre I remember the Spanish Ambassador, Baron and Baroness de Reuter, Sir Hussey and Lady Vivian, Sir Edward Lawson, Mr. Augustus Spalding, Mr. and Mrs. Beatty-Kingston, my wife, and many others who assisted to bring the celebrations to a brilliant conclusion.

I must not forget to mention that one night the theatre was converted, for the nonce, into a huge ball-room, by the elevation of the auditorium flooring to the level of the stage, at the back of which the orchestra was set up in an extemporised bower of flowers and evergreens, backed by the beautiful Nuremberg " cloth " of the garden scene in " Faust." The party broke up about 5 P. M., after having enjoyed a treat, I may venture to say, almost without precedent. I was assisted throughout by Mr. Hulley's able orchestra, and of the *tout ensemble* it would be impossible to speak in too high terms of praise.

After many of the guests and artists had left us, and we had hardly recovered from the excitement of the foregoing events, the agreeable news reached us that H. R. H. Prince Henry of Battenberg, whose yacht was stationed in Swansea Harbour, would honour the Castle with a visit to luncheon on the 21st of August, accompanied by Mr. Graham Vivian, of Clyne Castle, whose guest he was for the time being. Of course sundry telegrams were immediately despatched to recall the artists and orchestra, etc., and the greatest excitement prevailed generally while preparing for the Prince's visit.

The resources of the Castle were inexhaustible, and in spite of its remote situation in the heart of the wild Welsh

To my dear friend
Luigi Arditi
a souvenir of
sincere friendship from
Adelina Patti Nicolini
1896

hills, all the necessary decorations were forthcoming, — red cloths laid everywhere, a salute was prepared at the station for the arrival of the train, and the whole of the household establishment, consisting of forty or more servants, were drawn up in the courtyard to await the Prince's arrival.

Adelina Patti and her husband met their illustrious guest and his suite at the foot of the stairs; after which we repaired to the luncheon table, which was luxuriously laid out in the conservatory.

While the Prince, who was accompanied by Count Gleichen, Lord Royston, the Hon. Henry Bruce, and other distinguished people, was taking coffee and cigars in the winter garden, our host and hostess quickly retired to their dressing-rooms at the theatre to prepare themselves for a performance of the garden scene of " Faust." Needless to say that the " Queen of Song " strained every nerve in her desire to do honour to her royal guest, and, indeed, she sang superbly; Madame Giulia Valda and Signor Novara also sang with their accustomed artistic efficiency in their respective parts of Marta, Schwerlein, and Mephistopheles, and the Prince expressed his gratification and approval in the highest possible terms. During the interval Madame Patti sang two of my songs, and I cannot do better than quote the very words I jotted down in my diary at the conclusion of that ever-to-be-remembered day.

This is what I wrote: " *Adelina cantò 'Il Bacio' e 'Rosebuds' ed il Principe fu entusiasmato ; mi fece un complimento del quale ne fui fiero! . . .*"[1]

. . . .

After the performance, tea was served in the organ room, where the Prince listened with evident interest to

[1] " Adelina sang ' Il Bacio ' and ' Rosebuds.' The Prince was most enthusiastic, paying me a great compliment, of which I was most proud."— EDITOR.

the " Spirit of the Castle," as the huge organ is termed, and on taking leave expressed himself delighted with his visit.   How far from our minds at that gay gathering was the sad anticipation that we should never again set eyes upon the kindly handsome face and stalwart form of Prince Henry.

We intended leaving the Castle after the Prince's departure, but Adelina insisted on our remaining to accompany her to Swansea, where her annual Charity Concert was to take place.   The reception afforded to the Diva there was indeed a sight we were unprepared for.   On the arrival of our special train at Swansea the Mayor and his sheriff were in attendance at the station to receive us. Carriages having been provided for Madame Patti's guests, we drove slowly through the principal streets, which were gaily decked with triumphal arches, garlands of flowers, and banners, which bore such inscriptions as " Welcome," " God Bless the Queen of Song," " Long Live Adelina Patti," and a hundred other such devices, while every window was crowded with eager faces, and an excited populace surrounded the carriages to catch a glimpse of Madame Patti.

At the conclusion of Madame Patti's inaugural festivities at the Castle the Diva presented handsome gifts to all the artists.   I possess so many souvenirs of our various seasons that my standing remark to her on such occasions is invariably : " *Mille grazie ; spero che non sarà l'ultimo !* " [1]

After this, Virginia, my son, and I joined Madame Valleria's coaching concert tour, which was principally got up for the fun of a novel experience in touring, and without an attempt to cover more than our bare travelling expenses.   The company consisted of Madame Valleria, Miss E. Rees, Orlando Harley, Foli, and Luigi Arditi, Junior, as pianist.   Mr. Hutchinson (the husband

---

[1] " Thousand thanks.   I hope this will not be the last." — EDITOR.

of Madame Valleria), to whom the coach belonged, was the whip, Gigi sounding the post horn all along the journey and displaying quite an aptitude for that remarkably noisy instrument.

We accompanied the coaching party for a week or ten days, after which we returned to London, and I accepted a four weeks' engagement to conduct promenade concerts at Covent Garden for the late Sir Augustus Harris.

I had previously pledged my word to Lago, the Impresario, to conduct opera for him in case he should succeed in obtaining the Shaftesbury Theatre, which he confidently hoped to do; his expectations being shortly afterwards realised, I was compelled to leave the late Sir Augustus at that moment, an action on my part for which I believe he never forgave me.

This engagement I look back upon with the greatest satisfaction, for it enabled me to assist in bringing before the public one of the most successful of modern operas, the " Cavalleria Rusticana."

Every one who was present on the first night will remember the extraordinary enthusiasm with which Mascagni's work was received, and the success which artists and musicians alike achieved. Musiani was the original Santuzza in London, and but for the *tremolando* in her voice (a trait looked upon so unfavourably in vocalisation) she acquitted herself most efficiently. Francesco Vignàs made his *début* as Turiddu, and ere the curtain rose on the first act, his song (when he is heard *unseen*) was enough to establish him as an excellent tenor. The other parts were filled by Brombara, — how picturesque he looked as Alfio, the husband of Lola, and how well he sang, — Grace Damian, and Signora Brema, who has since won so distinguished a position. The *rôle* of Santuzza was consecutively taken by Mesdames Valda, Macintyre, and Elandi. I remember that when we were

honoured by a command to play the "Cavalleria" at
Windsor Castle the Hon. Alec Yorke came to the theatre
to personally select the *prima donna* for the part, and
decided upon Mdlle. Elandi.

On November the 27th, 1891, Lago's company was
bidden, as I said before, to perform "La Cavalleria Rusticana" before Her Majesty the Queen. It will be remembered that since the death of the lamented Prince
Consort no operatic representation had been given at the
Castle, consequently the excitement among our company
was all the greater in anticipation of being the first, after
so many years, to be honoured by Her Majesty's
command.

I publish a letter which Virginia wrote to America,
and in which she speaks of our visit to Windsor. I am
bound once more to leave its recital to her; for, as usual
on great occasions, all my powers were concentrated on
the performance itself.

". . . How can I give you an adequate idea of the wonderful
day we spent at Windsor Castle! The company started from
Paddington station in a special train, and on our arrival at Windsor several royal carriages were waiting to convey us to the
Castle.

"That most imposing of rooms, the Waterloo Chamber, was
fitted up as a theatre, opposite to which stood an enormous
platform with raised seats at the back to accommodate the invited guests. The throne room, partitioned off by screens, was
devoted to the lady artists, while the antechamber was taken for
the gentlemen as 'green room.' A beautiful luncheon was served
on our arrival in two separate rooms, the first being for the principal artists, and the second for the chorus and orchestra.

"When the artists retired to dress, I was free to roam about
the vast galleries filled with priceless works of art (unhampered
by a guide), a privilege which few visitors have enjoyed.

"Before the raising of the curtain I peeped through the opening of the heavy draperies, at which moment I was fortunate

enough to witness the entrance of Her Majesty into the music room.

"Never shall I forget the effect her presence made on me. There stood the Queen in her grandeur and stateliness; and yet, the simplicity and sweet womanliness so characteristic of Her Majesty's personality were omnipresent in every step she took and every gesture she made. The performance itself was a great success, Her Majesty frequently applauding, and at the conclusion the principal artists had the honour of being presented to the Queen. They subsequently received handsome souvenirs of the occasion.

"To Luigi she spoke most graciously, saying it was thirty-one years since she had heard an operatic performance, and that she was glad that he had directed the first music at the Castle, after so long a period.

"The royal guests who were present were the Prince and Princess Schleswig Holstein, the Princess Victoria of Schleswig Holstein, the Marchioness of Lorne, Prince and Princess Henry of Battenberg and their two eldest children, Princesses Victoria and Maud of Wales, Prince Alexander of Teck, and the Marquis of Lorne.

"After the performance the Queen and royal family proceeded to the drawing-room, where the invited guests were presented to Her Majesty.

"Refreshments were subsequently served for the artists in the dining-room, and so ended a memorable day for Luigi, and one which will ever remain among his brightest and happiest recollections."

CHAPTER XIX.

A THICK fog hung about the coast on the 23rd of December, 1892, when we started from Liverpool on the S. S. "Paris" for our operatic tour in the States. The passage was a fearful one, Christmas Day being spent by the members of the company in seclusion and wretchedness. It occurs to me that, as on another occasion, the captain and I were the only persons gifted with sea-legs; we walked about, vainly hoping to find some kindred spirits to converse with, but the exceptionally rough weather had rendered everybody not only unsociable but unapproachable.

We opened our concert season in New York on the 13th of January, and despite the counter attractions of the De Reskes and the regular Italian Opera Company (also under Abbey's management), our success was complete. Madame Patti was in splendid voice, and for the first time that season the theatre was full to overflowing.

At Boston and Philadelphia we had enormous houses, and were over and over again compelled to refuse money. There was such a rush for seats when the magic name of Patti was announced that even mechanics and labourers, clad in their working suits, came to the theatre with their money in hand, asking for standing room, if nothing more, *only to see Patti*.

Our company this time included Mesdames Patti, Fabbri, Signori Guille, Galassi, and Novara, — our concerts consisting of one act of an opera, given in full costume, and a miscellaneous programme for the second part.

Our visit to Buffalo, on the 22nd of January, was an interesting one. As we proceeded on our journey we passed the most magnificent and imposing scenery along the frozen shores of the Susquehanna river; everything was wrapped in a mantle of virgin snow, and huge icicles, ten to twenty feet in length, and giant waterfalls turned to glaciers, afforded some wonderfully picturesque effects.

Buffalo is situate about four hundred and thirty-two miles from New York, and is a very handsome town. The ladies of our company were amazed at the beauties of the shops and the elegance of their *étalages*, which, they said, were quite as fine as those of Regent Street.

The sleighing, too, was delightful. The drivers looked like Esquimaux in their heavy furs, and what with the opossum tails tied to iron rods, and the loud jangling of the shrill bells, the sleighs produced a startling effect.

One of our most remarkable experiences during that tour was a visit to the Niagara Falls. In summer time Niagara is a most charming resort, being surrounded by exquisite scenery, in which, among the splendid hotels, tiny cottages, looking like dolls' houses from the distance, are dotted here and there ; but to be seen in its fullest grandeur, Niagara must be visited in the depth of winter. The falls, one gigantic mass of ice and snow, viewed from the suspension bridge, are magnificent, and the enormous blocks of frozen water glistening in a radiant sunshine were dazzlingly beautiful.

We worked our way southwards, and found ourselves, much to my wife's delight, in Richmond, Virginia. There we gave a concert, and, as usual, the house was crammed.

I had suggested that the Diva should sing " Il Bacio " as an encore, if necessary, but Madame Patti informed me that her maid had left the score with other music in New York, or she would have been delighted to do so. When the time came, however, and the audience itself suggested the song in its reiterated calls for an encore, Patti caught my eye, and whispered, to my great astonishment and apprehension, " ' Il Bacio,' Arditi, as best we can." There was no time for any discussion, and the orchestra instantly struck up the melody. It was most plucky of the Diva to proceed as she did without faltering, singing the song fearlessly and fault-lessly to the very end, despite the false notes and wrong harmonies which proceeded from the orchestra, through their having to play without any copies. The audience soon became aware of our little *contretemps*, and expressed their approval in cheering and hearty applause.

At Washington, one of America's loveliest towns, we gave a similarly successful concert. During that stay the Hon. John Warwick Daniel (my wife's cousin) came to visit us, subsequently taking us all over that mag-nificent building, the Capitol, which cost fifty-seven millions of dollars.

One of Washington's most striking features is the extraordinary cleanliness of its streets. To use a familiar adage, one might almost eat off the ground. The huge avenues, with their fine broad walks and overshadowing trees, are delightful to stroll in, and the open cars afford pleasant drives.

That tour was a most successful one. Twenty-two of my own musicians always accompanied us (although we were obliged to rely on the co-operation of assistant players at each town, who were sometimes good and sometimes bad); to give an adequate idea of our daily booking, I may say that we never took *under* eight thousand dollars per night.

Previous to our departure for England we were surprised to learn that Marcus Meyer, by offering a higher sum than Abbey paid, had induced Madame Patti to accept an engagement for America with him for the 1893–94 season.

Chiquito, our little dog, had by this time become a well-known *habitué* of the opera, as well as a familiar member of the company. He had crossed the Atlantic five times, and I remember that the usual strict rule on board ship, which obliges passengers to part from their pets during the voyage, was one which we never had the heart to conform with.

On the homeward journey, in 1892, from the States, a concert was organised on board for some charity, and I was asked to officiate as conductor.

Virginia had been very unwell during the journey, but feeling better, she ventured upstairs and sat herself down on deck with Chiquito on her lap. Hitherto we had managed to smuggle the dog during the voyages, and the ship's officers, out of consideration for us, had been good enough to appear blind to the presence or our tiny charge. On this occasion, however, the captain fixed his eye ominously on Chiquito, and Virginia, anticipating some remark from him on the subject, said laughingly, " Now, Captain, don't you say anything about my dog; because I am Madame Arditi, and if you attempt to take him away from me *there will be no concert to-night! . . .*" Virginia's inspiration was a happy one, for the Captain, laughing most good-naturedly, immediately became oblivious of Chiquito, and the dog of course remained with us.

On our return to London I conducted the Patti concerts at the Albert Hall, we paid another visit to Craig-y-nos, and I again conducted opera for Lago at the Olympic Theatre. It was during that season that poor Oudin appeared in " Eugène Onegin," a work which, in spite of Lago's efforts, proved such a failure.

Poor Lago! How valiantly he strove to make his season a success, and how unfortunate it was that money failed him when he was most in need of it. He was such a thoroughly cultivated musician, too, that it was doubly sad for his efforts at that time to be so cruelly frustrated.

Ancona, excellent artist that he is, made his *début* under Lago's auspices during that season, a fact which also goes a long way to prove Lago's discernment in matters musical.

Towards the end of 1892 Virginia and I went to Brussels to conduct a series of concerts given at the Alhambra. Among the artists were Madame Melba

---

I remember a funny incident in connection with the visit to Craig-y-nos Castle.

We were seated in the theatre one evening as usual after dinner, and had been witnessing a dumb show and some comic recitations, when George, Mr. Nicolini's valet, who was very clever in pantomime, appeared on the scene, and being dressed as a woman began to sing " Il Bacio " in a high falsetto voice. This proved too much for Chiquito's nerves. The little dog had been seated on his mistress's lap, and was as a rule quite impervious to any kind of music ; but to hear his master's favourite composition massacred like that was more than the dog could stand. He jumped up and barked furiously and steadily until George was compelled to beat a retreat, amid much laughter from the company. — EDITOR.

(who sang " Rosebuds " with tremendous success), Mdlle. Leila, Guille the tenor, and others.

We enjoyed our visit to that delightful city immensely, and the engagement ended with a little complimentary oration to me, together with a presentation of flowers bearing a flattering inscription from the members of the orchestra.

The 1893–94 tour to the States, under Marcus Meyer, began inauspiciously and ended most unsatisfactorily.

It was the first time that the Diva did not travel in the same steamer as ourselves; for she elected to make the voyage in a new ship, the " Lucania," and there arose a good deal of speculation as to which vessel, the " Lucania " or the S. S. " Paris " (our boat), would enter the harbour first. I shall never forget Marcus Meyer's face when he came on board to tell us that, after all, we had arrived before the others. The " Lucania " was not even in sight, and when she did arrive, a few hours later, we heard, to our dismay, that the Diva had been seriously ill during the journey, and that she would not be able to sing for some time to come.

A more unfortunate season than this can hardly be imagined, — so much so that it almost seemed like an interposition of Providence to punish us for having left Abbey.

The postponement of Madame Patti's two concerts announced at New York was a serious loss to Meyer, as he was obliged to return more than £1,000 worth of tickets which had been sold. There had, moreover, been a money crisis in America, and business that year was disastrous in the extreme.

A feature of the tour was to be Pizzi's opera " Gabriella," which had been expressly written for Madame Patti, and being entirely a *one-part* opera, it consequently caused much discontent and ill-feeling among the artists of the company; a regrettable fact, since the music was decidedly clever and well written; the instrumentation was particularly admirable and the opera deserved a more conspicuous success. Guille, too, who was always a decided draw, had been omitted from the company, and the finishing touch to the trouble occurred when it was ascertained that the Diva had departed from New York on the eve of the last *matinée*, with which Meyer had hoped to recoup part of his losses.

The disappointment caused by the Diva's inability to sing was bitter in the extreme, for people had come from many of the neighbouring towns to be present at her farewell performance.

In all this trouble I must, however, do Marcus Meyer every justice. He behaved admirably to the members of his company, and in spite of our fears at one time that we might have to pay our own fares home, Meyer discharged himself of all his debts honourably and conscientiously.

During that last tour Nicolini developed a great passion for violins and violin playing. At every town he overhauled the old *bric-à-brac* shops in search of a Stradivarius, Amati, or a Guarnerius, and I was constantly being exhorted to give my opinion on one or another instrument. He even practised most assiduously, and in a very short time acquired quite a proficiency in playing. I must say he was always most good-natured when chaffed by his wife and myself, and, considering the monotony of his life on those tours, where he was absolutely without occupation, his choice of amusement deserves much praise.

And thus ends the record of my many visits to the country of my early triumphs, and the home of many of my steadfast and staunch friends. It is grievous to me that my last sojourn in the States was so conspicuously unfortunate, but I still live in hope that fate may once more guide my footsteps in the direction of America, for which country I have always entertained, and shall always continue to entertain, a feeling of grateful affection and respect.

CHAPTER XX.

MY task is now almost at an end. Two more important events will complete the record of my musical career up to the present time.

In August, 1894, the widow of my departed and deeply deplored friend, Carl Rosa, approached me with a view to securing my services for a tour of English opera in the provinces. Happy in being able to oblige her, I gladly acquiesced, the tour commencing at Blackpool, and lasting for three months, during which period we again visited Ireland and Scotland, returning to London at the end of November.

The company was well organised, and included such artists as Mesdames Duma, Esty, l'Allemand, Linck, and Meisslinger; Messrs. Barton McGuckin, Hedmondt, George March, Paul, Pringle, etc., etc. M. Jaquinot, formerly my leader in the Italian opera under Mapleson, shared the duties of conducting with me.

Here I must lay particular stress on the efficiency of the chorus, with which I was delighted. The voices were exceptionally fresh and young, and promised, individually, to make their mark in years to come. The "school" itself being an excellent one, put its scholars to the test by the hard tasks it set before them. The continual work imposed upon the English Opera Company undoubtedly taxed their powers more heavily than that which was allotted to the Italian opera artists.

Many times during the season two *matinées* a week were given besides the regular evening performances, and the singers were not only willing to be kept at their posts continuously, but were full of energy and *esprit de corps*.

Two novelties during that season call for special mention. " Santa Lucia," a charming opera by Taska, who is a composer of great refinement and elegance, was one of these novelties; and although this work did not, perhaps, meet with the success to which its intrinsic merits entitled it, it was admirably sustained by Mesdames Duma, Meisslinger, and Messrs. Hedmondt, Pringle, and others.

Taska's work was given three times, the third representation taking place at Manchester.

During the tour we revived Nicolai's admirable and spirited work, " The Merry Wives of Windsor," the dainty airs and lively concerted pieces of which were rendered with magnificent *élan*. We had full houses on each occasion, the audiences evincing evident delight and appreciation of the music.

The second novelty, produced at Edinburgh, was Mr. Hamish McCunn's Opera, " Jeanie Deans," which he conducted *in propria persona*, and which was most favourable received by the composer's countrymen. The score contains some charming passages, together with much ingenuity and delicacy, while the libretto, coming from the brilliant pen of Mr. Joseph Bennett, is written in the refined and elegant style which characterises all the productions of that most able and skilful of critics.

Of the tour itself it must be said that everything was arranged for the comfort of the company, especial care and attention being paid to every one by Mr. Friend, Mrs. Carl Rosa's manager. Mrs. Carl Rosa sometimes visited us in her capacity of " Lady Impresaria," and was a general favourite everywhere and with everybody.

While in the provinces I was asked to look over the score of Humperdinck's Fairy Opera, " Hänsel and Gretel," with a view to its production in London.

From the moment that my eyes lighted on that exquisite music, I knew it could not fail to become a sensational success. We had, however, great impediments to contend with prior to the production of the work, our principal trouble being the difficulty in finding a theatre. At last we arranged with George Edwards to take " Daly's " for three weeks, commencing on " Boxing night," and " Hänsel and Gretel " was put into active rehearsal immediately on my return to London. Ample opportunity was now afforded to me of renewing my former friendship with that charming and talented little artist, Jeanne Douste de Fortis, who as a child had made her *début* with me in America as a pianist in 1881, where she and her elder sister, Louise, had attained enormous popularity, It was somewhat of a surprise to me when I heard that Jeanne had decided to abandon the piano (for she was a brilliant player) in order to go on the stage. She had, however, another gift she was anxious to develop, to wit, a fresh and intensely sympathetic voice; and thus, by the kind intervention of my friend Signor Tosti, who had originally heard her sing and was the means of putting her before the notice of Mrs. Carl Rosa, she was engaged to impersonate the *rôle* of " Gretel," a task of which she acquitted herself to the full satisfaction of every one who heard her. Before passing to another subject I would like to say a word in praise of the exceptionally energetic and painstaking efforts the two sisters have always displayed in their work and studies. Their attachment to their profession is only equalled by their love for one another and their devotion to their parents; and the ardour with which they have striven to attain the pinnacle of success ought to serve as a pattern of artistic conduct to youthful aspirants seeking distinction in the vocal and instrumental branches of the musical profession.

Speaking of Jeanne in the capacity of singer reminds me of a pretty story illustrative of her grateful recognition of the kindness of a friend. Madame Johnson, the wife of the late representative of the Paris "Figaro" in London, took a deep interest in the little girls, and was really the original means of introducing Jeanne to Signor Tosti. Unhappily she died ere she was able to see the fruits of her kind intervention on behalf of her *protégées*, for the first concert given by the Sisters Douste, on the occasion of Jeanne's appearance as a vocalist, took place several months after Madame Johnson's death. Needless to say that the pretty concert hall was crowded to overflowing with enthusiastic and admiring friends, and the platform literally covered with floral offerings and souvenirs.

At the close of the concert a four-wheeler was called, into which the sisters packed all their bouquets. A friend who was seeing them off heard Jeanne direct the cabman to drive to a certain cemetery, and being surprised at these singular instructions asked Jeanne to explain.

"We are going to place all our flowers on the grave of the kind friend," she replied, "who was the means of my originally learning to sing. She was *so* good to us."

Mdlle. Elba, as "Hänsel," also sang delightfully; in

fact, one cannot imagine a more perfect little couple than Mesdames Elba and Douste as "Hänsel and Gretel;" and that reminds me that Mdlle. Elba also sang in "La poupée de Nuremberg," at the Grosvenor Club with great success, on the occasion of one of the performances which I directed in Bond Street. All the other parts in Humperdinck's opera were well sustained by Mesdames Julia Lennox, Edith Miller (a capital witch), Jessie Huddleston, Marie du Bedat, and Charles Copland.

Of the music of "Hänsel and Gretel" I can only say that I love every note of it, and that I discovered a fresh delight, a new charm, each time I conducted the opera. It was, however, no easy task to handle a local orchestra accustomed to burlesque and light opera, nor was it an agreeable experience to have to train four different sets of instrumentalists, the "extras" of which were constantly changing, since our original three weeks' run expanded into six months, and we were obliged to migrate four several times from one theatre to another.

À propos of that fact a very humourous sketch appeared in the "Entr'acte," in which I am represented holding the two children by the hand, while the following words are put into my mouth: "Well, my dears, we have knocked about from pillar to post quite long enough; it is to be hoped that we shall soon settle down somewhere! . . ."

Before concluding the chapter just a word about "Bastien and Bastienne," a one-act opera from the

---

The composer of "Hänsel and Gretel" forwarded his portrait to Mr. Arditi, in recognition of the success which attended the excellent conductor's labours on behalf of that opera. Humperdinck's photograph is appropriately inscribed, and written on the margin are the opening bars of the second act. — EDITOR.

youthful pen of Mozart, which was brought out simultaneously with " Hänsel and Gretel."

The extraordinary simplicity of this little work contrasted strangely with Humperdinck's elaborate and fascinating instrumentation, and the *débutante*, Miss Huddleston, enlisted general approbation.

L'ENVOI.

————•————

HAVING, to the best of my ability, given an account of the chief incidents in my life, I now desire to cast a retrospective glance on such characteristics, in connection with Impresari, the press, artists, and last, but not least, old friends of the past, as I have hitherto mentioned very briefly or not at all.

Taking my principal Impresari individually, I have come to the conclusion that Don Francisco Marty (my first) was the most generous of men, and Max Maretzeck the cleverest; Benjamin Lumley was the most courteous and gentlemanly, and E. T. Smith the least so. Colonel Mapleson was decidedly the astutest of directors, and Frederick Gye the most respected; the late Sir Augustus Harris the most ambitious and successful; while to Henry Abbey must be attributed every straightforward and honourable quality. Maurice Grau was the cleverest of *entrepreneurs*, and Lago the most cultivated and musicianly; while my relations with the Brothers Gatti and Freeman Thomas have always been of an entirely cordial nature.

Bright thoughts fill my mind when looking back upon the cheery days spent in Vienna and St. Petersburg in the company of my kind colleague, the late Eugene Merelli, a man whose amiable characteristics and honest dealings never failed to imbue the members of his company with feelings of security and confidence.

A whole host of people now occur to me, to each one of whom I should like to express some little *gracieuseté*, but whom I must content myself by mentioning cursorily. There was James Gordon Bennett, most kind and just of critics, and the late J. W. Davidson, of brilliant capabilities, whose brother Duncan, I am glad to say, is still in our midst. Dr. Hueffer, too, who, with all his ardent attachment to Wagner's music never depreciated the Italian school, was an invaluable journalist; so was the late-lamented Dr. W. A. Barrett; likewise the late Henry Hersee, Campbell Clarke, Sutherland Edwards, Edward Hanslick, one of the greatest of German critics, Beatty-Kingston, and Joseph Bennett, both men of letters, for many years intimately connected with the "Daily Telegraph," all of whom were or are old and valued friends of mine.

Of conductors, Bottesini comes nearest to my heart; for his artistic life and mine were very closely connected in the commencement of our musical career.

Franco Faccio recalls many pleasant reminiscences, beside that of his visit to London, when at the production of Verdi's " Othello " he conducted a performance so masterly that it has never, to my mind, been surpassed. We spent three days together at Madame Valleria Hutchinson's hospitable house at Bosworth, where, alas, he already showed signs of the fatal malady which eventually took him from us in the prime of life.

That accomplished conductor, pianist, and composer, Frederick Cowen, is too well-known in musical circles to need an introduction from me, although, curiously enough, it was I who placed a bâton in his hand, when presenting him to the orchestra on the occasion of his conducting his first rehearsal at Her Majesty's Theatre!

Then genial Dr. Hans Richter! I shall often think of those wonderful nights at Vienna, when, with an hour or so of leisure to spare, I found myself seated in a corner of the opera house listening with delight to the splendid orchestra directed with the fervency and dramatic power so characteristic of that masterly musician. He has ever since been my beau ideal of a great conductor, while it is pleasant to remember the courtesy and kindness he is always ready and eager to show to musical strangers who visit his country.

My friend, August Manns, a veteran like myself, as valiant and hard-working a musician as I know, might well be designated the Richter of England; he has done much for his art in this country, and is well-beloved among his professional colleagues.

Carl Rosa, that shrewdest and cleverest of men, was an organiser and conductor *par excellence*. He was animated by high and just principles, as well as by a kind heart, and he possessed that rarest of rare faculties, the power of "saying the right things to the right person, at the right moment."

Among those musicians who have been associated with me in the capacity of *maestri di piano*, Bevignani stands first and foremost. He soon, however, abandoned the piano for the bâton, and has, ever since, maintained his position among distinguished conductors.

Bisaccia ranks next in my estimation; he is a good and faithful friend. Then follow Rasori, Bimboni, Sapio, and Mascheroni.

Cordialities and greetings to Tito Mattei, whose talent as pianist and composer has become a household word, and the same to my brother collaborateur Wilhelm Kuhe, with reciprocated compliments and thanks for the friendly recollections of me contained in his interesting book.

A grateful acknowledgment is due to Mr. Oscar Beringer, as well as to the Chevalier Bach, for the valuable tuition both musicians bestowed upon my son, and the kind interest they have always shown in his welfare.

Next a compliment to Theodore Thomas, who is now at the head of and directs one of the finest orchestras in America, the Philharmonic at Chicago. I recollect that he used to be my *chef d'attaque* at New York when I conducted there in days gone by, and I was then already delighted with his musical abilities, never doubting that he would ultimately achieve a great success.

There are many masters of English music, such as the late Sterndale Bennett, Sir Joseph Barnby, Sir A. Mackenzie, Sir G. Macfarren, Hubert Parry, Villiers Stanford, Fred Cliffe, and many others, whose works I have always admired despite the fact that I was rarely fortunate enough to conduct them, with one conspicuous exception, however, for I am happy to say that the conducting of several selections from Sir Arthur Sullivan's compositions has fallen to my lot.

Rivière still directs as well and as painstakingly as ever; long may he continue to do so. Likewise that elegant composer of ballet music, Jacobi, of the Alhambra, where his energy and artistic skill at once found their proper sphere, while Wilhelm Ganz, whose familiar presence and popular compositions are always in demand, has often shared my professional duties.

It would be impossible to mention individually all the tenors with whom I have maintained an intimate friendship. Mongini, my chum of old, Campanini, and Gardoni (who used to dress so perfectly that even Englishmen, the leaders of fashion all over the world, were constantly enquiring, enviously, " Who is his tailor? "), and Naudin (whose dainty little artistic gatherings at Homburg will be gladly remembered by those who were present, apart from the pleasure which his singing always afforded me) — all these occupy a large corner of my heart.

And now to recall a few more phenomenal voices, such as those of Tamberlik, Mierswinski, Prevost, Wachtel, Tamagno, and Guille. And *à propos* of Guille, I am reminded of a good story. I was dining with the popular singer one day, with other friends, and during the course of dinner the conversation turned on the subject of cooking. Guille, who never made a secret of his origin, appeared to be so particularly *au fait* in the preparing of special dishes that someone jestingly remarked to him : " *Vous paraissez être connoisseur de la cuisine, Monsieur ?* " Guille, who has ever been commended for his frank outspokenness, replied in his usual suave manner : " *Cela vous étonne, Madame ? Par bleu, c'est mon métier !* "

To the greatest of living violinists and violoncellists, Joachim and Piatti, let me pay a tribute of sincere affection and respect. There do not live artists who are endowed with more thorough uprightness, firmness of character, and earnestness of purpose than they, nor any whose beneficent influence has raised them to a standard of greater moral power in the musical world. Speaking of Joachim recalls Sivori, who, in my opinion, was an almost perfect exponent of the Italian school of violin-playing. I conducted many of his concerts in New York and Havana, while our friendship was a close and lasting one.

Also my cordial greetings to Wilhelmj, whose brilliant execution and masterly command over the resources of his violin has often delighted me. He encouraged me, in the first instance, to bring before the public those selections from Wagner's music which afterwards became so popular, not, however, before they had been subjected to some public controversy in the outset. Mr. Joseph Bennett told me of a curious instance of this. One day at a concert in Hanover Square, which I was conducting, my friend was seated next to a stranger, who persisted in applauding every selection vehemently, although, to all appearances, his enthusiasm was not the outcome of real appreciation or knowledge of music.

Mr. Bennett grew somewhat weary of his neighbor's noisy commendation, and finally asked him why he applauded so steadfastly. " Oh, I don't know," was the answer he received, " I suppose it's because they are making such a jolly row! . . ."

Two charming and cultivated artists, whose hospitality I have often enjoyed, are Mesdames Etelka Gerster, and Desirée Artot. The former lady possesses a lovely villa near Bologna, in Italy, where I have stayed, and the latter has frequently entertained me in her Berlin residence.

Of Madame Valleria, whose home is as familiarly dear to me as though it were my own, I have spoken at some length in the earlier pages of this book ; while her father-in-law, the late Mr. Hopwood Hutchinson, was one of my greatest friends. His beautiful home, Tenter House, is still, I am happy to say, hospitably presided over by his widow.

A grateful compliment to Madame Sembrich, not only a charming singer, but also a brilliant pianist and violinist who has made some of my compositions most popular. I have often regretted not having been afforded the pleasure of conducting for her, and beg to be numbered among her sincere admirers.

The late Sir Charles Hallé and his wife, whose names have been felicitously connected with this country for years past, also rank conspicuously among my long list of good friends.

I must not omit a word of regret for the many missing

faces which gathered round us of yore in our home in Albany Street.

There was Pellegrini, a host in himself; Frederick Lablache and his wife; Corney Grain and Arthur Cecil, who were always ready to entertain and delight our friends; Virginia Gabriel, Prince Poniatowski, Trebelli, Luigi Caracciolo, Charles Mapleson, and many, many more. Of those who are happily still living I am glad to mention Paolo Tosti, that most fascinating of song writers, Denza, Alberto Raimo, Visetti, Carpi, Meiners, De Lara, Mazzoni, Lennox Browne, the friend of all singers, and Louis Fagan, the author of that cleverly-written book, " The Life of Sir Anthony Panizzi," who, by the way, first suggested to my wife the desirability of collecting notes from the British Museum for this work.

I feel I have well-nigh exhausted my repertory of comrades and friends, but will not lay my pen aside without paying my affectionate respects to England's most popular musician, Sir Arthur Sullivan.

Of all careers that I have watched, his has undoubtedly been one of the most successful, and there is no one for whom I entertain a more profound admiration.

.   .   .   .

And thus I find myself at the end of my last chapter, and I, who have so often had occasion to thank the public for their warm applause and appreciation of my efforts, trust, with all my heart, that my readers will receive these Reminiscences in the same kind spirit.

If I have succeeded in amusing them for a while, my self-imposed task will be wholly gratifying and satisfactory to me, and in this profound hope I now bid the public and my friends (*they are one and the same*) a cordial farewell.

APPENDIX.

———•———

A T the request of my publishers and other friends I here add
a complete list of my compositions, arrangements, etc.,
together with the names of the conductors, composers, and
many of the singers, violinists, and pianists with whom I have
been brought into close personal contact, or who have appeared
under my direction during the last fifty years.

I know that this list is far from being complete; indeed, were
it possible for me to make it so from memory, it might be
almost indefinitely extended, but a glance at the names here
given will suffice to indicate a fifty years' retrospect, which, as
my readers will understand, cannot but be to me remarkably
comprehensive and very full of interest. — L. A.

COMPLETE LIST OF MY COMPOSITIONS
FROM 1838 TO 1896.

OVERTURE — Campestre.

OVERTURE — Dedicated to Count Renato Borromeo.

I BRIGANTI — Opera in One Act.

SEXTET — For Strings.

SOUVENIR DE DONIZETTI — " Lucia and Betly." Scherzo
Brillante for two Violins, with accompaniment for Pianoforte. (Arditi and Yotti.)

DUO — for two Violins, on Airs from the Opera, " Bianca
Santa Fiora," dedicated to Count Litta, and performed by
the Sisters Milanollo at La Scala, Milan. (Arditi and
Yotti.)

MASS and TANTUM ERGO — For Tenor and Bass, executed in the Church of the Madonna del Palazzo at Crescentino, with the celebrated Orchestra of Turin.

FANTASIA (in A) for Violin, dedicated to the Duke Litta.

LES SONNETTES D'AMOUR — Scherzo for Violin.

GRAN DUET — On Airs from the Opera " I Puritani," for Violin and Double-Bass. (Arditi and Bottesini.)

SCHERZO — On Cuban Melodies, for Violin and Double-Bass. (Arditi and Bottesini.)

THE CARNIVAL OF VENICE — For Violin and Double-Bass. (Arditi and Bottesini.)

IL CORSARO — Spanish Opera in One Act, performed in the Tacon Theatre, Havana.

NORMA di Bellini — Caprice for Violin and Pianoforte, dedicated to my master, B. Ferrara.

IL TROVATORE di Verdi — Fantasia for Violin with Pianoforte.

CUBAN DANCES — " L' Avvisador," " Le Streghe," " Los Tamburos," " L' Incendio," " L' Olandesa," " Los Ojos Azules," dedicated to Count Narciso de Penalvér, and " La Sirena," dedicated to Madame Bosio, etc.

SCHERZO BRILLANTE — On American National Airs. For Violin with Pianoforte.

LUCREZIA BORGIA — Fantasia for Violin and Pianoforte.

FUNERAL MARCH — For Military Bands, composed and performed in New York on the death of Henry Clay.

VARIATIONS — Dedicated and sung by Marietta Alboni.

RONDO — For Soprano, sung by Angiolina Bosio.

NEW YEAR'S TRIO — Dedicated to the daughters of Mario and Grisi.

LA SPIA — " The Spy," Opera in Three Acts, performed at the Academy of Music, New York.

TURKISH HYMN — Dedicated to H. M. the Sultan Abdul Medjed, performed at his Palace in Constantinople.

DUETTINO — For M. S. and T., sung by Signor and Madame Trebelli Bettini.

ROMANCE — " Colli Nativi," from " La Spia," sung by Giuglini, Mongini, Naudin, and Capoul.

IL DESIO — Duet, dedicated and sung by the Sisters Marchisio.

IL BACIO — Valse, dedicated to Marietta Piccolomini.

BOLÉRO — Sung by Désirée Artôt, Elisa Volpini, and Erminia Novara.

L' ARDITA — Valse sung by Eufrosina Parepa, Marie Roze, and Louise Dotti.

LA FARFALLETTA — Mazurka, dedicated to Rossini, sung by Trebelli.

L' ESTASI — Valse, dedicated and sung by Clarice Sinico, Adelina Patti, Desirée Artôt, and Etelka Gerster.

LA STELLA — Valse, dedicated and sung by Thérèse Titiens.

ROMANCE — " La Tradita," for Soprano.

SONG — " La Capinera di Lombardia," dedicated to Giulia Grisi.

DUO — " Una notte a Venezia," sung by Louisa Pyne and Sims Reeves.

ILMA — Valse, dedicated and sung by Ilma de Murska.

DUET — " Trema, o Vil," sung by Giulia Grisi and Paolina Viardot.

DUO — For Pianoforte and Violin, on the Opera " Dinorah," of Meyerbeer, dedicated to H. M. Isabella II., Queen of Spain. (Benedict and Arditi.)

SONG — " The Stirrup Cup," dedicated and sung by Charles Santley.

REMINISCENCES — Dedicated to Angiolina Bosio.

SCHERZO — " L' Orologio," " Tic-tic-tic," sung by Laura Harris and Ida Cristino.

LA GARIBALDINA — Dedicated to General Garibaldi.

SONG — " L' Orfanella," for Soprano.

RONDO — Sung by Thérèse Titiens in Nicolai's Opera, " Merry Wives of Windsor."

ROMANCE — " La Povera," dedicated to H. M. The Empress of Russia, sung by Trebelli.

MADRE ITALIA — National Song, with Chorus, performed at the Crystal Palace in honour of General Garibaldi.

SONG — " Life's Curfew Bell," sung by Santley.

HYMN — Dedicated to Vittorio Emanuele.

QUARTET — " Invito al Mar," sung by Kellogg, Trebelli, Bettini, and Santley.

BALLAD — " They ask me why I love her," sung by Signor Foli and Signor Vetta.

INTERNATIONAL SONG — With Chorus, " Though seas between us roar," dedicated to His Excellency Major-

General Robt. C. Schenck, United States Minister at London.

THE DRUMMER BOY'S POLKA — Dedicated to my little son.

QUICKSTEP — "I Bersaglieri," for Orchestra and Military Band.

SONG — "Il Gitano," sung by Antonio Galassi.

THE POPULAR POLKA — For Orchestra and Piano.

LES BELLES VIENNOISES — Valse for Orchestra, and *idem* for Soprano Voice, dedicated and sung by Madame Albani.

LE TORTORELLE — Valse, dedicated and sung by Etelka Gerster.

ORIENTAL CANTATA — Dedicated and performed before H. M. The Sultan, Abdul Hazis Khan, at the Crystal Palace.

ROMANCE — "Ah! se degg' io lasciarti," for Tenor, sung by Signor Alberto de Bassini.

SONG — "O vezzosa Giovinetta," for Soprano.

SONG — "Let me love thee," sung by Ch. Santley, and Ch. Copland.

THE PAGE'S SONG — Sung by José Sherrington, Bianca Bianchi, and Rose Hersee.

BALLAD — "True," sung by Helene Arnin.

LAMENTO — "Mi compiangi, o Giovinetta," dedicated to H. M. L'Imperatrice di Russia.

VALSE — "L'Incontro," dedicated to my pupil Alvina Valleria.

FOROSETTA — "Tarantella," dedicated and sung by Adelina Patti.

CANTATA — "Salve, o Prenci," performed at the marriage of Her Royal and Imperial Highness the Duchess of Edinburgh. Mesdames Adelina Patti, Emma Albani, Urban, and Sofia Scalchi; Messrs. Nicolini, Naudin, Graziani, Mendioroz, Bagagiolo; orchestre and chorus.

CAPRICCIO–MAZURKA — Dedicated and sung by Christine Nilsson and Bianca Bianchi.

OPHÉLIE–VALSE —Composed on the Airs of "Hamlet," A. Thomas, sung by Christine Nilsson.

POLKA CANTABILE — "Fior di Margherita," sung by Etelka Gerster and Nikita.

VALSE — "L' Incantatrice," dedicated to H. M. the Queen of Italy, sung by Adelina Patti.

GAVOTTE —" L'Ingénue," for Orchestra.

SONG — "What is love?" (" L' Ingénue), dedicated and sung by Alvina Valleria and Marie de Lido.

WEDDING MARCH — For Military Band, dedicated to my daughter Giulietta on the occasion of her marriage.

BALLAD — "What shall I sing?" sung by Santley.

VALSE — "Parla," sung by Mesdames Sembrick, Minnie Hauk, Paolina Rossini, and Arnoldson.

LE CAVALIER NOIR — Romance for Tenor, sung by Naudin, Capoul, Tom Hohler, and Guille.

BALLAD — "The nearest way home."

VALSE — "Gloria alla Beltà," sung by Mdlle. Leila — arranged likewise as a Trio for S., M. S., and Contralto.

SONG — "Love's Presence."

QUICKSTEP — For Orchestra.

SACRED SONG — Sung by Giuglini.

SONG — "The gift and the giver," sung by Santley.

BARCAROLA —For Strings only. Written expressly for the Italian Orchestra of the Regio Theatre of Turin, and performed for the first time at the Paris Exhibition in 1878.

VALSE — "Se saran Rose" (Rosebuds). Words by P. Mazzoni. Dedicated to Adelina Patti, and sung by Nellie Melba and Emma Albani.

QUICKSTEP MARCH — "The Tower Hamlets," dedicated to Col. T. H. Mapleson.

BALLABILE — For Orchestra, "The Fair Americans."

DAWN — ("L' Alba") Valse Song. Dedicated and sung by Mdlle. Nikita. Words by Mowbray Marras.

OPERATIC SELECTIONS ARRANGED BY ME.

LOHENGRIN . . . . *Wagner*

TANNHÄUSER . . . . "

THE FLYING DUTCHMAN . . . . "

UN BALLO IN MASCHERA . . . . *Verdi.*

AÏDA . . . . "

MOSÈ IN EGITTO . . . . *Rossini.*

CINQ MARS . . . . *Gounod.*

DIE WALKÜRE (New) . . . . *Wagner.*

PRODUCED FOR THE FIRST TIME IN LONDON
AT THE PROMENADE CONCERTS, (A. & S.
GATTI) UNDER MY DIRECTION.

DANSE MACABRE (First Time) . . . . *Saint-Saëns.*

LARGO (For String Instruments) . . . . . . *Handel.*

Violin Solo — HERR WILHELMJ.

FUNERAL MARCH of A. MARIONETTE . . . *Gounod.*

MINUET (String Instruments only) . . . . . *Bolzoni.*

SALTARELLO . . . . *Gounod.*

OPERAS FIRST PRODUCED IN ENGLAND UNDER MY DIRECTION.

MEDEA (Recitatives by ARDITI) . . . . . . *Cherubini.*
IPHIGENIA IN TAURIS (Recitatives by ARDITI) *Gluck.*
IL SERAGLIO . . . . *Mozart.*
L'OCA DEL CAIRO (Recitatives by BOTTESINI) "
ABU HASSAN (Recitatives by ARDITI) . . . . *Weber.*
LA SERVA PADRONA . . . . *Pergolesi.*
I VESPRI SICILIANI . . . . *Verdi.*
LA FORZA DEL DESTINO . . . . "
UN BALLO IN MASCHERA . . . . "
MEFISTOFELE . . . . *Boito.*
FAUST . . . . *Gounod.*
MIRELLA . . . . "
HAMLET . . . . *A. Thomas.*
MIGNON . . . . "
MERRY WIVES OF WINDSOR (Recit. by Arditi) *Nicolai.*
IL VASCELLO FANTASMA . . . . *Wagner.*
NICOLÒ DE' LAPI . . . . *Schira.*
LARA . . . . *Maillard.*
LA ZINGARA (The Bohemian Girl) . . . . . *Balfe.*
ALMINA . . . . *Campana.*
LA POUPÉE DE NUREMBERG . . . . *Adolph Adam.*
CAVALLERIA RUSTICANA . . . . . . *Mascagni.*
HÄNSEL AND GRETEL . . . . . . *Humperdinck's.*
BASTIEN AND BASTIENNE . . . . *Mozart.*
MESSE SOLENNELLE . . . . *Rossini.*
CANTATA . . . . *Verdi.*
LE DÉSERT . . . . *Félicien David.*

COMPOSERS WHOM I HAVE PERSONALLY KNOWN, AND WHOSE OPERAS I HAVE CONDUCTED.

Rossini.
Donizetti.
Verdi.
Vaccay.
Wagner.
Meyerbeer.
Auber.
Gounod.
Thomas, Ambroise.
Boito.
Massenet.
Pacini.
Flotow.
Rossi, Lauro.

Delibes, Léo.
Maillard.
Petrella.
Balfe.
Wallace.
Bottesini.
Cagnoni.
Meiners.
Pedrotti.
Campana.
Schira.
Mascagni.
Pizzi.
Mazzucato.

Humperdinck.

COMPOSERS WHOM I HAVE PERSONALLY KNOWN, SOME OF WHOSE WORKS I HAVE CONDUCTED.

Arrieta.
Auteri.
Albeniz.

Benedict.
Barnby, Joseph.
Bazzini, Antonio.
Barnett, J. F.
Bach, Emile.
Burgmein, J.
Bucallossi.
Braga.
Barrett.
Blumenthal.
Badia.
Benberg.
Bevignani, Enrico.
Bimboni.

Costa, Sir Michael.
Cowen, F. H.
Clay, F.
Catalani, A.
Cliffe, Frederic.
Coronaro.
Cellier, Alfred.
Caryll, Ivan.
Caracciolo, L.

David, Félicien.
De-Lara.
Denza.

Eckert.

Faccio.
Foroni.
Farhbach.

Ghevart.
Gomez, Carlo.
Gorin, Thomas.
Goldschmidt, Otto.
Gabriel, Virginia.
Gung'l.
Ganz, Wilhelm.
Giorza.
Gallico, R. C.

Henschel, George.
Hullah.
Hamish, McGunn.
Higgs, H. M.

Jacobi.

Leoncavallo.
Li Calsi.

Mariani, Angelo.
Massé, Victor.
Mackenzie, Sir A. C.
Marchetti.
Macfarren, Sir George.
Mancinelli, Luigi.

Mattei, Tito.
Macfarren, Walter.
Marras.
Mascheroni.
Mazzoni, Pietro.

Offenbach.
Oakeley, Dr.

Ponchielli.
Peri, Achille.
Pinsuti.

Rubinstein, Antoine.
Russell, William.
Randegger, Alberto.
Rottoli.
Rossari, Carlo.
Rasori.
Raimo, Alberto.

Saint-Saëns.
Suppé.
Sullivan, Sir Arthur.
Sgambati.
Stanford, Dr. C. Villiers.
Strauss, Johann.
Strauss, Edward.
Sydney Jones.
Silas.
Sapio.
Scuderi.

Tosti, Paolo.

Usiglio.

Visetti, Alberto.

Wenzel.

Zardo.

CONDUCTORS I HAVE PERSONALLY KNOWN.

Armbruster, Carl.
Anshutz.
Accerbi.
Archambaud.

Bottesini, Giovanni.
Benedict, Sir Julius.
Barnby, Sir Joseph.
Bassi, Nicola.
Bevignani.
Baveri.
Bertuzzi.
Bimboni.
Bolelli.
Betjemann.

Costa, Sir Michael.
Cowen, F.
Colonne.
Cavallini, Eugenio.
Cusins, Sir W. G.
Cummings, W. H.
Crowe.
Campanini, Cleofonte.

Damrosch, Leopold.
Dupont.
Damrosch, Walter.
Dami.

Eckert.

Faccio, Franco.
Ferrara, Bernardo.
Feld.

Ghebart.
Gung'l.
Glover, J. M.
Ganz, W.

Hallé, Sir Charles.
Henschel, G.

Jullien.
Jacobi.
Jaquinot.

Lamoureux.
Li Calsi.
Lutz, Meyer.
Levi.
Logheder.
Levi, Edgardo.

Mariani, Angelo.
Mottl, Felix.
Mackenzie, Sir A. C.
Manns, August.

Maretzech, Max.
Mancinelli, Luigi.
Martucci.
Muzio.
Mount, George.
Mellon, Alfred.
Mengone.
Mascheroni, Angelo.

Orsini, Orsino.

Polledro.
Pollitzer.

Richter, Hans.
Rosa, Carl.
Randegger.
Rivière.
Romili.

Seidl.
Strauss, J.
Strauss, E.
Sapio.
Seppilli.
Slapoffski, G.

Thomas, Theodore.

Usiglio.

Vianesi.
Visetti, Alberto.

Wylde, Dr.
Wood, J. Henry.
Wenzel.

SINGERS WHO HAVE APPEARED UNDER MY DIRECTION.

SOPRANI.

Adelina Patti.
Albani.
Adini, Ada.
Artôt, Desirée.
Ambrè.
Abbott, Emma.
Alameda.

Bosio.
Bishop, Anna.
Benza.
Barbòt.
Bertucca, Maretzech.
Barili, Clotilde.
Bianchi, Bianca.
Balfe, Victoire.
Brock, Jenny.
Bauermeister.

Chapuy, Margherite.
Carranti.
Carradori.
Colombo, Mattei.
Cristino, Ida.
Colombati.
Corani, Elena.
Corani, Ida.
Cobianchi.

Conneau.
Crosmond.

De Lagrange.
De Giuli.
De Murska, Ilma.
De Vries, Rose.
Donadio, Bianca.
De Luzzan, Zelie.
Donatelli, Salvini.
Derevis.
Dotti, Louise.
Duval.
De Lido, Marie.
Drog.
Duma, Marie.
Decca.
Douste, Jeanne.
De Vigne.
Donovani.
De Vernet.
Dorani.
Dollaro.
Domenici.
Dagmar.

Engel, Marie.
Elandi.

Esty, Alice.
Elba.

Fürsch, Madi.
Fricci.
Ferni.
Fohstrom.
Farini, Daria.

Grisi, Giulia.
Gerster, Etelka.
Galletti.
Gabbi.
Guerrabella.
Giovannoni, Zacchi.
Gassier, Madame.
Gargano.
Gambogi.
Galassi, Giuditta.
Gerli.
Gherslen.

Hauk, Minnie.
Hensler.
Harris, Zagury.
Hersee, Rose.
Heilbron.
Huddleston.
Hunt.

Juck, Emma.
Joran, Pauline.

Kellogg, Louise.
Kruls.

Lucca, Pauline.
Lehmann, Lilli.
Liebhart, Louise.

Leila.
Litvinoff.
Laborde.
Levitsky.
Lablache, Louise.
Le Brun.
Lennox.
L'Allemand.
Litta, Marie.
Larkom, Agnes.
Link.

Melba.
Marchisio, Carlotta.
Marimon.
Murio, Celli.
Macintyre.
Monbelli.
Musiani.
Michell.
Moody, Fanny.
Miller, Edith.

Nilsson, Christine.
Nordica.
Nevada.
Nikita.
Norini.
Novara, Erminia.

Ortolani, Tiberini.

Piccolomini, Marietta.
Patti, Carlotta.
Penco.
Parepa Rosa.
Parodi.
Pyne, Louisa.
Pappenheim.

Ponti.
Palmieri.
Pettigiani.
Peri.
Pernini.

Russell, Ella.
Roze, Marie.
Rossini, Paolina.
Ravogli, Sofia.
Rolla.
Ruddersdorff.
Rubini, Scalisi.
Rosavella.
Reboux.
Raimondi.
Redi.

Sontag, Contessa Rossi.
Steffenone.
Spezia, Aldighieri.
Salla.
Sessi.
Sinico.
Sarolta.
Sedlazech.
Sherrington, Lemmens.
Sherrington, José.
Synnerberg.
Stromfeld.

Savertal.
Scotti.
Switcher.
Samuell, Clara.
Simmondi.
Siedinburgh.

Titiens, Thérèse.
Tedesco, Fortunata.
Truffi.
Tagliana.

Urban.

Valleria, Alvina.
Van Zandt.
Volpini, Elisa.
Valda.
Varesi, Elena.
Vaneri, De Filippi.
Vachot.
Vanzini.
Vitali.
Valerga.

Wipern, Harriers.
Wynne, Edith.
Winttrop.
Warwick, Julia.

Zoja, etc.

MEZZO-SOPRANI E CONTRALTI.

Alboni.
Arnin.

Borghi, Mamo.
Bettelheim.
Belocca.

Brema.
Borchardt.
Belle-Cole.

Cary.
Celega.

Dolby, Sainton.
Desvignes.
Damian.

Fernandez.
Fabbri, Guerina.
Fairman, Alice.

Guarducci.
Grossi.
Gomez, Alice.

Hastreiter.

Jansen, Agnes.

Lablache, Demeric.
Lemaire.
Laura, Lilian.

Marchisio, Barbara.
Macvitz.

Meislinger.
Moody, Lily.

Pyne, Susan.
Patti, Strakosch.
Patey.
Pisani.

Ravogli, Giulia.

Scalchi.
Sanz.
Steinback.
Sterling, Antoinette.
Saunier.

Trebelli.
Tremelli.

Vestvali.
Vietti, Vertiprach.

Yorke, Josephine.

Zeiss.

TENORI.

Aramburo.
Armandi.
Anastasi.
Adams.

Braham, Charles.
Bettini, Geremia.
Brignoli.
Belart.
Baldanza.
Bettini, Alessandro.
Bulterini.
Benedetti.

Bolcioni.
Bertini.
Baragli.
Bentham.
Brophy, R.
Bignardi.

Campanini.
Cuzzani.
Cardinali.
Capoul.
Ciaffei.
Corsi, Achille.
Carrion, Emmanuele.

Cooper, Wilbye.
Candidus.
Chinelli.

Davies, Ben.
De Bassini.
De Falco.
Dimitresco.
Daniele.
Dorini.

Errani.

Fraschini.
Fancelli.
Frapolli.
Fernando.

Giuglini.
Gayarre.
Gardoni.
Graziani, Lodovico.
Giannini.
Guille.
Goula.
Gillandi.
Gunz.
Guetary.

Hohler, Tom.
Harrison.
Hedmondt.
Harley, Orlando.

Lloyd, Edward.
Lorini.
Lucchesi.
Lazzarini.
Lely.

Lestellier.
Lyall.

Mario.
Masini.
Mongini.
Mirate.
Marconi.
Mierzwinshy.
Malvezzi.
Massimi.
Marini.
Mazzoleni.
Manzocchi.
McGuckin, Barton.
Maas, Joseph.
Morini.
Montariol.

Nicolini.
Neri.
Naudin.
Neri, Baraldi.

Oxilia.

Pozzolini.
Perotti.
Perelli.
Prevost.
Pattierno.
Perugini.
Perrin.
Palladini.
Parravicini.
Paoletti.
Palmieri.
Parisotti.
Piercy, Henry.

Ravelli.
Runcio.
Ronzi.
Rigby, Vernon.

Salvi.
Stagno.
Sims Reeves.
San Giovanni.
Sani.
Sirchia.
Shakespeare.
Stephens.
Scovello.
Suane.
Swift.
Severi.
Sabatier.
Smith, Valentine.

Tamberlik.
Tamagno.

Tiberini.
Tasca.
Talasach.
Tombesi.
Talbò.
Tecchi.

Urio.

Vignas.
Valero.
Vicini.
Volpini.
Vietti.
Vizzani.

Wachtel.
Walter.

Zona.
Zerni.

BARITONI.

Agnesi.
Aldighieri.
Amodio.
Ancona.

Badiali, Cesare.
Belletti.
Beneventano.
Blanchard.
Bonetti.
Bispham.
Black.
Buti.
Brombara.

Cotogni.
Corsi, Giovanni.
Colonnese.
Ciabatta.
Carpi.
Cresci.
Cima.
Caravoglia.
Colletti, Domenico.
Ciampi, Celai.
Celli.
Copland.
Campobello.
Colmenghi.
Claus.

De Bassini.
Delle Sedie.
D' Andrade, Francesco.
De Soria.
Del Puente.
Del Negro.
De Anna.
De Lara.
Du Breuil.
Dome.
De Pasqualis.

Everardi.

Faure.
Fiori.
Ferri.
Fagotti.
Fiegna.
Ferranti.
Federici.
Foote, Barrington.
Fox.
Farkoa.

Graziani.
Galassi.
Gassier.
Gillardoni.
Ghislansoni.
Gnone.
Garcia, Gustave.

Lassalle.
Lhérie.

Maurel.
Morelli.

Moriami.
Mendioroz.
Marchesi.
Medica.
Mariscalchi.
Marcassa.
Maybrick.
Marsh.

Neri.

Oudin.
Orlandi.

Pandolfini.
Padilla.
Pantaleoni.
Pini-Corsi.
Paltrinieri.
Paull.

Ronconi, Giorgio.
Rota.
Roudil.
Raguer.
Rossato.
Rodriguez.

Santley.
Strozzi.
Sterbini.
Sparapani.
Snazelle.
Sauvestre.
Saxe.

Taffanelli.
Tagliafico.

Varesi.
Vita.
Verger.

Valdeck.
Vaselli.
Valcheri.

Zacchi.
Zardo.

BASSI PROFONDI.

Antonucci.
Amati.
Abramoff.
Antonelli.

Bagagiolo.
Behrens.
Belval.
Bossi.
Barili.

Castelmary.
Cherubini.
Costa.
Capponi.

Duval.
David.
Dondi.

Formes.
Foli.
Fricker.

Junca.

Lombardelli.
Lanzoni.

Marini, Ignazio.
Mitrowick.
Miller.
Medini.
Monti.
Müller.
Miranda.

Nanetti.
Novara.
Navarini.
Novelli.

Ordinas.

Pollonnini.
Patey.
Perkins.
Pettit.
Pringle.

Rokitanski.
Rosa.

Susini.
Schmidt, Dr.
Serbolini.

Vialetti.
Vidal.
Vecchioni.
Vetta.

Weiss.
Wohnrelth.
Worlock.
Winogradon.

BASSI COMICI.

Bottero.
Borella.
Bonafous.

Rovere.
Rocco.
Rossi.

Cambiagio.
Ciampi.
Corsini.
Carbone.
Caracciolo.

Scalese.
Soáres.
Scheggi.
San-Quirico.

Fiorini.

Tierry.
Tebaldo.

Massetti.
Meroles.
Migliara.

Vianelli.

Pappini.

Zucchini.
Zoboli.

VIOLINISTS I HAVE PERSONALLY KNOWN.

Arditi, Emilia.

Bazzini, Antonio.
Boulanger, Marie.
Bassi, Nicola.
Blagrove, Henry.
Busiau.
Burnett, Alfred.
Bocchi.

Carpenter, Nettie.
Carrodus, J. T.
Caldera.
Corbellini, Vincenzo.
Cremaschi.
Contin, G.

Douglas, Marie.
De Angelis.

Eissler, Marianne.
Erba.

Ferni, Virginia & Teresina.
Ferrara Bernardo.
Frontali.

Ghebart.

Hellmeisberger.
Hollander.

Hill, Weist.
Heyman, Henry.
Hamn, Carl.

Joachim, Dr. Joseph.
Jullien, Paul.

Levallois, Mdlle.
Lipinski.

Milanollo, Teresa & Maria.
Molique.
Musin.
Maurer.

Neruda (Lady Hallé).
Nachéz, Tivadar.
Nahan, Franko.

Ole Bull.

Pommereul.
Polledro.
Papini.
Patti, Carlo.
Parker, Frye.
Pollitzer.

Rolla, Alessandro.
Rapetti.
Remeny.

Rosa, Carl.
Rovelli, Emanuele.
Robbio.
Resigari.

Sivori, Camillo.
Sarasate.
Sainton, P.
Sauret, Emil.
Simonetti.
Strauss, Ludovic.
Scuderi.
Slapoffski, G.

Toricelli, Mataura.
Thomas, Theodore.

Urso, Camilla.

Vieuxtemps.
Viotti, Collins.

Wilhelmj.
Wienianski.
Wolff, Johannes.

Ysaye.
Yotti, Luigi.

PIANISTS I HAVE PERSONALLY KNOWN.

Anderson, Mrs.
Andreoli, Andrea.
Andreoli, Carlo.
Albanesi, Carlo.
Arditi, Luigi, Junior.

Bulow, Hans.
Bach, Emil.
Beringer, Oscar.
Bendall.
Bird, Henry.
Berger, F.
Bisaccia.
Bending.

Carreno, Madame.
Cerasoli-Rosina and Bice.
Cambiasi, Branca Cirilla.
Clerici.
Cusins, Sir W. G.

De-Konstki.
Desvernine, Paolo.
Davies, Fanny.
Douste, Louise.
Debillemont, Jane.
De-Pachmann, Margherite.
De-Pachmann, Vladimir.

Essipoff, Annette.

Fumagalli, Adolfo.
Fumagalli, Disma.
Fumagalli, Luca.
Foroni.
Fasanotti, Filippo.
Fishoff, Roberto.

Goddard, Arabella.
Gottschalk.
Ganz, W.

Herz, Henry.
Hallé, Sir Charles.
Haas, Madame.

Jaell, Alfred.

Ketten, Henry.
Kuhe, W.

Liszt.

Mayer, Leopoldo de.
Miclòs, Madam Roger.
Mattei, Tito.

Mehlig, Anna.
Martucci.
Maton.

Osborne.

Paderewski.
Pratt, S. G.
Palmieri.

Rubinstein.
Rendano.

Sgambati.
Saint-Saëns.
Schiller, Madeline.
Stœger.
Schlosser.

Thalberg.

Waud, Florence.
Wieniawski.
Wehli, James M.

Zimmermann, Agnes.